# THE EVOLVING UNITED NATIONS: A PROSPECT FOR PEACE?

# THE EVOLVING UNITED NATIONS: A PROSPECT FOR PEACE?

Edited by

KENNETH J. TWITCHETT

Foreword by

LORD CARADON

*Former British Minister at the United Nations*

Published for

The David Davies Memorial Institute of International Studies

By

ST. MARTIN'S PRESS
NEW YORK

For information, write:
St. Martin's Press, Inc., 175 Fifth Avenue, New York, N.Y. 10010

Printed in Great Britain

Library of Congress Catalog Card Number: 70-178037

First published in the United States of America in 1971



*AFFILIATED PUBLISHERS:*
*Macmillan & Company, Limited, London - also at*
*Bombay, Calcutta, Madras, and Melbourne*
*The Macmillan Company of Canada, Limited, Toronto*

# *Foreword*

THIS book comes at a good time. Beset by troubles at home and bewildered by terrible news from abroad there is, so it seems, a turning away in British public opinion from the outside world, a disinclination to favour any initiative in international affairs, a cynical indifference or antagonism towards the United Nations, a concentration instead on domestic and local anxieties.

The prevailing public mood might be summed up in the old verse:

> Void of strong desire and fear
> Life's wide ocean trust no more
> Strive thy little bark to steer
> With the tide and near the shore.

This bad patch of disillusion, weariness, ingrowing selfishness is perhaps natural enough. Only twenty-five years ago Britain administered a quarter of the population of the world. In a quarter of a century we have performed the gigantic task of converting a subject empire into a free commonwealth. It was a revolutionary and on the whole an admirable achievement – and not surprising that the older people in this country should feel that after the winding up of the greatest empire the world has known, and two world wars, that is enough for one generation.

Even the possibility of entry into Europe, in any event only half-heartedly supported, is by many looked upon as an escape from dangerous diversions in the wider world, rather than an opportunity to make a more constructive contribution to international peace and prosperity.

This bad patch may not be surprising, but it is certainly sad – sad because it seems to me that the United Kingdom now has a unique opportunity to take a proud share in world leadership. The new lead would derive not from arms or force but from a readiness to work with others through the UN for peaceful settlement of conflicts and disputes, and for making the peace tolerable to those millions who now live in fear and want.

The United Kingdom with its traditions of tolerance and fair play and democratic government, and with its world-wide experience and interests, and its dependence on world trade, and its Commonwealth associations, has, so I maintain, an unrivalled opportunity to take a lead in the search for common ground of international agreement.

No longer a super power and no longer an imperial power, the United Kingdom can and should become an outstanding leader in international co-operation.

The older generation may be too tired or too selfish to seize such opportunities, or even to see them. But there is real hope, I believe, in the new generation. It is in these international questions that the greatest generation gap grows. The younger generation does care, so I believe, about the new frontier subjects of race, poverty and population. Old men may become isolationists. Young ones are instinctively internationalists.

What has this to do with the subject of this book? Everything, I think. Here is a book written by acknowledged experts on a variety of different aspects of the international scene. All are concerned with international co-operation. What they write is authoritative. It is also provocative. I myself do not agree with everything written in these papers; to much of it I have reservations or even objections. But I recognise that this is a most important collection of the comments of writers who have undisputed knowledge of their subjects and enjoy wide international respect. I warmly congratulate those who have given us such a substantial feast of expert assessment and stimulating opinion on the main international questions of our time.

To those who are about to read this series of impressive essays I make some preliminary suggestions.

Look out, let me suggest, for five trends and developments which I think I can distinguish from my own decade of practical experience working in or for the UN.

First, there is the slow thawing of the Cold War, dreadfully slow it is true, proceeding at no more than glacier pace, but with welcome change perceptible. The massive obstruction of the Soviet Union and its satellites is slowly easing.

Second, consider what the impact of the admission of mainland China would be to the Security Council and the Assembly. I myself fear that the entry of communist China will continue to be blocked (by a two-China move) but better sense may prevail. No one doubts that her arrival to take the Chinese seat in Council and Assembly (with a veto in the Council) would create a period of serious difficulty. Perhaps on a number of issues it would lead to deadlock. But the arrival of the Chinese from Peking would also, it is permissible to hope, open out the prospect of making the international community more vigorous, more effective and making the world much more safe from nuclear war.

Third, although in many matters the two super powers of the United States and the Soviet Union now appear to dominate the world, it is a mistake to underrate the influence of middle powers and even small powers in the new parliamentary diplomacy of the UN. The two muscle-bound giants are often slow and clumsy in working for agreement, even when they want to avoid continuing confrontation and conflict. It is often the initiative of a lesser power, or a group of them, which can show the way to escape from an impasse, and not even the super powers can profitably or for long flout and disregard the opinion of the great majority.

Fourth, look out for the subjects which now increasingly command world attention – environment, poverty, population. Keeping the peace must always come first, but it is almost equally important to make the peace tolerable. Economic development is increasingly the principal activity of the UN, and economic development without population control and without environment control too is a delusion. Of the four functions of the UN – an instrument for peace, a forum for world opinion, a centre for international diplomacy, and a machine for multilateral economic development, the last may yet prove to be the most successful of all international enterprises.

Fifth, do not doubt that the UN system is here to stay. No country is powerful enough to destroy it. Those who fail to make use of the instrument or stand out against overwhelming world opinion (on racial issues for instance) will do so to their own detriment.

I repeatedly say that there is nothing wrong with the UN except the members. The instrument is keen, powerful. It can be used effectively whenever there is agreement, but agreement seldom comes without a great deal of negotiating work. This is the work in which I trust that our country can take the lead. This is the true British interest. This is a challenge which we must not neglect or refuse.

If we are to make our contribution in the UN effective and take a worthy British lead in international affairs we must not only be ready and anxious to use the instrument which the UN provides, but we must know it and be skilled in its use. This book should help us to do so and be so.

*April* 1971 CARADON

# *Acknowledgements*

I WISH to acknowledge the courtesy and kind co-operation of Lord Caradon and the other contributors to this book. My thanks also go to Mary Sibthorp, Executive Secretary of the David Davies Memorial Institute of International Studies and her assistant, Esme Allen, Walter Simon and Jane Carroll of Europa Publications, and the Librarian at the London Office of the United Nations Information Service. A special debt of gratitude is owed to my wife, Carol Ann Cosgrove, for her invaluable assistance in compiling and editing this book.

The chapters by D. W. Bowett, Rupert Emerson, J. E. S. Fawcett, Geoffrey L. Goodwin, Ernst B. Haas and David Mitrany were first published as articles in the special November 1970 edition of *International Relations*, the journal of the David Davies Memorial Institute, on the twenty-fifth anniversary of the United Nations.

*April* 1971 KENNETH J. TWITCHETT
(*Editor*)

## *Contents*

*Foreword* by Lord Caradon v

*Acknowledgements* viii

*Abbreviations* xii

*Editor's Preface* xv

1. THE INTERNATIONAL DRAMA: THE UNITED NATIONS ON THE WORLD STAGE 1
   *Kenneth J. Twitchett*
   The International Perspective
   The Birth and Evolution of the United Nations
   The United Nations and the International Legal System
   The Security Functions of the United Nations
   International Responsibility for Dependent Peoples
   International Economic Co-operation and the United Nations
   From Globalism to Regionalism
   The Powers and the United Nations
   An Overall Survey

2. THE UNITED NATIONS: EXPECTATIONS AND EXPERIENCE 28
   *Geoffrey L. Goodwin*
   San Francisco and the Founding Fathers
   Twenty-Five Years on Trial
   Who Wants What and Who Gets What?
   Prospects

3. THE UNITED NATIONS AND INTERNATIONAL LAW 57
   *J. E. S. Fawcett*
   The United Nations as a Legal and Political Unit
   General Assembly Resolutions and the United Nations as a Primitive Legislature
   The Codification of International Law

4. UNITED NATIONS PEACE-KEEPING 71

*D. W. Bowett*

Constitutional Authority to Establish a Force
Finance
Consent to the Presence of a United Nations Peace-Keeping Force
The Principle of Non-Intervention
Political Direction and Control
Limitation of Force to the Exercise of Self-Defence
A Headquarters Military Planning Staff

5. THE UNITED NATIONS AND COLONIALISM 83

*Rupert Emerson*

The Trusteeship System
Non-Self-Governing Territories
The 1960 Declaration on the Granting of Colonial Independence
The Committee of Twenty-Four
Conclusions

6. THE UNITED NATIONS AND INTERNATIONAL ECONOMIC RELATIONS 100

*Susan Strange*

Concepts, Hopes and Premises
The United Nations Factor
Conclusions and Prognoses

7. THE UNITED NATIONS AND REGIONALISM 120

*Ernst B. Haas*

The Phenomenon of Regionalism
The United Nations, Regionalism and the Maintenance of Peace
Regionalism and Economic Development
Regionalism and Global Integration
List of Disputes Involving Regional Action

8. BRITAIN AND THE UNITED NATIONS 141

*F. S. Northedge*

British Diplomatic Style and the United Nations
Party Attitudes to the Organization
Britain's Record at the United Nations
British Responsibilities

9. THE UNITED NATIONS IN HISTORICAL PERSPECTIVE 157
*David Mitrany*
The Nature of the Organization
The United Nations and the Three-fold Revolution
Charter Revision and Political Division
Regional and Functional Devolution
Law-Making for the World
The Historical Task
The Present Realities of World Politics
Winds of Change and the Prospects

APPENDIX I: The Covenant of the League of Nations 191

APPENDIX II: The Charter of the United Nations 201

APPENDIX III: Membership in the United Nations 225

*Notes on Contributors* 227

*Select Bibliography* 229

## *Abbreviations*

| | |
|---|---|
| AJIL | American Journal of International Law |
| ANZUS | Pacific Security Treaty (between Australia, New Zealand and the United States) |
| CENTO | Central Treaty Organization |
| DAC | Development Assistance Committee (of OECD) |
| ECA | UN Economic Commission for Africa |
| ECAFE | UN Economic Commision for Asia and the Far East |
| ECE | UN Economic Commission for Europe |
| ECLA | UN Economic Commission for Latin America |
| ECOSOC | UN Economic and Social Council |
| ECSC | European Coal and Steel Community |
| EEC | European Economic Community |
| EFTA | European Free Trade Association |
| EPTA | Expanded Programme of Technical Assistance |
| FAO | Food and Agriculture Organization |
| GA | UN General Assembly |
| GATT | General Agreement on Tariffs and Trade |
| ICAO | International Civil Aviation Organization |
| ICBM | Inter-Continental Ballistic Missile |
| ICJ | International Court of Justice |
| IDA | International Development Association |
| IFC | International Finance Corporation |
| ILO | International Labour Organisation |
| IMF | International Monetary Fund |
| IPKO | International Information Centre on Peace-Keeping Operations |
| ITO | International Trade Organization |
| LAFTA | Latin American Free Trade Association |
| LDC | Less-Developed Country |
| NATO | North Atlantic Treaty Organization |
| OCAM | Organisation Commune Africaine et Malgache |
| OAS | Organization of American States |
| OAU | Organization of African Unity |
| OECD | Organization for Economic Co-operation and Development |
| OEEC | Organization for European Economic Co-operation |
| ONUC | UN Operations in the Congo |
| PCIJ | Permanent Court of International Justice |

| | |
|---|---|
| SDR | Special Drawing Rights (of IMF) |
| SEATO | South-East Asia Treaty Organization |
| UAM | Union Africaine et Malgache |
| UNA | United Nations Association |
| UNCTAD | UN Conference on Trade and Development |
| UNDD | UN Development Decade |
| UNDP | UN Development Programme |
| UNEF | UN Emergency Force |
| UNESCO | UN Educational, Scientific and Cultural Organization |
| UNFICYP | UN Force in Cyprus |
| UNIDO | UN Industrial Development Organization |
| UNITAR | UN Institute for Training and Research |
| UNMOGIP | UN Military Observer Group for India and Pakistan |
| UNOGIL | UN Observer Group in the Lebanon |
| UNRRA | UN Relief and Rehabilitation Agency |
| UNTSO | UN Truce Supervision Organization (in Palestine) |
| UNYOM | UN Yemen Observation Mission |
| WHO | World Health Organization |
| WLR | World Law Review |

# *Editor's Preface*

DURING the quarter of a century since the Second World War, the United Nations has become an established feature of the international scene. Although a very different organisation from that originally envisaged in the Charter and operating in a very different international environment from that of 1945, it has become a much more important focal point for international activity than did the League of Nations. Unlike the League, the UN is a truly global organisation although not yet universal in its membership. Its early aspirations have not been fulfilled, aspirations more wide-ranging but much less idealistic perhaps than those held by some of the League's founding fathers at the Versailles peace conference in 1919. Yet the UN has had a definite if not wholly tangible impact on the conduct of inter-state relations during the last twenty-five years or so.

The vast range of the UN's involvement in inter-state relations is demonstrated by the contributions to this book. The contributors start from differing viewpoints and consider very different aspects of the UN's activities. Our approach is analytical and diagnostic rather than prescriptive and by and large we are neither unduly enthusiastic about the Organization's achievements nor optimistic regarding its future prospects. But we all accept that the UN is an integral feature of the international system as we know it today, one which does offer a much needed prospect for peace. That prospect itself can only be utilised by the member states. It is up to the reader to decide whether our collective diagnosis is too pessimistic or perhaps even too optimistic.

*Aberdeen, April* 1971

KENNETH J. TWITCHETT

# 1. THE INTERNATIONAL DRAMA: THE UNITED NATIONS ON THE WORLD STAGE

Kenneth J. Twitchett

THE purposes of the United Nations are set forth in Article I of its Charter. The Organization was intended "to be a centre for harmonising the actions" of states in maintaining international peace and security, developing "the principle of equal rights and self-determination of peoples", furthering international co-operation in economic, social, cultural and humanitarian matters, and "encouraging respect for human rights and for fundamental freedoms for all without distinction as to race, sex, language, or religion". The basic objective was the furtherance of international peace and security – all other objectives were essentially secondary, or rather, contributory, to this central objective.

This chapter examines the extent to which the UN's purposes have been realised in the light of the Organization's impact on inter-state affairs. The UN's impact is placed within the changing international environment in which the Organization has operated and, in passing, compared with that of the League of Nations. The chapter also introduces and comments on the other eight contributions to this book. The ideas and views contained in it are my own unless explicitly attributed to the other contributors. In fact, many of their ideas are similar if not identical to my own, and I have used them in developing my own argument. The responsibility for any misinterpretation of their points of view is, of course, mine alone.

## The International Perspective

The UN as we know it today is in many respects a completely different entity from that envisaged by its founding fathers at the San Francisco Conference in 1945. Although the Charter remains the same, apart from some relatively minor revisions,[1] many of its provisions are now interpreted very differently. Many original hopes have been dashed and the UN has assumed functions unforeseen by most of the delegates at San Francisco.

[1] In particular, Chapter V has been revised to increase the Security Council's membership from eleven to fifteen, while Chapter X has been revised to increase the Economic and Social Council's membership from eighteen to twenty-seven. For further details see Appendix II.

The actual working of the Organization itself has been transformed – due in large measure to an expansion of its membership from the original 51 to 127 in 1970.[2] These new member states, the majority from Africa and Asia, have very different historical experiences and traditions, economic and political capacities, and hopes and aspirations from those of the founding fathers. Some of them do not so much contribute to the work of the UN as constitute a drain on its resources. The Organization itself has never been a *club* in quite the same way as the European-dominated League of Nations.

Most importantly, the international system within which the UN exists is very different from that envisaged in 1945. The victorious Allied wartime coalition, institutionalised by permanent seats on and veto rights in the Security Council, did not really even survive the San Francisco Conference itself. In the immediate aftermath of the war, world politics and hence the global organisation became dominated by the cold war rivalry of the Soviet Union and the United States. These two super powers are now apparently moving towards an uneasy and suspicious détente, by no means towards a whole-hearted *rapprochement*. A third potential super power looms large on the horizon. China is a member of the UN, but the Chinese seat is occupied by the nationalist rump based on Formosa, not the Communist regime in Peking. Britain and France still retain the great power trappings of permanent Security Council membership. Yet even they apparently recognise, albeit tardily and reluctantly, that their world roles are now reduced.

The former Axis powers have rejoined the international community. Italy and Japan are now full UN members, but not so Germany – she remains outside and divided along with Korea and Viet-Nam. In international economic terms both Japan and West Germany have become as important, if not more so, than Britain and France. Italy and West Germany are now joined with their erstwhile enemies, France and the Benelux, and perhaps soon Britain and the Scandinavian countries, in the European Economic Community. The potential source of international conflict is no longer seen as stemming from German or Japanese ambitions, or, indeed, even from the hot rivalries of the two super powers, but rather from a resurgent China and from the instability and antagonisms of many of the new states of Africa and Asia. The threat of Fascism as an aggressive creed has been largely if not wholly replaced by opposing capitalist and Communist ideologies, colonialism and anti-colonialism, and by racial hatreds.

There are new dangers to the very existence of organised life on this

[2] For further details of the UN's membership, see Appendix III.

planet. The tremendous post-1945 scientific and technological revolution has witnessed the beginning of mankind's conquest of space; it has also brought in its wake a more menacing danger from the destruction and pollution of the natural environment. The activities of organised non-state terrorist groups, operating on the national and international planes, in some respects pose an even more immediate threat than that of a nuclear holocaust. Hopefully nuclear war is extremely unlikely, but throughout the world there is an increase of aeroplane hi-jacking and the kidnapping of diplomatic personnel. Such terrorism is not easily detected before society is held to ransom.

In 1945 the emphasis was on post-war reconstruction and the establishment of an economic system between industrialised states which would avoid the vicissitudes of the 1930's. The latter still awaits construction, the task being more complicated now due to Western European integration and the emergence of the EEC as a new international economic giant. Awareness of the endemic problems of poverty confronting most Third World states is a new international feature. Massive bilateral and multilateral aid to these states to assist them in tackling their complex tasks of modernisation is a new dimension almost wholly unforeseen at San Francisco.

European nationalism is no longer so potent a force as previously, but nationalism is rampant throughout much of the Third World. The post-1945 world has witnessed the tortuous winding up of most of the great European overseas colonial empires and the emergence of a virulent brand of Afro-Asian anti-colonialism. Suspicion of European-type colonialism has been overlaid with a hatred of so-called white neo-colonialism. The invidious brand of 'colonial' rule practised by the Soviet Union in Eastern Europe has been largely ignored by most of the leaders of the Third World. The international aspects of human rights and racial questions have also assumed a new, more potent guise. The Israeli problem has replaced the Jewish one, and, looming above all, are the racial antagonisms between white and non-white and, more tragically, among the non-whites themselves.

The inadequacies of the nation-state in the modern age have brought about an expansion of international co-operation, much of it at the regional rather than the global level. The proliferation of regional institutions during the last twenty years or so has been due as much to the nature of many of the problems themselves as to the inadequacies of the UN system. The inadequacies of the UN's security system were largely responsible for the establishment of the regional cold war alliances – NATO, SEATO, CENTO, and the Warsaw Pact – organisations which themselves have now perhaps become anachronisms. Yet the birth of such regional political organisations as the OAU or economic ones like the EEC are as much to do with the aspirations of their member states as the deficiencies of globalism. Chapter VIII of the UN Charter itself allows for and permits regional devolution. The UN's founding fathers, however, had in mind organisations like the Arab League, the OAS, and the OAU rather than ones like NATO and the Warsaw Pact or Comecon and the EEC.

## The Birth and Evolution of the United Nations

Geoffrey Goodwin points out that in the case of the UN not only have expectations and experience failed to coincide, but that the expectations themselves reflect three very different conceptions of the Organization: the first views the UN as evidence of an embryonic world community; the second conceives it as a functional response to increasing inter-dependence in a world of sovereign states; and the third characterises it as a diplomatic instrument for coercion rather than for collaboration. Professor Goodwin contends that all three conceptions were present in 1945 and are indispensable for understanding the UN's evolution since then.

At a very early stage in the Second World War it was decided by the Allied powers that a new post-war organisation would be required to assist in keeping the peace. They rejected suggestions that the League of Nations should be kept in being, either in its existing form or even with drastic modifications. The League was tainted with failure and its believed imperfections too well known. In the United States it was regarded with suspicion, stemming in large measure from the American failure to join the League. Such was American suspicion of the League that at the Atlantic Charter meeting in August 1941, Franklin Roosevelt rejected Winston Churchill's proposal that they include reference to "effective international organisation" in the Atlantic Charter.[3] Most significantly of all, to attempt to resurrect the League would have been an insult to the Soviet Union. Her membership of any new international organisation was deemed essential by both Britain and the United States. Almost the last act of the enfeebled League had been the expulsion of the Soviet Union for its attack on Finland in 1939. The Axis powers had left the League of their own volition.

The immensely detailed and long-term wartime planning for the envisaged post-war organisation, both within the United States and Britain and among the Allies as a whole, was in marked contrast to the lack of planning and inter-allied consultation regarding the establishment of the

[3] See Sumner Welles, *Where Are We Heading* (New York, 1946), p. 15. For an excellent discussion of the Atlantic Charter meeting, see Ruth B. Russell and Jeannette E. Muther, *A History of the United Nations Charter* (Washington, D.C., 1958), Chapter I.

League. While the UN can be regarded as being directed at the Axis powers, its founding fathers avoided one mistake of the Versailles negotiators. Unlike the League Covenant, the UN Charter was not attached to the postwar peace settlement. Of course, after the Second World War there was not a formal peace treaty on the lines of the Versailles model. Professor Goodwin highlights the role of the United States as the UN's chief architect, the Dumbarton Oaks negotiations, and the importance of the Yalta formula regarding Security Council voting.

The small states endeavoured to amend the proposals brought to the San Francisco Conference by the Big Three. Nevertheless, although when the conference opened in April 1945 the strains among them had become more evident, this did not unduly extend the scope for small power initiative. In fact, the Australian attack on the proposed Security Council privileges of the permanent members merely drove them together. The draft proposals of the great powers were changed in certain aspects, in particular those regarding the Economic and Social Council, human rights, and trust and non-self-governing territories. But the San Francisco Conference did not radically alter the Organization, especially its security functions, as set out in the Dumbarton Oaks and Yalta formulas. In essence, the smaller powers had no choice but to accept the *diktat* of the great powers.

In examining the UN's experience to date, Professor Goodwin points out that the world in which the Organization has existed has been marked by both fragmentation and integration; these world pressures being reflected in the changing relations between the UN's principal organs. It is against this background that he looks at power and responsibility within the UN and investigates such problems as the impact of its expanded membership, voting patterns, and the cost of universality. In terms of membership and functions the UN is more of a universal organisation than the League ever was – as Inis Claude has pointed out, the League became in fact a restricted European organisation.[4]

The institutional similarities between the League and the UN are more apparent than real. Although of limited value, the Trusteeship Council is a principal organ of the UN unlike the Permanent Mandates Commission under the League system, while no equivalent of the Economic and Social Council was to be found under the League. In both the UN and the League institutional structures, there are *assemblies* of all the members and *councils* of the privileged few. But beyond this superficial level the respective institutional structures are very different. The League unanimity principle is absent from the UN, and with the latter the functions of the Security

[4] See Inis Claude, Jr., *European Organisation in the Global Context* (Brussels, 1965).

Council and the General Assembly are more clearly delineated in the Charter than was the case with the League Council and Assembly. The extent to which the General Assembly has challenged and encroached upon the prerogatives of the Security Council is probed by Professor Goodwin.

Professor Goodwin also investigates the extent to which the UN can be regarded as representing a burgeoning world community, especially whether its Secretariat symbolises such a community. It was given a more prominent role to play under the Charter than was its League equivalent under the Covenant. In practice, however, the Secretariat's role has depended more on the positive emphasis placed by individuals on their functions and the opportunities for initiative afforded by unique circumstances than on constitutional provisions. Moreover, in many respects its impact has been administrative rather than political in origin.[5] The Secretariat's capacity to influence has been utilised with varying degrees of effectiveness in UN peace-keeping operations, the Organization's involvement in the decolonisation process, and in its economic activities. The symbolic aspect of its activities are possibly more important than their tangible impact.

## The United Nations and the International Legal System

Whereas Geoffrey Goodwin looks at the UN in terms of political relationships, James Fawcett examines its influence in legal terms. He points out that the Organization has been recognised under international law "as a body politic distinct from its members, as a legal person on the international plane, and as the principal for its servants and agents". He suggests that this recognition of the UN as a corporate body has had a number of important political as well as legal consequences, especially regarding the domestic jurisdiction requirements of Article 2 (7) of the Charter.

The argument should not be taken too far, however, as even in the international legal system the UN's role is restricted. Unlike the Commission of the European Communities within the Europe of the Six, neither the UN itself nor any of its principal organs may be a plaintiff before the International Court of Justice, only states may so act. The UN nexus may only ask for Advisory Opinions, a right which has been infrequently exercised. Moreover, on the strictly political plane and again unlike the institutions of the European Communities, the UN is not a supranational organisation in the sense of one whose member states have given its central

[5] The administrative inefficiencies in the UN machine are examined briefly in the section on economic co-operation when discussing the Jackson Report.

institutions the right and the ability to exercise functions and to take decisions independently of and even in spite of the member states in fields traditionally within their preserve.[6] As I have argued in another context, however, the UN does possess an autonomous decision-making ability which contributes towards its role as an international actor, having an impact different from but coincidental with that of states.[7]

Mr Fawcett examines an important characteristic of the UN as an international entity – the status of General Assembly resolutions and the Organization as a primitive legislature in legal terms. He suggests that Assembly resolutions coming within the purview of international law fall into two broad categories: "those which elaborate, formulate or declare standards and principles of state conduct, and those which are specifically designed to further the codification of international law". The first category is important, but perhaps should not be unduly stressed as international legal norms are by no means always readily obeyed or enforced. Even if a majority of states favours an Assembly resolution, that majority might only be a numerical one rather than a majority in terms of population, wealth, or international influence. Mr Fawcett argues that while it is natural to ask what are the effects of Assembly resolutions, this is not the right question. Instead, one should ask what is their cause? He maintains that "on this approach at least, those resolutions, which meet a felt need to declare agreed principles in concise and comprehensible terms, function as a part of international law and are likely to be observed as such".

In considering the codification of international law, Mr Fawcett is especially concerned with the two UN Covenants on Civil and Political Rights, and on Economic, Social and Cultural Rights. His conclusion is that the UN has played a role as a centre for the harmonisation of international law, but that progress has been and is likely to continue to be slow. One disadvantage of the Organization is that it may attempt to formulate rules on a global basis which are only workable, if at all, in more limited confines.

Is there, in fact, a global system of international law? The use of the word *law* to describe both international and metropolitan rules can perhaps itself be misleading in so far as it encourages analogies between inter-state legal processes and those within stable states. Not only are there very different orders of consensus and enforcement, but in the diplomatic milieu there are numerous legal traditions and no universally accepted international legal code. Traditional international law and the international institutions

[6] The *legislative* powers given to the Security Council under Chapter VII of the Charter are considered in the next section on security issues.

[7] See Carol Ann Cosgrove and Kenneth J. Twitchett (eds.), *The New International Actors: the UN and the EEC* (London, 1970), pp. 21–6.

which assist in binding and underpinning the international system are primarily the outcome of the synthesis of the Roman Empire's legal code, the Roman Catholic Church's canon law, the scholastic doctrines associated with Saint Thomas Aquinas, and the rules and practices of the European system of sovereign states. It is no easy task to reconcile this Western-oriented legal heritage with the Communist states' perceptions of law. The Afro-Asian march to nationhood during the last twenty years or so has further complicated matters in that it has culminated in a diplomatic milieu composed largely of states having no deep cultural, sociological, and religious roots in Western civilisation.

Moreover, the functions, competences, and powers of such inter-state judicial authorities as the International Court of Justice, the European Court of Human Rights, and the Court of the European Communities, differ widely. They are superficially similar only in that all are *courts*! Traditionally only states are the subjects of international law, but at least in Western Europe since the Second World War individiduals, business corporations, and international institutions can, in certain circumstances, come under its purview. This essentially emerging regional system is divorced from any emerging global one. The Western European experience is by no means being repeated at other regional levels, although some attempts have been made to do so.

The ICJ is the only principal organ of the UN almost wholly modelled on its League predecessor, the Permanent Court of International Justice. Since he does not consider that the ICJ has made a significant contribution to the UN's role in international law, Mr Fawcett rightly devotes the minimum of analysis to it. The failure to utilise the Court more fully since 1945 is not in itself necessarily a bad thing. The need in many if not most international disputes is political conciliation rather than a legal judgement.

## The Security Functions of the United Nations

The UN's founding fathers intended the Organization to have a leading role in preserving and enforcing international security, this responsibility being vested in the Security Council. Its security functions were based on an institutionalisation of the Allied wartime coalition rather than on the collective security club envisaged by the League Covenant.[8] Although the practice of the League did not conform to the collective security ideal, its collective security provisions (Articles X to XVI) were intended to be the

[8] For a cogent analysis of the UN's security system as originally envisaged, see Inis Claude, Jr., "The Management of Power in the Changing United Nations", *International Organization*, XV. ii (Spring, 1961), pp. 219–35.

heart of the Covenant.[9] But no League institution possessed the explicit autonomous decision-making capacity for maintaining international peace and security given to the Security Council by the UN's founding fathers.

While Chapter VI of the Charter gave the Council the right only to recommend measures for peacefully settling international disputes, Chapter VII gave it the right to undertake direct positive action by ordering the imposition of economic sanctions, the disruption of communications, the severance of diplomatic relations, and the use of military force to prevent or to terminate threats to peace, breaches of the peace and acts of aggression. Such rights were not given to the General Assembly or to the Secretariat, and the Council itself could only *legislate* if there was unanimous agreement among its five permanent members. These veto rights were based on a recognition of the Allied wartime coalition's preponderance of military power. In actual practice it would be absurd if not dangerous to the whole delicate fabric of global security for the Council to attempt to legislate against the wishes of the great powers, particularly the Soviet Union and the United States.

Although this decision-making capacity was to be exercised by an élite group of states rather than the UN as such, it represented a considerable advance on the League system. The latter's Council was hamstrung by the need for unanimity among all its members and had only a limited constitutional role. Article X of the Covenant permitted it merely to "advise" on the means whereby League members were to fulfil their collective security obligations. The provision in Article 47 of the Charter for a Military Staff Committee was another advance on the League system. It was "to advise and assist the Security Council on all questions relating" to its security functions. While intended to provide the Security Council with the executive arm lacked by the League, the Committee was not intended to be an independent supranational body – it was composed of representatives of the Security Council's permanent members.

The Security Council and, indeed, the UN itself have not, however, played the prominent role in preserving international security which was envisaged in 1945, due primarily to the coming of the Cold War and the absence of great power unity. The Military Staff Committee has been dormant since 1947 and the Council's decision-making capacity largely unutilised except for limited and somewhat ineffective economic sanctions regarding Rhodesia's unilateral declaration of independence. The Korean operation was not so much a UN as an American action which only came

[9] For a discussion of the working and deficiencies of the League security system, see C. A. W. Manning, "The 'Failure' of the League of Nations", *Agenda*, I. i (1942). Reproduced in *The New International Actors*, pp. 105–23.

under the UN umbrella as a consequence of the Soviet Union's temporary boycott of the Organization. In fact, the chief lesson of the Korean operation was that a repetition would almost certainly destroy the UN "as it could not again appear to side with one super power in an enflamed conflict of vital Cold War significance".[10]

The operation itself was not authorised by the Security Council, but was recommended by the General Assembly under the American-sponsored Uniting for Peace Resolution of 1950, after the United States had already intervened on the South Korean side. This Resolution did not transfer the Council's primacy in security matters to the Assembly. Chapter IV of the Charter permits the Assembly to make recommendations on security matters only if so requested by the Council or if an issue is not before the Council. The Uniting for Peace Resolution merely permitted the Assembly to make such recommendations if the Council were paralysed by the veto: the Assembly can only recommend, it has never possessed or acquired the right to make binding decisions. The smaller states, however, have attempted to give Assembly resolutions the appearance of bindingness and compulsion by prefacing them with titles like *Declaration*. The great expansion of Assembly membership in the early 1960's conferred a large measure of verbal confidence on these efforts. But the initiative itself was an important factor in deciding the great powers to rely more on a limited use of Security Council procedures. Moreover, the rapid expansion in membership has reacted against the Assembly's acquisition of meaningful decision-making powers in that it has become "a cumbersome, unpredictable, and unmanageable voting machine".[11]

The original security functions of the UN have been augmented if not replaced by the development of UN peace-keeping forces, whether possessing a Council or an Assembly mandate, such as UNEF, ONUC, and UNFICYP. The role of such forces is examined by D. W. Bowett. He points out that whereas many observers in the early 1960's seriously contemplated an expansion of such activities, few would now anticipate much development in the foreseeable future. He investigates the reasons for the *malaise* surrounding these forces and suggests that the failure to develop them has diminished the UN's standing and influence in the world. Dr Bowett does not favour the abandonment of such enterprises as they have a clear advantage in settling certain types of international conflict. U Thant's possibly precipitate withdrawal of UNEF in 1967 and the immediate outbreak of the June war between the Arabs and Israel does not necessarily prove the ineffectiveness of such forces – after all, UNEF did

[10] *The New International Actors, op. cit.*, p. 22.
[11] See Geoffrey Goodwin, "The General Assembly of the United Nations" in E. Luard (ed.), *Evolution of International Organizations* (London, 1966), pp. 42–67.

contribute towards keeping the Egyptians and the Israelis apart during the previous decade.

The bulk of Dr Bowett's chapter is concerned with examining some of the basic issues regarding peace-keeping forces which may need re-thinking if they are to be utilised in the future. He pays particular attention to the constitutional authority necessary to establish a force, the problem of finance, consent to the presence of a force, the principle of non-intervention in intra-state disputes, problems of direction and control, and the limitation of coercion to the exercise of self-defence. His conclusion is that efforts should be made to retain some of the original impetus behind UN peace-keeping forces. "Circumstances, and government policies, can change very rapidly and the possibilities for a new and important UN peace-keeping role in the foreseeable future are quite real enough to make the effort of re-appraisal worthwhile". So far, however, the effectiveness and international impact of UN peace-keeping forces has been limited. They have usually been confined to a few conflict situations either directly or indirectly resulting from decolonisation in which the two super powers have wished to limit their involvement.

## International Responsibility for Dependent Peoples

The UN was not designed as an instrument of decolonisation, at least in the eyes of the European colonial metropoles. Moreover, as Rupert Emerson points out, the UN itself has had a very restricted role in the winding up of the great European colonial empires. UN debates and Afro-Asian anti-colonial pressure within the Organization, however, have played a significant part in creating an international climate of opinion in which European rule over non-white peoples overseas is almost universally condemned, at least with lip service. But neither this change in the acceptability of colonialism nor Afro-Asian pressure at the UN should be over-estimated. Portugal, by far the weakest of the colonial metropoles, has so far managed to retain control over her African empire in the face of both a fierce anti-colonial onslaught at the UN and, more significantly, pressure from her Western allies. In fact it could be argued that UN pressure has perhaps only served to make the white regimes of southern Africa more intransigent than might otherwise have been the case.[12]

In many ways the League of Nations mandates system was more of an innovation than the UN trusteeship system as for the first time definite international machinery was created to oversee the conduct of colonial

[12] For a fuller discussion of this point, see K. J. Twitchett, "African Modernisation and International Institutions", *Orbis*, XIV. iv (Winter, 1971).

administration. The mandates system only applied to some of the colonial spoils of war, not the empires of the victorious allies of the First World War. The only reference to the latter in the Covenant was the obligation in Article 23 (b) whereby League members undertook "to secure just treatment of the native inhabitants of territories under their control".

Under the mandates system the League had the right to receive reports from the administering powers and receive petitions from the indigenous inhabitants. The League's principal overseer, the Permanent Mandates Commission, was drawn from eminent private individuals, not governmental representatives as is the practice of the UN Trusteeship Council. The importance of this League provision is to be seen by the fact that a British citizen, Lord Lugard, vigorously criticised Australia's application of the 'whites only' immigration policy in her mandates.

Nevertheless, the mandates system lacked teeth. Woodrow Wilson's original suggestion that small powers, not the major colonial ones, assume responsibility for the mandates was not really acted upon. Belgium assumed the mandate for Ruanda-Urundi, but the remaining mandates were allotted to Britain, her white Commonwealth, France and Japan – the very states who had conquered these territories, some of whom had desired to annex them outright. The administering powers were in a strong position due to the fact that they conducted the day-to-day administration and League supervision was nominal to say the least. By and large League probing of their administration was not very effective, while apart from the Jewish agency in Palestine, all petitions from the indigenous inhabitants to the League had to be approved by the requisite mandatory. Unlike the UN trusteeship system, there was no provision for League visiting missions to inspect the mandates. Most significantly, the mandates system operated during an era when colonialism was accepted as part of the natural order of things. In Western Europe at least, the prevailing philosophy saw colonialism as merely one facet of the white man's manifest duty to assume the guardianship of his non-white brethren. The one advanced state, the United States, who perhaps might have criticised this colonial ethos, refused both to accept mandatory responsibilities and, indeed, to join the League of Nations itself.

The emphasis of the mandates system was on good government in the sense of law and order rather than on self-government or independence. Positive welfare government was somewhat alien to colonial rule at this time – the philosophy of the welfare state being not yet fashionable even in Western Europe. Article 22 of the Covenant envisaged independence for the Arab nationalities under "A" class mandates. But while Iraq did achieve independence during the League's existence, the remaining vestiges of British control would now be denounced as neo-colonialism rather than true independence. Although independence for the African territories under "B" class mandates was a possibility, this was only envisaged after many generations of continued colonial tutelage. Independence for the "C" class mandates was not really contemplated. They were administered as integral parts of the mandataries' metropolitan territory and even President Wilson apparently countenanced their eventual annexation.

Professor Emerson points out that at the San Francisco Conference the European colonial powers at least did not intend the UN to have a much greater say in colonial administration than had the League. He counsels against over-estimating the UN's role in the evolution towards independence of both trust and non-self-governing territories, but suggests that the ever-increasing anti-colonial group in the General Assembly has from the very start of the Organization's existence used its numerical voting strength to discredit colonial rule. These efforts culminated in December 1960 with the passing of Resolution 1514 (XV) on the *Granting of Independence to Colonial Countries and Peoples* which enshrined the thesis that self-government is intrinsically superior to good government by an alien metropole.[13] Resolution 2105 (XX) of 1965 went so far as to maintain that colonial rule threatened international peace and security and constituted a crime against humanity. Indeed, the fourteenth General Principle of the 1964 UNCTAD declared that colonial status was incompatible with material progress.[14]

Professor Emerson shows how the anti-colonialists have used their voting majority in the General Assembly to attempt to bridge the constitutional gap in the Charter between the UN's functions over trust territories (Chapters XII and XIII) and those regarding non-self-governing territories (Chapter XI). He highlights the activities of the Committee of Twenty-Four, the UN institutional innovation intended to bridge that constitutional gap and to oversee the prompt implementation of Resolution 1514 (XV). In particular, he underlines that the Committee has "furnished the anti-colonials with a meeting place and machinery to co-ordinate their efforts and an invaluable platform from which to broadcast their views to the world at large". He is sceptical regarding both the Committee's achievements and the degree of responsibility exhibited by its members and by the anti-colonial group in the UN as a whole. Overall, it could well be argued that the more virulent brand of anti-colonialism exhibited at the UN has

[13] In particular, "Inadequacy of political, economic, social or educational preparedness should never serve as a pretext for delaying independence".

[14] "Complete decolonisation, in compliance with the United Nations Declaration on the Granting of Independence to Colonial Countries and Peoples and the liquidation of the remnants of colonialism in all its forms, is a necessary condition for economic development and the exercise of sovereign rights over natural resources."

served to aggravate racial tensions by encouraging the striking of postures which place whites on the one side and non-whites on the other. In fact, while the Organization has been used to undermine the ethos of the European model of colonial rule and served as a necessary focal point for the anti-colonial crusade, the actual anti-colonial impact has not always been very constructive.

## International Economic Co-operation and the United Nations

The furtherance of international economic co-operation was proclaimed to be one of the UN's primary objectives in Article I (3) of the Charter. The Organization's intended role in this field was set forth in Chapter IX on "International Economic and Social Co-operation" and in Chapter X setting up the Economic and Social Council. This emphasis on economic co-operation was in marked contrast to the League. Articles XXIII–XXV of the Covenant established only a vague basis for League activities in the general functional area. Apart from the ILO's autonomy, the League system was subject to the central control and direction of the Council. The League undertook some useful work in matters like the control of the traffic in dangerous drugs, but played no real part in attempts to resolve the vexed international economic questions of the inter-war period. The Bruce Committee in 1939 recommended a thorough revision of the League system which envisaged creating a new organ free from Council control and placing greater emphasis on the development of economic and social activities.[15] Although coming too late to have an impact on League developments, the Bruce Report did contribute to the corpus of ideas influencing the founders of the UN.

The concepts, hopes and premises which underlie the UN's excursion into the economic field are examined by Susan Strange. Perhaps the most important contributory factor was the widespread general belief that political security depended in large measure on economic security. The economic uncertainties and instabilities of the 1930's were held to have directly contributed towards the political rivalries and antagonisms which brought about the Second World War. The Anglo-Saxons took the lead in establishing the UN system, but whereas the League's mandate in the functional field was primarily due to British initiative, the United States played the leading role in the Charter's new emphasis on economic and other non-political co-operation. The role of Secretary of State Cordell Hull was particularly prominent in committing the new organisation to

[15] For details of the Bruce Report, see Special Supplement to the *Monthly Summary of the League of Nations*, August, 1939.

the multilateralist conception of the free trade principle and the elimination of discriminatory barriers to international trade. The UN system as it emerged from the San Francisco Conference was based essentially on economic intercourse between industrialised states and designed to tackle the international economic problems of the 1930's. The overall primary goal was security and there was little awareness that the UN would become involved in long-term efforts to aid countries which at that time were still under some form of colonial domination.

Miss Strange scrutinises the impact of the UN and its associated agencies on international economic relations since 1945 and suggests that for the most part this has been merely symbolic. She believes that so far as the West is concerned, the UN's economic system is primarily an instrument for preserving the *status quo* rather than transforming it. Wherever and whenever the accelerating Western economy has needed mechanisms of adjustment, the response has mostly come from outside the UN. But the Western states have made use of UN agencies like the IMF which they control through their financial contributions giving them the deciding voting power. Indeed, the member states collectively, not the institution as such, have sometimes exercised great, even decisive, influence on domestic economic policy. For instance, the deliberations of the IMF's Group of Ten regarding support for sterling in the mid-1960's had far more impact on the British economy than the activities of the so-called Gnomes of Zurich. While the Group of Ten had no formal or direct veto on British economic policy, note had to be taken of their recommendations and criticisms if Westminster wanted continued support for the pound sterling. Overall, however, the Western economic system has been more influenced by regional developments than by the UN system; in particular, by the growth of the EEC.

Miss Strange points out that the UN system has had minimal influence on economic relations between the Communist countries. With regard to East–West economic relations, her submission is that the UN has been impotent and unable to prevent the continued separation of these groups of industrialised states into two international monetary and, in large part, commercial systems. The Organization has certainly not served as a bridge to increase economic co-operation between them.

Miss Strange accepts that the strong and rich states now at least pay lip service to a public responsibility towards the weak and poor countries and that some progress has been made under the UN's auspices to further economic relations between the West and the developing countries. She maintains, however, that the developing countries are not really the partners of the West and that the ethos surrounding the Pearson Report and other references to *Partners in Development* is misleading if not positively harmful.[16] The developing countries are rather the supplicants of the West – they can only cajole not force potential donors to give aid via the UNDP or to grant special preferences under the auspices of UNCTAD. A thin crust of pretension hides a very real inequality.

Miss Strange's cautionary note, as she herself indicates, should not detract from the fact that the recognition of the problems of the developing countries has added a new dimension to UN economic activity. The developing countries want special rather than equal treatment to enable them to tackle their problems of modernisation. The UN provides some assistance which might not be forthcoming if it did not exist. Perhaps more importantly, the Organization provides the developing countries with a forum from which to make the West more aware of their interests and needs. The intrusion of the new dynamic, that of development, into an institutional framework not designed for that purpose, has intensified the UN's growing pains. GATT, the IMF and the World Bank were established with developed rather than developing countries in mind. UN machinery has been modified and new institutions created to take account of the developing countries' problems. ECOSOC has had its membership expanded from eighteen to twenty-seven and has itself become overshadowed by the General Assembly and UNCTAD. Yet while there has been a large expansion of UN multilateral aid and technical co-operation, its volume is still relatively small compared with non-UN multilateral assistance and, more importantly, with bilateral aid programmes.

The impact of UN aid itself is diminished because of deficiencies in the administering machinery. The Jackson Report emphasised that at the headquarters level there is "No 'Headpiece' – no central co-ordinating organisation – which could exercise effective control". The member states have created a UN machine which now extends its activities throughout the world, but "This 'Machine' now has a marked identity of its own and its power is so great that the question must be asked: 'Who controls this "Machine"?' So far, the evidence suggests that governments do not, and also that the machine is incapable of intelligently controlling itself." Although accepting that the Western-controlled IMF and World Bank are "well managed", the Report maintains that the UN's specialised agencies are mostly "the equivalent of principalities, free from any centralised control".[17]

Third World control of such forums as UNDP and UNCTAD has also served to undermine their usefulness in tackling world poverty. The

[16] See Lester B. Pearson, *et al.*, *Partners in Development* (London, 1969), and Lester B. Pearson, *The Crisis of Development* (London, 1970).

[17] See United Nations, *A Study of the Capacity of the United Nations Development System* (Geneva, 1969), vol. I, pp. iii and v.

developing countries have utilised their voting power to set up these institutions and to pass by large majorities resolutions favouring their special needs, but have been unable to compel the industrialised countries to place the bulk, or even a large proportion, of their aid efforts under UN direction. The Western states themselves tend to use OECD rather than the UN framework as a forum for co-ordinating their aid programmes and considering UNCTAD-type proposals. Most of the UN development agencies which have had the greatest success are still Western-controlled, voting power being based on the size of financial contributions rather than on the principle of one state, one vote. These agencies, moreover, have been comparatively free from emotional political issues, unlike UNCTAD and specialised agencies such as the FAO and WHO who perhaps have devoted too much time to condemning the white supremacy regimes of southern Africa.

Another consideration is that the UN system has tended to benefit the more advanced developing countries rather than the more backward ones. For such countries as Chad and Upper Volta it is French bilateral aid supplemented by the benefits of their association with the EEC which contributes most towards their material progress, not the UN system.[18] The needs and interests of the developing countries differ widely and a global approach might not be the answer to all their problems. The UN itself has adopted a regional approach along side its global one – first with the ECE and later with the ECA, ECAFE, and ECLA. Indeed, Robert Gardiner, the ECA's Executive Secretary, has fostered the notion that African economic co-operation should take place on a sub-continental rather than a continental basis. Perhaps what is needed are dialogues and agreements between regional UNCTADs and industrialised states under general UN co-ordination.

Nevertheless, the UN system has made a useful contribution towards making the industrialised states more aware of the needs of the developing ones. While it is true that in some respects only lip-service is paid to the UN's role in the attack on world poverty, this itself is perhaps preferable to that role being openly denied. At the same time, Miss Strange is undoubtedly correct in warning against undue optimism regarding the actual prospects for the UN's Second Development Decade in view of the disappointments of the first one. Yet, as the Jackson Report maintains, the UN system has enormous potential, especially in the twin fields of technical co-operation and pre-investment surveys – potential which might well not be realised because of failures of control and direction in the UN system.

[18] For an examination of African association with the EEC, see Carol Ann Cosgrove and Kenneth J. Twitchett, "The Second Yaoundé Convention in Perspective", *International Relations*, III. ix (May 1970), pp. 679–89.

"It is not that large sums of money are involved – technical co-operation is probably the most economical of all methods of assisting development. The real reason is the great inertia of this elaborate administrative structure which no one, it seems, can change . . . change is now imperative."[19]

## From Globalism to Regionalism

The proliferation of regional institutions during the last twenty years or so has transformed the international system and, as has already been indicated, had a considerable impact on the UN. The UN Charter itself makes far more concessions to the regional impetus than did the League Covenant. Although the League became in effect a European regional organisation half-heartedly undertaking a supposedly global role, the Covenant rejected regionalism, due in large measure to "the Wilsonian tendency to identify regionalism with war-breeding competitive alliances".[20]

The survival of this Wilsonian attitude was primarily responsible for the Charter being based on globalist principles – world peace and economic co-operation being believed to be indivisible. Despite President Roosevelt's early flirtation with the regional premises underlying his conception of the great powers acting as world policemen, the United States played the leading role in the apparent victory of globalism. Cordell Hull, in particular, believed that not to adopt a global approach could leave the way open for the United States to slip back into isolation through concentrating on policing the Western Hemisphere. Nevertheless, the globalists were forced to reach an uneasy compromise with the regionalists. Concessions had to be made to Winston Churchill's belief in reliance upon regional groupings as the "massive pillars" of the new world organisation. He advocated a two-tier UN with a central organ at the global level underpinned by regional arrangements.

Moreover, at the San Francisco Conference there was a demand from some regionally committed states for recognition of their existing arrangements – notably from the participants in the Arab League, the British Commonwealth, and the inter-American system. But, as Inis Claude has pointed out, "The Charter reflected the premise that the United Nations should be supreme, and accepted regionalism conditionally, with evidence of anxious concern that lesser agencies should be subordinated to and harmonised with the United Nations".[21] This philosophy underlies the Charter's references to regional arrangements in Article 51, Chapter VIII

[19] *A Study of the Capacity of the United Nations Development System*, vol. I, p. ii.
[20] See Inis L. Claude, Jr., *Swords into Plowshares*, 3rd rev. ed. (London, 1965), p. 106.
[21] *ibid.*

(Articles 52–4), and Article 103. Charter obligations were to prevail in the event of conflict with regional ones.

The phenomenon of regionalism and the underlying factors which have led to the mushrooming of regional institutions in the postwar world are examined by Ernst Haas. He investigates the significance of regional arrangements for world peace, world economic welfare, and global cohesiveness as a whole. His overall conclusion is that regionalism does not necessarily detract from the UN's importance. Regional peace-keeping activities themselves, he believes, are likely to decline in importance whereas economic ones are likely to become even more important in the future.

The UN itself, as has already been indicated, has adopted a partial regional approach in the economic and other functional fields. Moreover, throughout the North Atlantic area generally, Latin America, the Arab world, and Black Africa, there are numerous mechanisms for the peaceful settlement of international disputes whose constitutions make general references to the supremacy of UN procedures. But when quarrels between the members of such organisations as the OAU reach the UN, this is usually only after regional procedures have been exhausted. In fact, in some respects the UN has become the disposal bin for regional insolubles. In the Western Hemisphere, the United States has taken care to ensure that threats to American interests are dealt with in the OAS where her view is almost certain to prevail rather than in the UN where she might be criticised severely, if not out-voted.

The fragmentation of the contemporary world combined with the regional impetus has led to a partial resurrection of Winston Churchill's wartime proposals for a two-tier UN. Lester Pearson made suggestions along these lines in his 1968 Reith Lectures. Mr Pearson based his ideas partly on the precedent provided by the fact that "in the economic and social field, the practice has been growing of delegating responsibility and authority to United Nations regional commissions". One objection to his proposals, as he himself recognised, is that such a Charter revision "would require an amendment to the Charter" and "the veto operates in respect of amendments".[22]

Another objection is that while such proposals "are at least theoretically realisable in Western Europe, possibly Latin America, and even Black Africa, for a long time to come they will probably be unrealisable for the Middle East and South East Asia. In these two areas particularly, there is minimal consensus among the leading states and the major threats to security come from within the regional systems themselves".[23] Indeed,

[22] See Lester Pearson, *Peace in the Family of Man* (London, 1969), pp. 85–6.
[23] See Kenneth J. Twitchett, (ed.), *International Security: Reflections on Survival and Stability* (London, 1971), p. 43.

apart from the Europe of the Six and perhaps Western Europe as a whole, it is doubtful whether any other regional systems possess sufficiently developed "core areas" for viable "security communities" to evolve in the foreseeable future.[24] But who thirty years ago would have foreseen the EEC, let alone the OAU? In so far as regional institutions exist, and especially if they develop further, they are likely to undermine the global approach to world politics even more than they have already done.[25]

## The Powers and the United Nations

The impact of the UN on the international system is primarily a function of the importance which states attach to it in the formation of their foreign policies. Much will obviously depend on the historical traditions and interests of particular states, the internal and external pressures acting on them at any one time, and their responses to what are essentially a series of unique events. Two general points can be made.

The first is that almost all states attach some importance to membership of the Organization, even if only because the UN is useful as a diplomatic sounding board. Many states who, for a variety of reasons, are not members, have observer status, contacts with the specialised agencies, and are parties to the Statute of the ICJ. South Africa remains a UN member in spite of constant vilification in the General Assembly and suspension from the work of many of the specialised agencies, as departure would leave her even more isolated than she is already. Unlike their practice with regard to the League of Nations, no great powers have left the UN, despite misgivings about its apparent objectives and the direction in which they were evolving. The United States' initiative over Korea in 1950 demonstrated that it was not in the Soviet Union's interest to be absent, even if only temporarily. For the majority if not all of the new Afro-Asian states, moreover, UN membership is a jealously regarded symbol of their sovereignty.

The second is that while the UN budget is primarily financed by a handful of industrialised states, most states devote a considerable amount of money, skilled personnel, and time to UN affairs. The Western in-

[24] Ernst Haas has ably probed the importance and significance of the *core area*. His pioneering work is reproduced in *The New International Actors*, pp. 76–92. I use the term *security community* as existing when there is an absence of violence between two or more states who have attained a feeling of community in both the *Gemeinschaft* and *Gesellschaft* senses, sufficient for them to develop "institutions and practices strong enough to ensure, for a 'long time', dependable expectations of 'peaceful change' " among them. My definition is adapted from that used by Karl Deutsch and his associates in *Political Community and the North Atlantic Area* (Princeton, 1957), p. 5.

[25] This aspect is discussed by David Mitrany in the last chapter of this book.

dustrialised states, for example, spend more of these resources on UN affairs than they do on relations with, say, Nepal, Nicaragua, and Niger. For many of the developing states who cannot afford to maintain diplomatic representation throughout the world, the UN is *the* forum for their international diplomacy. It has provided them with a platform from which to exercise a collective influence they would not otherwise possess.

League membership was not valued so highly. Although Germany during the early years of the Weimar Republic attached considerable importance to obtaining membership, following the American failure to join the League none of the leading states of the inter-war period gave it a very high priority in foreign policy formation. Even in the case of the Weimar Republic it was not League membership *per se* which was important, but rather the international acceptability that it would represent. Britain and France were the only two great powers to be members of the League throughout its existence. While some small states perhaps attached more importance to League membership, their interests and actions were of little account compared with those of the great powers during the inter-war period.

The importance which the varying groups of UN member states attach to the Organization is discussed by Geoffrey Goodwin. He suggests that the West has been inclined to use the UN to multilateralise and to legitimise its differing interests. Despite some of their more idealistic if not hypocritical declarations, the success and welfare of the Organization has not become a core value in their actual foreign policy formation. While they dislike adverse UN criticism, the passing of favourable resolutions in the General Assembly is a relatively minor policy objective. Professor Goodwin describes Soviet ambivalences towards the UN and points out that it is probably not very important in Communist eyes. For Moscow, it does not represent an embryonic international community which should be encouraged to grow, but is rather a treaty relationship among states which has come to be useful as a platform for criticising the West and for wooing the new Afro-Asian states. He argues that the latter have exerted pressure in three main directions since the early 1960's: to attack racial discrimination and to assert the right to self-determination, to use their voting power to attempt to secure concessions from the industrialised states, and to exert pressure against Western European colonial rule and the white regimes of southern Africa.

F. S. Northedge scrutinises Britain's role in the UN's development and the importance attached to it in the making of British foreign policy. He points out that League supporters in Britain were more fervent and intense in their enthusiasm than UN supporters have been. But while there has not been a notable positive identification, there is a negative commitment in the sense that Britain is a *status quo* power who stands to gain from international institutions designed to inhibit violent international change. Her role in such institutions, however, has been diminished coincidently with her declining status as a world power. In particular, whereas Britain along with France dominated the League system, both have played essentially secondary roles at the UN.

Professor Northedge illuminates the underlying importance of the British diplomatic style in Britain's responses to UN developments and pressures. The makers of British foreign policy do not place much faith in the *forensic* diplomatic style. The employment of emotional propaganda in 'goldfish bowl diplomacy' is alien to the British diplomatic tradition, whether in the form of Communist uses of the UN to vilify the West, or African endeavours to use the Organization to condemn utterly the remaining vestiges of Western European colonialism and the white regimes of southern Africa. He then examines another important related facet of the British tradition – the belief that "in the last resort it is the mutual relations between the greatest powers of the day, not the speech-making or the votes of a host of small and weak countries" which determine "the outcome of the supreme issues in world affairs".

The domestic considerations influencing British policy-stands at the UN are also probed by Professor Northedge. He pays particular attention to differences of nuance between the Conservative and Labour parties and points out that while neither actually questions British membership of the UN, there is an underlying difference in the public utterances of the Conservative and Labour leaders. Traditionally the Labour party has been committed to internationalism, whereas the Conservative party has been inclined to put British interests first and to emphasise that it was for Britain alone to determine whether her policies were in accord with obligations under the UN Charter. Of course, the actual practice of the Labour party when in office has not departed from this line, except perhaps in style or lip-service paid to internationalism.

Edward Heath's speech at the commemorative session for the UN's twenty-fifth anniversary, was based on the underlying premise that Britain's Charter obligations would be interpreted by the British government, not by majority opinion in the General Assembly. His speech also reflected a general *malaise* regarding the UN's actual achievements and a distinct *ennui* regarding the value of its public deliberations.[26] This disillusion with the Organization is prevalent throughout the Western world. The interim report of President Nixon's commission for the observ-

[26] Speech delivered at New York on 23 October 1970. Official text distributed by the Central Office of Information, 1970.

ance of the twenty-fifth anniversary stated bluntly that the UN "is becoming increasingly incapable of dealing with the grave issues troubling the world". The report paid tribute to the Organization's achievements in promoting political, economic, and social development, but maintained that it did not possess the required means or vitality to tackle the graver underlying problems or those over which "the interests of the super powers clash". Overall, "too many national governments have either given lip-service to the principles of the Charter or interpreted them for petty advantage and narrow self-interest".[27]

This dissatisfaction with the UN is neither new nor confined to the Western states. The President of the General Assembly's twenty-fourth session, Miss Angie Brooks of Liberia, in her Presidential address reiterated the almost mandatory ritualistic account of the Organization's achievements and value, especially to small states. She also warned against the *mythology* of achievement – "there was a failure to realise that neither oratory nor agreements between delegations, nor resolutions or recommendations had had much impact on the course of world affairs".[28] The UN has provided the African and other Third World states with a central forum from which to exercise a collective vocal influence on world affairs, greater than if they had argued separately thousands of miles apart. The African states, in particular, have several remarkable achievements to their credit. Without large-scale African membership of the UN, for instance, such international *goods* as the Convention on the Elimination of All Forms of Racial Discrimination might not have come into existence. Conversely, African anti-colonial incantations at the UN, primarily directed at satisfying domestic elements of xenophobia, have contributed towards the growth of Western dissatisfaction with the Organization.

The African states themselves tend not to place so much importance on UN membership as they did formerly. It still symbolises their sovereign equality with the former colonial masters, but even the more militant African states now place less emphasis on the Churchillian drama of world affairs and concentrate more on their complex internal problems of modernisation. Concentration on day-to-day issues of development could well result in UN affairs as such being given a lower priority in African policy formation in the future. This is especially likely if African regional institutions become more capable of fulfilling their members' interests and needs than they have so far.[29]

[27] For the main conclusions of the interim report, see *The Times*, 14 September 1970.

[28] See *UN Monthly Chronicle*, VI. ix (October 1969), p. 35.

[29] For a fuller discussion of the importance of the UN to the African states, see Kenneth J. Twitchett, *op. cit.*

Such a down-grading of the UN in African policy formation would obviously have important repercussions for the work of the Organization. The impact, however, is unlikely to be so great as if the United States either reduced her commitment to the UN or withdrew it altogether. The Organization's achievements so far have largely rested on a combination of American moral support and massive financial contributions. A significant down-grading of the UN in American eyes has already been evidenced. The previously mentioned interim report to President Nixon pointed out that American public support for the UN had dropped considerably – "Five years ago, opinion polls showed that 84 per cent of the public regarded the Organization as the last best hope for peace. Today that figure has dropped to 51 per cent."[30] The American financial commitment to the UN system is scrutinised and criticised even more closely by Congress and the Nixon Administration than was so previously. The last American ambassador to the UN was an able career foreign service officer, Charles Yost, without the international or American national standing of his predecessors, Henry Cabot Lodge, Adlai Stevenson, and Arthur Goldberg. President Nixon has now nominated George Bush for the post – a minor Republican from Texas who was defeated in the 1970 Senate elections. President Nixon himself in his addresses and references to the Organization emphasises American interests rather than UN principles and achievements. Certainly, no American leader would now describe the UN as the *keystone* of American foreign policy as the late John Foster Dulles once did. Indeed, Mr Dulles's comment itself was one of ritualistic obeisance rather than conviction. American policy-makers are at least now more honest in their public utterances regarding the UN.

## An Overall Survey

The last chapter in this book is an assessment of the UN in historical perspective by David Mitrany, whose own teaching, writing and general expertise have contributed so much to twentieth-century efforts to build a more stable and peaceful world based on co-operation between states. Professor Mitrany was an early advocate of and worker for the establishment of the League of Nations, while his classic text, *A Working Peace System*, and other writings gave birth to a new school of thought on international co-operation – the functionalist school. He argued that "states find it worthwhile to co-operate in many non-political matters which could stimulate a closer consensus between them . . . [and] that to identify and capitalise on those functional areas where states co-operate is a more

[30] See *The Times*, 14 September 1970.

positive approach to the human predicament than merely negative attempts to avoid war".[31]

In his contribution to this book, Professor Mitrany begins by examining the origins of the state of crisis which appears to have become endemic in UN affairs. He distinguishes two separate sources – between difficulties arising from the Charter and hence the working of the UN itself and those brought about by events in the world outside. He then examines the problems attendant on revising the Charter, the regional impulse and functional devolution, and the authority of the UN in law-making for the world. In the light of this perspective he considers the UN's historical task to promote a truly global community and the realities of world politics, and concludes with a survey of the Organization's future prospects.

Professor Mitrany's chapter commences by pointing out that "the UN might well claim 'I struggle, therefore I live', even if its state of crisis may appear to have become endemic". This apparent crisis has been a factor in causing the Organization's prospects to be viewed with increasing pessimism and gloom in recent years. But the UN is not the only political creation of man which now seems somewhat irrelevant to the needs of his ever-expanding scientific and technological capacity. Internal governmental procedures and even the very *raison d'être* of the nation-state itself are subject to increasingly critical scrutiny. In fact, while the UN may have been overtaken by progress in science and technology, even at the beginning of the twentieth century the truncated and restricted Organization which exists today would have been widely viewed as the revolutionary dream of idealists. For all its faults the UN has had a much greater international impact than the League of Nations ever did. Indeed, when seen in historical perspective, it is surprising that the UN has achieved so much in the mere twenty-five years or so of its existence.

The UN does represent an important centre of international activity, existing alongside but not dominating states. It has had a significant impact on the international system coincidental with that of states – the impact being primarily symbolic and a function of its all-pervading role. Its functions have shifted in the general flux of world politics. Like its predecessor the League, the UN was originally designed primarily to preserve the international *status quo*, but has become more of a barometer for registering evolutionary global transformations, especially in issues relating to colonialism and international economic co-operation. It has had only a marginal, though significant, role in preserving international peace and security. Yet UN peace-keeping in particular does rest on an implicit

[31] Quoted from *The New International Actors, op. cit.*, p. 16.

rudimentary consensus that events should neither be dominated by the great powers alone nor be allowed to run their *natural* course.

The UN's global role is diminished by the general lack of consensus and deep cleavages of interest between its member states. In turn this has been a principal cause of the growth of regional institutions outside the UN framework on whose well-being many states place a higher priority. Certainly, there is not the community consciousness which can sometimes be detected at the regional level, especially in the Europe of the Six. Some European League of Nations societies, albeit unsuccessfully, did press their national governments to base their international relations on Covenant principles. At present, however, there is a lack of influential pressure groups who endeavour to persuade their governments to give the UN interest precedence over separate national ones. Such groups as the Campaign for Nuclear Disarmament, the anti-Vietnam War and anti-apartheid movements, and the numerous organisations pressing for a more meaningful attack on world poverty, unfortunately appear to believe that the UN as it exists is largely irrelevant for promoting their particular cause.

Is the UN as we know it today appropriate for the contemporary world? The interim report to President Nixon maintained that "the UN may not be in danger of immediate collapse, but that co-operation among the permanent members of the Security Council is vital to the Charter".[32] Nevertheless, in some respects it is perhaps fortunate that the Soviet Union and the United States do not have too much faith in the Organization as an international instrument for furthering their policy objectives. Already as the General Assembly has become unwieldy with the growth of small power membership, the emphasis of UN affairs has shifted back to the Security Council where American and Soviet views tend to be paramount. The Brazilian Foreign Minister, José de Magalhaes Pinto, warned against this development in the General Debate of the twenty-fourth session of the General Assembly: "Often an issue is transferred from the General Assembly to the smaller Security Council, because the idea prevails that, in the final analysis, it might be more advisable and realistic to leave the matter to the discretion of the super-Powers, as if a new world directorate had already been established."[33] The United Nations might well become more effective if the emerging détente between the Soviet Union and the United States should grow into a *rapprochement* such that they become close enough to use the Organization as either an instrument of or a cloak for their joint actions. But this effectiveness might well be in the form of a tyranny. Admittedly improbable, although still possible.

[32] *The Times*, 14 September 1970.
[33] See *UN Monthly Chronicle*, VI. ix (October 1969), p. 115.

If Peking should eventually take the Chinese seat in the Security Council, this would almost certainly detract from any American-Soviet efforts to use the UN as the instrument of their joint rule. But could the UN survive the likely disruptive effects of Communist China's admission, coming as it would after the disruption caused by East-West cold war rivalries and the militant anti-colonialism of the Third World states? In fact, should the Organization be a more representative and effective instrument of world government? It was certainly not designed as one. Is not the UN of more international value as it is now – a partial microcosm of world politics in which member states go through the motions of co-operation, largely symbolic but also making a significant if marginal contribution to international well-being?

The UN has often been condemned for inactivity and lack of achievement, not only regarding the fundamental questions of peace and war and the attack on world poverty, but also regarding the recent spate of international hijacking of civilian aeroplanes by individual malcontents and by organised terrorist groups. But we cannot blame the UN as such for this lack of achievement; the responsibility rests squarely with the member states. Yet if the Organization should stand still and fail to keep abreast with the challenges presented by the changing world, like all creations of man it will stultify and wither. Although the scientific and technological revolutions have added to the strains of the UN, they also offer possibilities of challenging new spheres for international co-operation and action in fields like the conservation of the natural environment, dealing with drug abuse and the hijacking of civilian aeroplanes, and as a centre for harmonising international relief regarding natural disasters such as the 1970 Peruvian earthquakes and the floods in East Pakistan.

Obviously, the existing UN structure is not adequate for fulfilling all the Organization's existing functions, and needs some refashioning especially if it is to be given new functions. For example, should the UN be re-structured to gain added strength from rather than be weakened by the forces of regional devolution as at present? Unfortunately, it is much easier to suggest what should be done than to agree on criteria for change, let alone obtain the member states' acceptance of proposed changes. But the possibilities and opportunities for change must be considered. So long as the UN struggles, it survives; it might one day succeed in becoming the basis for a truly more peaceful world. At the moment it does offer a prospect for peace.

# 2. THE UNITED NATIONS: EXPECTATIONS AND EXPERIENCE

Geoffrey L. Goodwin

EXPECTATIONS and experience rarely coincide. Nor have they in the case of the United Nations. Moreover, in this case expectations reflected three quite differing conceptions of the character of the Organization. Thus one set of expectations supposed that it was part of the institutional infrastructure of a burgeoning world community. Just as General Smuts had seen the League of Nations as "not merely a paper constitution, but a living human society", so in 1945 the constitution of the UN, buttressed by a thickening network of technical or specialised agencies and international non-governmental organisations, was held to demonstrate the existence of a nascent *Gemeinschaft* whose members would be increasingly tied together in "an intimacy of conduct, an interdependence of welfare, and a mutuality of vulnerability". As its instrument and expression the Organization was to be an "entity in itself, a synthetic but separate actor on the international stage, created by states and dependent upon them for its survival but capable of acting in its own right".[1]

A second view of the UN was that it constituted a response to the tensions inherent in a twentieth century diplomatic system; a system marked by a growing degree of technological interdependence, but still politically based upon the sovereign state. The tensions between technological interdependence and political fragmentation necessitated instruments or mechanisms for collaborative action between states. But their proliferation testified not to the emergence of a modicum of community mindedness amongst the members of the international political system, but to their continued attachment to state sovereignty, an attachment qualified only by their reluctant recognition of the sheer inconvenience – and often risks – of a refusal to collaborate on a wide range of day-to-day matters ranging from postal charges to air traffic rules. Collaboration was seen, therefore, as the price of co-existence, not as a step to closer community.

[1] Inis L. Claude, Jr., "The United Nations, the United States and the Maintenance of Peace" in Lawrence S. Finkelstein (ed.), *The United States and International Organization* (Cambridge, Mass., and London, 1969), p. 71. See also Carol Ann Cosgrove and Kenneth J. Twitchett (eds.), *The New International Actors: The UN and the EEC* (London, 1970).

A later and harsher variant on this instrumentalist or mechanistic view of the UN was to see it as a diplomatic instrument not for collaboration but for coercion, a cloak for the attempted dominance by one state or group of states over others, or, conversely, as a diplomatic lever manipulated by the powerless to extract concessions from the powerful. In both cases the Organization was pictured as an arena of competition in which the requirements of collaboration had to take second place to the particular state or ideological interests of the contestants.

It is the contention of this chapter that all three views of the Organization were operative in 1945 and are indispensable to an understanding of its experience over the last twenty-five years.

## SAN FRANCISCO AND THE FOUNDING FATHERS

In the early 1940's as the whole world became engulfed in war, the sense of "the pity of war and the pity war distilled" strengthened the passionate concern "to save succeeding generations from the scourge of war" and to fashion a future international order no longer so prone to human folly and human greed. The sense of horror evoked by the bestialities of genocide and the flagrant disregard of human rights by the Nazi regime strengthened the search for a 'common law of mankind' under which the rights of the human person, whether individual or in association with his fellows, could be more effectively protected.

Little less vivid were the memories of the human waste and degradation of the 'Great Depression' of the 1930's, which was also held to have contributed to the psychological conditions conducive to the growth of militarism and totalitarianism; to the spread of an economic nationalism which had helped to exacerbate international political relations; and to a failure to heed the pleas of the economic 'have-nots' which were held to have encouraged them to turn to military means to attain their ends. Consequently much of the initial planning for the future peace was focused on the economic foundations of that peace. This was reflected not merely in the setting up of the United Nations Relief and Rehabilitation Administration, but also in the United Nations Conference on Food and Agriculture in May 1943, in the Bretton Woods meeting of July 1944 to set up the new monetary and financial institutions, and in the International Labour Organisation's Philadelphia Conference of May 1943.

The blueprints that emerged from these conferences reflected not only the expectation of eventual victory, but also the supposition that in the post-war world there would be a far greater disposition to collaborate amongst the war-time allies than had obtained in the past. In any case, whatever private doubts they may have harboured, most Allied leaders well knew that in order to sustain morale amongst a weary and often battered population such expectations of better things had to be sedulously cultivated if the war effort was to be maintained.

Initially, Allied thinking focused on the notion of a continuing grand alliance which would be supported by a number of regional councils subordinated to it. This grand alliance, in Winston Churchill's words the 'Supreme World Council', or the 'Four Policemen' as Franklin Roosevelt termed it, would assume responsibility for ensuring that the defeated Axis powers never again threatened the peace and for maintaining that peace in what was anticipated to be an otherwise very largely disarmed world. Fears that the stress on regional councils might encourage renewed American isolationism deprived the regional emphasis of much of its attraction. Nevertheless, in the Dumbarton Oaks proposals of 1944 the continuing 'Armed Concert' of the victorious Allied powers which was to be invested with supreme responsibility for the maintenance of peace was not only to be embedded in a "larger organisation and subjected to the restraints of an orderly constitution",[2] but it was also to be buttressed by regional arrangements.

For the United States the planning of the future international organisation had a high priority – possibly too high. President Roosevelt, having been weaned away from his earlier preference for regionalism, was now persuaded that the new Security Council might help to draw the Soviet Union more effectively into the collective handling of all the myriad problems that would arise in the post-war world – an aim of supreme importance to him. The Dumbarton Oaks proposals for special agreements, later to become Article 43 of the Charter, under which each state would undertake to make available armed forces and facilities to the Security Council, would also ensure that the United States would not have to take the full burden of any military action called for by the Council. The economic and social provisions, together with the proposals of the Bretton Woods Conference, would serve as a step towards the post-war multilateral world trade and payments system which could put an end to the discriminatory arrangements which had grown up in the 1930's; Secretary of State Cordell Hull and many Americans denounced these arrangements as not merely an impediment to American economic and trading interests, but also as a potential source of international political conflict.

Britain's most immediate and special concern was with the future of Europe. Yet it was clearly incumbent on Britain to do everything possible to preserve and strengthen the close wartime co-operation between the

[2] Sir Charles Webster, *The Making of the Charter of the United Nations* (Creighton Lecture, University of London, 1946), p. 21.

United States and herself and also as far as possible to encourage the Soviet Union to remain in close association with both. Whatever doubts there might be about particular American proposals,[3] to accept American leadership in post-war planning might commit the United States more firmly to an active part in the post-war world. The spectre of renewed American isolationism or policies of 'back to normalcy' was never absent from British thinking. Thus the British proposal for a military staff committee (later Article 47) was motivated in part by the desire to perpetuate the exceptionally close co-operation that had been achieved during the war between the United States and Britain and in the hope that Soviet membership might reduce the barriers to effective military liaison which had been so frustrating during the wartime operations.

Soviet attitudes must, of course, be more a matter of conjecture. The main Soviet preoccupation appears to have been to ensure that the new organisation could not be turned into an instrument of the capitalist imperialist powers against the socialist camp and, even if it were, that the Soviet Union could effectively safeguard its interests. Otherwise, the Soviet Union's interest was to preserve the Grand Alliance (in the form of the Security Council) against a possibly resurgent Germany and to gain an entrée into Anglo-American military planning through the abortive Soviet proposal for bases for United Nations use and the successful proposal (later Article 45) for national air force contingents to be immediately available for combined international enforcement action.

The Dumbarton Oaks proposals therefore reflected the widespread concern to build a peace worth fighting for; the concept of a continuing 'armed concert' of Allied powers which would exercise collective responsibility for maintaining that peace; and the particular and in many ways diverging interests of the negotiating countries. That these interests could be effectively reconciled owed a great deal to two major factors. The first was that at the time the main threat to international peace in the post-war world was expected to come from the existing enemy states, in particular Germany. To guard against such an eventuality was a matter of common concern to all the Allied powers. The second factor was that the manner in which the new Security Council was to arrive at its decisions was not agreed upon at Dumbarton Oaks. It was not therefore clear under what circumstances the elaborate machinery for economic and military sanctions could be set into operation. Was the new 'armed concert' to be able to act only against resurgent enemy powers and against an occasional refractory small state or could it be brought to bear against one of its own members? The

[3] For instance, the American proposal for a separate Economic and Social Council was questioned; see Geoffrey L. Goodwin, *Britain and the United Nations* (London, 1957), pp. 17–8.

former view was embodied in the Yalta Agreement of February 1945 under which a distinction was drawn between recommendations for the peaceful adjustment of disputes and decisions relating to the use of enforcement measures. No great power (i.e. permanent member) could on its own prevent discussion of a dispute to which it was a party; but no great power could be subjected to enforcement measures (Article 27). This distinction had been proposed by the United States and its acceptance reflected a considerable concession on the part of the Soviet Union. The privileged position now accorded to the great powers might arouse misgivings, but it was the price that had to be paid to secure American and Soviet participation in the new organisation.

At the San Francisco Conference which opened in April 1945 the strains in the wartime alliance had become increasingly evident. Yet a concerted attack on the privileged position of the five great powers[4] on the Security Council, led by Dr Evatt of Australia, merely drove them together in defence of that position and led them to spell out the implications of the Yalta voting formula in a manner which in effect extended the unanimity principle to a rather wider area of voting. Not all the smaller powers deplored the veto provisions. To some they provided a safeguard against their own involvement on the side of one great power or group of great powers against another great power. The veto could also put a premium on negotiations between the five permanent members which might redound to the advantage of all.

Nevertheless, the growing realisation that in the event of dissension between the permanent members the security provisions of the Charter could not be relied upon, inevitably provoked a search for alternative security measures which would not be subject to the authority of a divided Council. One approach was to exempt action against any ex-enemy state (Article 107) or measures of individual or collective self-defence[5] against armed attack (Article 51) from prior Security Council authorisation. Another was to enhance the powers of the General Assembly, which was given the right to discuss and to make recommendations upon any questions or any matters within the scope of the Charter, subject only to recognition of the primary responsibility of the Security Council in matters of international peace and security (Article 12). *Power* might be held to reside in the Security Council under the Charter and it would be incumbent upon members to carry out its decisions (Article 25); but if the Council were

[4] France had joined the private discussions of the four (i.e. including China) sponsoring powers of the San Francisco Conference, though she had refused to become one herself.

[5] Including measures under regional pacts such as the Act of Chapultepec concluded in March 1945 between Latin American states.

hamstrung the Assembly, as the "town meeting of tomorrow's world", could provide an alternative forum for security issues and also encourage a more dynamic approach to the problems of peaceful change.

The status of the Economic and Social Council was also enhanced and a good deal more stress was placed upon the provisions on human rights. And it was, of course, at the San Francisco Conference that the provisions for trust territories and for all non-self-governing territories were added. These reflected a compromise between the anti-colonialist pressures which made themselves more keenly felt than at Dumbarton Oaks and the determination of the colonial powers not to allow their responsibilities to be diluted whilst accepting an obligation to *account* to the Organization for the manner in which they exercised those responsibilities.

The declaration on non-self-governing territories embodied in Chapter XI was designed in part to meet the pressure to bring all such territories under UN surveillance. But in other respects the trusteeship provisions did not differ very materially from the corresponding mandate provisions of the League of Nations (other than in the exclusion of strategic areas at the insistence of the American Defense Department). Yet the debates did indicate how very different the atmosphere for the discussion of these issues was likely to be from that in the League of Nations. In the latter the colonial powers' influence predominated; in the UN the two leading members, the United States and the Soviet Union, were avowedly anti-colonialist and there was a growing number of other members who could be expected to be openly critical of any form of European colonialism. At that stage anti-colonialist pressure might be muted, but it was already beginning to make its weight felt.

The San Francisco Conference did not radically change the shape of the Organization as set out in the Dumbarton Oaks proposals. The permanent members were able to get their way – not merely on the issue of their voting rights in the Security Council, but on virtually every other issue on which they were agreed.

Reactions to the San Francisco Charter were mixed. In the United States there was some inclination to think of the new organisation and its institutions as "devices to make the world safe for basically peaceful, satisfied, and progressive – if not entirely democratic – nations; the UN Charter implied the American Way of Life writ large".[6] Yet neither in the United States nor elsewhere was the Charter received with unqualified approbation. It was very widely realised that whatever additional powers had been given to the Assembly or to the Economic and Social Council, the

[6] Ernst B. Haas, *The Web of Interdependence: The United States and International Organizations* (New Jersey, 1970), p. 3.

Charter security system was built around a continuing armed concert, the members of which seemed increasingly to be at variance with each other. Moreover, although the advent of the atomic bomb seemed to emphasise the need for such an organisation the question now was whether in a nuclear world the conceptions and assumptions on which delegates had worked at San Francisco were still valid.

## TWENTY-FIVE YEARS ON TRIAL

### A World of Change: Fragmentation and Integration

At the same time the world in which the UN was to function was expected to be, if not the 'One World' of Wendell Wilkie, at least a more integrated and peaceful one than that of the pre-war period. The Organization would be upheld, it was widely supposed, by the continued common interest of the victorious powers in preserving peace; by the growing economic and technological interdependence of mankind; and by general acceptance of the principle of national self-determination for dependent peoples both as an act of justice and as a contribution to world order. All three suppositions have in practice proved of questionable validity over the last twenty-five years or so.

Not only was the 'armed concert' torn asunder by the pressures of the Cold War with only a brief interval after victory, but with the demise of European imperialism and the rise of Asian and African peoples to full statehood, the world has become politically, culturally and ideologically increasingly fragmented. In 1945 there were 51 original members of the UN; by 1970 with the influx of Asian and African states its membership has risen to 127. This political atomisation of the world has been accompanied by the cultural fragmentation of world society – as indigenous cultural systems have revived and Western-trained élites have seen the reins of power and influence slip steadily from their grasp. The consequent strains on the international system have been accentuated by the clash of ideologies which purport to ignore national frontiers, but whose very doctrinal rigidity is apt to thwart any but the most modest attempts at international collaboration.

To some extent this process of fragmentation has been paralleled by forces which have made for integration. Dag Hammarskjöld could in 1961 cite the pledge in the Charter "to save succeeding generations from the scourge of war" – a pledge given urgency by the advent of nuclear weapons – and members' acceptance of the principles of equal political rights and economic opportunities as giving substance to the notion of an incipient international community. True the notion itself might be only fitfully reflected in the behaviour of states. Yet the strains inherent in the bipolar system which has characterised much of the last twenty-five years have been mitigated by the sense of a common peril posed by the nuclear arms race; few have been able to escape the pressures of technological change which have propagated a common economic ethos of industrialisation and in the realm of communications have made for a political awareness which can link a riot in Berlin or Tokyo or Kent, Ohio, with a "tactical excursion" into Cambodia or can turn a policy of *apartheid* in South Africa into a matter of international concern. Few in 1968 would have dared to speak of the crisis in Czechoslovakia, as Chamberlain did in 1938, as a "quarrel in a faraway country, between people of whom we know nothing". There has, therefore, been a process of integration as well as of fragmentation. Integration psychologically and technologically; fragmentation: politically, culturally and ideologically.

Yet it is the processes of fragmentation which have been reflected most markedly within the UN itself. Apart from the early demise of the 'armed concert' of great powers, the rapid influx in the late 1950's and especially early 1960's of the newly independent Asian and African states into the Organization, most of them with very differing interests and priorities from those of both the West and the Soviet Union and a massive voting power which could ensure that these interests could not go unregarded, has turned the UN into a much more complicated, unwieldy, and often cantankerous body than could have been envisaged in 1945.

It is true that the preponderant influence of the United States – and its allies – in the first ten years of the Organization's existence did somewhat conceal the implications of this process of fragmentation. This was the period in which the UN became, especially during the Korean War from 1950 to 1953, very much a vehicle for the "multilateralisation of American national interests". As thereafter the process of decolonisation began to accelerate the UN became an arena of competition between the West and the Soviet Union for the sympathies of the still largely non-aligned Third World. In the process it became the beneficiary of the concessions which the United States and, to a less extent, the Soviet Union were willing to make in order to cultivate the sympathies of, or 'fraternal association' with, this increasingly numerous Asian and African membership, for it was through the UN that the latter sought to make their presence felt. Yet this period of 'competitive co-existence', though it gave a certain coherence to the bargaining process in New York and elsewhere, did tend to over-estimate the sensitivity of the central balance to Third World pressures and to under-estimate both the tensions and divisions within the Third World itself and the volatile and unpredictable character of politics within so many Third World countries. As this has become evident the UN's ability to act as an instrument for the powerless in wresting concessions from the powerful has tended to diminish or at least been called into question.

## Continuity and Change in the United Nations Structure

### *The Security Council and the General Assembly – rivals or partners?*

These changing world pressures have been reflected in the changing relationships between the principal organs of the Organization. The early period of Cold War brought about the near disintegration of the Security Council and ensured that the Chapter VII machinery of the Charter with its Military Staff Committee and military agreements was virtually set aside in favour of alliance systems sheltering under the umbrella of Articles 51 and 107. There were exceptions. The Security Council played a role in helping to secure a ceasefire in Kashmir in 1949 and armistice agreements in the aftermath of the Palestine War in 1948–9. And a truncated Security Council endorsed President Truman's decision of 27 June 1950 to commit American air and sea forces to the defence of South Korea. One important *de facto* revision of the Charter was also introduced, it should be noted, by the Soviet Union, namely the practice of not counting the abstention of a permanent member as a negative vote.[7]

Nevertheless, the plight of the Security Council inevitably led to moves to shift some of its responsibilities on to the General Assembly. The 'Uniting for Peace' resolution of 3 November 1950 in effect tried to build within the ambit of the General Assembly machinery which, although only recommendatory, could be invoked if the Security Council itself was hamstrung by great power dissension. The General Assembly's enhanced status did provide greater scope for mediation both by the Arab-Asian group during the Korean War and by others during the Suez crisis, but for the most part Assembly majorities were used to give Western policies legitimacy – and so wider diplomatic and domestic support – in the eyes of as many United Nations members as possible.[8]

However, with the influx of Asian and African states in the late 1950's and 1960's, the balance of voting power within the General Assembly began steadily to undermine the position of the Western powers and particularly of the European colonial powers. General Assembly resolutions became less concerned with the issues of what to most appeared to be a dying Cold War and more with accelerating the process of European de-colonisation and

[7] The Soviet Union initiated the practice in April 1946 when it abstained on a resolution to consider whether Franco's Spain constituted a threat to international peace.

[8] Ernst B. Haas, *op. cit.*, p. 38.

with affirming the illegitimacy of all forms of Western racism or colonialism. "The Western 'mechanical majorities' of which the Soviet had so long complained were replaced by Afro-Asian 'non-aligned' majorities which, on the one hand, for the most part refused to endorse any action to which either the United States or the Soviet Union strongly objected and, on the other, showed an increasing disposition to recommend far-reaching measures in certain fields of primary concern to themselves – Southern Africa, human rights, development and trade – even if they lacked the authority or the resources actually to carry out these measures."[9] Ultimately, however, the effectiveness of Afro-Asian pressures turned on the sensitivity of the Western powers to them. By the later 1960's, as the central balance became more stable and power generally more diffused, that sensitivity appeared to be on the wane. In any case, the realisation was growing that although the General Assembly might prove a useful instrument of pressure and barometer of diplomatic moods and needs, only the Security Council could serve as an effective vehicle for collective action by the great powers, and especially by Washington and Moscow, to implement many of the measures sought by the Afro-Asians as well as to safeguard world peace.

The 1960's therefore were to see a certain reversion to the Security Council. Thus the initial resolutions for setting up the Congo force of July 1960, the Cyprus force of April 1964, the calls for a ceasefire in the Indo-Pakistan War of 1965 and in the Six-Day War in the Middle East in June 1967, as well as the resolution of 21 November 1967 looking to a longer-term settlement of the Middle East dispute, all emerged from the Security Council rather than from the General Assembly. Even over Southern Africa attention has been shifting from the General Assembly's condemnatory resolutions to the much more difficult question of whether the Security Council's permanent members are prepared seriously to consider how these resolutions might be implemented.

Experience suggests that when there is an element of détente in great power relations the permanent members' veto powers do put a premium on negotiation and on arriving at consensus. Moreover, the Security Council, as compared with the General Assembly, is, in Ambassador Goldberg's words, a "negotiating body and not a debating society" for in it power and responsibility are much more closely linked. The dominant position of the United States and the Soviet Union is generally acknowledged, even if sometimes resented, while the rather special position of the other two effective permanent members, Britain and France, is certainly not al-

[9] RFD, "Unilateral and Multilateral Options in Foreign Policy", in Lawrence S. Finkelstein, *op. cit.*, p. 189.

together ignored. It is true that as a result of the expansion of the Security Council in 1966 there are now more elected members – ten out of fifteen instead of six out of eleven as previously. Nevertheless, the elected members do often in effect speak for particular groups of states who are thereby given some voice, if only indirectly, in the Council's deliberations. A consensus on the Security Council is, of course, no guarantee of compliance – far from it. Nevertheless, in many ways in the 1960's there has been a steady reversion to the original Dumbarton Oaks concept of a Security Council embodying an 'armed concert' of great powers with primary responsibility for safeguarding world peace. There is indeed renewed interest in resuscitating a modified Military Staff Committee and military agreement procedure (Article 43) to strengthen the collective role of the great powers in peace-keeping matters. The General Assembly would remain a body of last resort, but would otherwise be mainly a diplomatic sounding board and 'kindergarten in peace'.

### *The Economic and Social Council – An Essay in Fatuity?*

Originally intended as a "separate, technically competent, but political level body to deal with economic affairs"[10] and elevated at San Francisco to a 'principal organ' of the UN, the Economic and Social Council has been beset by the increasing tendency to fragmentation in the world economy. It has only rarely shown signs of a level of technical competence comparable to that found in most of the Specialised Agencies. Moreover, it has been increasingly overshadowed by the General Assembly's second (Economic) and third (Social) Committees, and by semi-autonomous bodies such as the United Nations Conference on Trade and Development and the United Nations Industrial Development Organization set up by the Assembly itself, to the point where it retains little more than the tattered mantle of a 'principal organ'.

The picture is not wholly bleak. The Council played a leading part in setting up the system of regional economic commissions and has helped towards a reasonably satisfactory balance of responsibilities between these commissions and the headquarters in New York and Geneva. It has convened conferences, such as the World Population Conference in Belgrade in 1965, of real research and educative value and it can claim some credit for putting the Organization's development (mainly pre-investment and technical assistance) activities on a rather more viable footing.

[10] A State Department proposal of 1943 quoted in Walter R. Sharp, *The United Nations Economic and Social Council* (New York, 1969), p. 72.

Nevertheless, the Council has suffered so acutely from the steady trend towards more limited regional arrangements (whether in the Organisation for European Economic Co-operation, the Organisation for Economic Co-operation and Development, the European Economic Community, or the Latin American Free Trade Area) and from the relatively greater operational significance of the Specialised Agencies, that it has been virtually by-passed by the main stream of international economic relations. In addition, its capacity to 'co-ordinate' the activities of the Specialised Agencies has almost foundered on the twin rocks of the Council members' evident incompetence to give coherence and point to their own activities and of the determination of most of the agencies to guard their autonomous status as jealously as any sovereign state.

Nor has the Council been free from the 'forensic diplomacy' so common in the General Assembly, while the influx of new states from Asia, and particularly Africa, in the 1960's led to long and heated denunciations that the Council was unrepresentative of the now expanded membership of the UN and to the setting up of such bodies as UNCTAD (as a rival to the General Agreement on Tariffs and Trade), UNIDO and the virtually still-born United Nations Capital Development Fund as more or less autonomous bodies accountable primarily to the General Assembly. Nor has the enlargement of the Council's membership in 1966 from 18 to 27 or the holding of meetings at a ministerial level done much to arrest this steady diminution of its authority.

The vacuity of the general debates, the insatiable demand of some delegates (especially from the less developed countries) for yet more documentation (the volume usually being in inverse proportion to its quality and relevance) and their inclination to deal with problems by setting up yet another committee or conference – providing more soft jobs and tourist jaunts – suggests that the problem for some time past has been less with re-invigorating the Council than with 'damage prevention' to really worthwhile bodies like the United Nations Development Programme and with exploring ways by which the unwieldy Assembly committees could be enabled to handle their economic and social responsibilities more effectively.

### *The General Assembly and Colonialism – The End of the Road?*

In the 1960's, however, economic and social matters (other than economic aid which is seen as a form of restitution for past colonial exploitation, and human rights which are interpreted almost exclusively in terms of the right to national self-determination or to racial equality) have had generally to take second place to the preoccupation of the Afro-Asian majority in the

General Assembly with eradicating the 'scourge of colonialism and white racism'. As colonialism is the subject of Professor Emerson's chapter, this is not the occasion to examine the United Nations' part in accelerating – or possibly complicating – the 'contraction of Europe'. Suffice it to say that in the process the UN has acted as both 'midwife' and 'wet-nurse' and the General Assembly has acted as a focus of discontent, a standard by which to measure the shortcomings, real or imaginary, of the colonial powers. By and large, most of the Western colonial powers have accepted, reluctantly in some instances no doubt (as in the case of South-East Asia and Algeria) the eventual goal of independence for their overseas dependent peoples. Differences have more often been over timing – important though that is – than over long-term objectives. The situation in Southern Africa is, for obvious reasons, very different. The present white-majority regimes in power intend to hold on to that power, by hook or by crook. And the receptivity of those Western powers who alone might be able to weaken their hold to Afro-Asian pressures, whether inside or outside the United Nations, is closely circumscribed by economic and strategic considerations. Here is a ready-made formula for mounting frustration and exasperation – and a consequent turning away from the UN on the part both of those under pressure and those exerting pressure – while the situation within Southern Africa itself steadily deteriorates. Nor does experience so far suggest that recourse to the Security Council is likely materially to change the situation. One outcome is that the opportunities for other forms of external intervention may well multiply.

## Power and Responsibility

### *The Impact of Expanding Membership*

In any international organisation most members will tend to seize upon those aims – set out in this case in the Purposes and Principles of the Charter – most closely in line with their own particular national interests. The organisation is there, as they see it, primarily to further or to legitimise those interests rather than to propagate some rather nebulous concept of the 'general interest'. All that can be expected – though it is, in fact, to expect a great deal – is that in their understanding, interpretation and pursuit of these interests they will not be so short-sighted and egotistical as altogether to preclude a concern for the interests of their fellow members – a sense of 'good neighbourliness' if you like – even possibly a sensitivity to the needs of what a handful might acknowledge to be a burgeoning world community. It is inevitable, therefore, that the objectives of a General Assembly of 127 members (70 of which are Afro-Asians) will be very different from those current at the time of the San Francisco Conference.

Each new member will, in fact, inject its own particular aspirations and anxieties into the Organization together with a determination to see that they do not go unregarded. As its membership has grown, so therefore has the list of problems with which the UN is expected to deal and the range and diversity of views as to the appropriate means for doing so. The problems of scale are as pertinent at the international as at the domestic level. Not only is any initial homogeneity of outlook and approach unlikely to survive a rapid process of expansion, but with the admission of a succession of mini-states the hierarchy of power becomes more sharply differentiated, the sense of alienation between powerful and powerless more marked, and the gulf between the experienced craftsman and the raw apprentice painfully apparent. That the General Assembly has not been more volatile and unpredictable as a result of its rapid expansion owes a great deal to the growth of groups whose voting patterns show some consistency of approach. Within these groups some preliminary adjustment of views is also easier to achieve and an apprentice newcomer can briefly shelter to learn his craft.

Acute problems, both of size and structure, remain however. The sheer size of the General Assembly puts a premium on exhortatory resolutions supposedly expressing a diplomatic consensus – even, some would dare to claim, the 'opinion of mankind' – but often cast in such vapid generalities as to defy respect. In its committees close and detailed scrutiny of concrete problems is easily overlaid by the verbosities of ill-informed demagogues intent on self-advertisement or of manipulators concerned with vote-catching rather than with substantive issues. Problems of structure are no less acute. The Western powers' resentment at the antics of the Committee on Colonialism and the less developed countries' continual suspicion of even an enlarged ECOSOC inhibits effective sifting of these issues before they reach the Assembly committees as a whole, while the very plethora of specialist sub-committees and other bodies with more limited membership tends both to create a sense of confusion and to overtax the resources of all but the dozen or so well-endowed delegations. The wonder is that so many General Assembly resolutions make a good deal of sense. But they are, of course, only recommendations which states have to weigh alongside other considerations – assuming that they pay any attention to them at all. At present the General Assembly's conduct of business is in such disrepute that the weight most of the resolutions carry is minimal. A drastic overhaul of the Assembly's structures and procedures aimed at encouraging a greater sense of responsibility and seriousness of purpose is essential if there is to be a greater readiness on the part of member states to treat its resolutions seriously.

The impact of expanding membership is most acutely felt in the General

Assembly, but the Security Council has not been altogether immune. Since the Council's own membership was expanded from eleven to fifteen in 1966 it is theoretically possible on a procedural issue for the ten elected members to outvote the five permanent members.[11] More serious is the situation where, as Richard Gardner points out, "despite the Charter stipulation that members be chosen with regard to their contribution to the maintenance of international peace and security, six of the ten elected members (in 1970) currently pay the minimum 0.04 per cent towards the expenses of the Organization".[12] This is both another argument for the creation of semi-permanent seats (as in the League Council) for middle powers such as Japan, India and Brazil, and another instance of the great disparity between voting power and real responsibility for implementing decisions which stem from the egalitarianism of the "one state, one vote" principle at the UN – of the United States and the Maldives, each having one vote.

### *Voting – An Irremediable Scandal?*

The anomalies of this voting system are well known. They are, of course, compounded by the introduction of majority voting into the UN (as compared with the unanimity rule in the League of Nations) and by the analogy so often misleadingly drawn between majority rule within a parliamentary democracy and majority rule in an international institution.[13] The difficulties are particularly acute when the majority (whether the United States and some of its allies in the early 1950's or many of the Afro-Asians in the 1960's) use their numerical voting power to steam-roller a resolution through with little regard to minority interests or, indeed, to the likelihood of compliance. However obvious it may seem in the outside world, the distinction between voting power and real responsibility for implementing recommendations or decisions tends to become blurred in the corridors of the UN, where even an 'illusory voting victory' can give a welcome boost to a delegation's ego. There is also the absurd situation of "taxation without adequate representation" as Richard Gardner points out, whereby "the five permanent members plus Japan pay two-thirds of the United Nations' costs, yet members whose total contributions equal 4½ per cent of the budget control two-thirds of the votes".[14]

Nevertheless, whatever the intrinsic merits of the alternative of weighted

[11] Nine votes instead of seven now constitute a majority on the Security Council.
[12] Richard N. Gardner, "Can the United Nations be Revived?", *Foreign Affairs* (July 1970), p. 666.
[13] Geoffrey L. Goodwin, *op. cit.*, pp. 211–20.
[14] Richard N. Gardner, *op. cit.*, p. 671.

voting (as found in the International Monetary Fund and World Bank), it would be extremely difficult to obtain agreement on the precise weighting. Which criteria should be used in computing voting strength – population, national or per capita income, territorial area, etc.? If the weighting were based on a single factor only it would give an entirely false picture of the relative importance of states. If several factors were taken into account, how much importance should be attached to each? And so on and so forth. At least the present majority voting system prevents UN bodies (other than the Security Council) from being hamstrung by the calculated obstructionism of a small minority. There is also in practice a great deal of 'mental weighting'. That is, delegates look very carefully at the composition of the votes behind resolutions to assess the diplomatic weight of the majority and the extent and intensity of the minority's opposition. This mental weighting needs to be supported, however, by setting the membership of subsidiary bodies of the UN (such as UNCTAD) so as to allow for a careful balancing of group interests and by providing within such bodies (as again in UNCTAD) procedures for 'consensus' and 'conciliation' which can mitigate the vagaries of majority rule.[15]

### *The Cost of Universality*

At San Francisco, original membership was limited to those who had participated in the struggle against the Axis powers. Subsequent applicants were expected to satisfy both two-thirds of the General Assembly and the Security Council (where the veto would be operative) that they must (a) be states, (b) be peace-loving, (c) accept the obligations of the Charter, (d) be able and (e) be willing to carry them out. Up to the package-deal of 9 December 1955 only nine new members had been admitted and twenty-one states had had their applications rejected (mostly as a result of Soviet vetoes). Thereafter as the process of decolonisation accelerated the flood gates were open. Virtually every newly independent state demanded membership as of right and others paid little heed to the obligations it entails. One result has been to admit well over a dozen 'mini-states' with populations of under 500,000 who cannot in any real sense meet all the criteria of Article 4 (1) of the Charter. And there may be quite a few to come. The presence of such states further aggravates the gap between voting power and real power. The mini-states have usually added to Afro-Asian voting power, which is already strong enough to block any down-grading of their status. Nevertheless, "one measure already under consideration would be to offer the mini-states associate membership in the Organization with the privilege of circulating documents and addressing

[15] Ernst B. Haas, *op. cit.*, p. 82.

meetings, but without the privilege of voting and the burden of paying a share of UN expenses".[16]

Even with the presence of the mini-states the UN remains a *would-be* world organisation. The seating of the People's Republic of China, accompanied or followed by the admission of the divided states of Germany, Korea and Viet-Nam, would turn it into a more authentic diplomatic meeting place and mirror of world trends – even of an embryonic world community. Inevitably these states' absence lends an air of unreality to debates on, for instance, disarmament or European and Asian security issues. Yet the price of admission might be high. Each would bring with them an array of new issues which could prove highly disruptive. In particular, Communist China's (and probably North Korea's and North Viet-Nam's) basic objectives and approach appear as yet to be fundamentally different from those of the Charter and indeed from those of the great majority of present members. This may change; if not, Communist China's presence on the Security Council would almost certainly destroy the fragile consensus – based on a measure of accord between Washington and Moscow – that has recently emerged. In that case the General Assembly might be drawn back into the centre of the stage, even on security matters. It is not an encouraging prospect, for so long as the present discrepancies between voting power and real power – between votes and responsibilities – persist, the Assembly's voice is liable to be badly out of tune with – and the UN to be a very distorted mirror of – realities in the world at large.

## WHO WANTS WHAT AND WHO GETS WHAT?

### An Instrumentalist View

To those who see world institutions as essentially diplomatic artifacts – diplomatic instruments – used by member states primarily to further their own particular national objectives, it is what states actually do rather than the evolving pattern of institutional relations that matter most. The question then is whether a would-be world institution such as the UN is able to encourage member states to pursue their interests with some consideration for the interests of others or whether it tends to excite and accentuate their more self-seeking and egotistical inclinations.

#### *The 'Multilateralisation' of Western Interests*

In the first decade of the Organization the United States often seemed to think of the UN as little more than a supplementary arm of Western defence. Although several countries, Britain in particular, clung to the hope

[16] Richard N. Gardner, *op. cit.*, p. 666.

that it could serve as a centre for conciliation and mediation in East-West relations, the Western powers for the most part 'used' the UN in four main ways: (a) to legitimise Western policies, (b) to act as the West's 'proxy' in near-crisis situations, (c) as a face-saving device, and (d) as a depository for unresolved or embarrassing problems.

The first is illustrated by the way the initial wrangles at the UN over Iran and Greece demonstrated publicly the marked deterioration in great power relations and so eased the way to the enunciation of the Truman doctrine and to the legitimisation of that doctrine by enabling it to be presented as both consonant with the Charter's aim and yet necessitated by the demise of the Charter's security system. The Security Council's endorsement in June 1950 of President Truman's decision to commit air and sea and then land forces to the defence of South Korea and the resolution of 7 July setting up the unified 'United Nations' command conferred legitimacy on that operation and so helped to allay uneasy domestic questioning within the West and to mobilise wider diplomatic support. In more recent years Britain's attempts to secure the imprint of legitimacy on successor regimes in Malaysia and South Arabia came to naught, but various UN plebiscite supervisory groups helped to give a certain temporary legitimacy to post-colonial regimes in West and Central Africa. The price of securing legitimacy is to accord others a minor leverage over the policy legitimised. This price has usually been both modest and salutary.

The Western powers have, in the second instance, been able to use the UN as their 'proxy' by supporting the Organization's intervention in situations where their interests appeared to be threatened, but not to the extent of warranting unilateral intervention. The United Nations Observer Group sent to the Lebanon in June 1958 could be described as a less embarrassing alternative to the landing of American troops (as was to happen little over a month later) to bolster up an American-favoured regime in the face of alleged Syrian infiltration. Indeed, American support (especially logistic and financial support) has been so crucial both in mounting and in shaping the style and course of several UN peace-keeping operations (particularly that in the Congo) as to make them appear little more than an adjunct to United States diplomacy.

The UN has, in the third instance, acted as a face-saving device for the West, as in November 1956 when the formation of the United Nations Emergency Force opened up a respectable line of retreat for Britain and France. In the late summer of 1958 the General Assembly greatly facilitated the withdrawal of American forces from the Lebanon and British forces from Jordan. Over West Irian the Dutch arrived at a face-saving formula for their withdrawal through the intermediary of the UN.

In the fourth and last instance the UN has been used as a dumping ground for apparently insoluble problems. Thus in 1947 Britain unloaded the question of the future of Palestine on to the General Assembly and subsequently shunned virtually all responsibility for the outcome of its action. To refer a problem to the UN may, of course, hold out a reasonable possibility of solution, as did the Council of Foreign Ministers reference to it in 1948 of the future of the former Italian colonies. The danger is that only too often the states concerned use the UN as a camouflage for the absence of any coherent policy or cast upon the Organization tasks of great difficulty and then deny it the means to handle them.

No positive action may, of course, be desired. Western intervention in the case of the Hungarian crisis in 1956 was far too perilous to be seriously contemplated. Yet domestic public opinion in the West was incensed by the brutality of the Soviet occupation; mere passivity would have brought a torrent of criticism on their political leaders. By seizing the UN of the matter and by securing a suitable condemnation of the Soviet action public pressure could be allayed. Similar considerations obtained in January 1968 at the time of North Korea's seizure of the USS *Pueblo* and during the Soviet occupation of Czechoslovakia in August 1968. This use of the UN helped to give the impression something positive was being done and so helped to siphon off pressure which might have damaged the slow process of détente between Moscow and Washington which was otherwise beginning to emerge.

Attitudes within the Western world, both within and between states, have often differed sharply on a wide range of issues, especially on issues of colonialism. Nevertheless, broadly speaking most Western states in the first decade or more saw the UN as, in a sense, 'their' Organization which could help preserve an international order of which they were the main beneficiaries. Although it was occasionally used by them in a one-sided (e.g. anti-Soviet) and irresponsible (e.g. Palestine 1948) manner, they had in the process to define their interests in a manner as consonant as possible with the objectives of the Charter and with the wishes of the majorities whose support they sought. In the 1960's, as the Organization's expansion – and growing diversity of purpose – undermined earlier Western pre-eminence they have had to 'learn' to redefine their objectives and tactics accordingly. In this the United States has been more successful than most. Nor should it be forgotten that the fact "that the Organization exists and functions at all is due more to the United States than to any single nation".[17]

[17] H. G. Nicholas, "The United Nations in Crisis", in *International Affairs* (July 1965), p. 443.

*Soviet Ambivalences*

In Soviet eyes the UN is probably of no great significance. From its early minority position the Soviet Union constantly stressed that the Organization was not an "embryonic form of world government which should be encouraged to grow", but rather a "treaty relationship between the powers, and particularly between the Great Powers, which should be held within a strict construction of its contractual terms". Consequently, it insisted on strict adherence to the Charter and particularly on the preservation of the primary, even the exclusive, responsibility of the Security Council in the realm of international peace and security.[18] Attempts by the West to extend the General Assembly's authority were denounced as "an unsubtle attempt by the United States to conceal its imperialist manipulation of the world by a transparent international screen". Similarly, the Soviet Union has seen the Secretary-General as more the servant of governments than the *persona* or executive head of a world body.

There are, of course, ambivalences and contradictions in Soviet attitudes to the UN as in those of any other power; and the precise role of ideology in Soviet policies is difficult to assess. Yet even in an era of co-existence there still appears to be a revolutionist perception of the UN as merely one arena for the struggle between the capitalist and socialist camps in which the contradictions between the capitalist imperialist powers and also the contradictions between those powers and the emergent forces of the Afro-Asian world can be exploited. But it is a struggle inhibited by the mutual interest of the contestants in survival in a nuclear-charged world. Consequently, and especially in the peace-keeping field, the Soviet Union has been ready to turn occasionally to the UN as a possible means of reducing the risks of a nuclear confrontation as a result of the escalation of local conflicts.

Moreover, the influx of Afro-Asian states into the UN in the 1960's coincided with the Party directive to cultivate 'fraternal association' with the new Afro-Asian nations and to afford support for national liberation movements as a socialist international duty. The Soviet Union had not always appreciated that in the 1960's the UN occupied a rather more important place in the thinking and expectations of newly independent states than in those of the Soviet Union. But generally Soviet delegates have gained a good deal of diplomatic kudos by their support of Afro-Asian anti-colonial pressures and initiatives on Southern Africa and race issues generally. Moreover, just as in the days of decolonisation the Soviet Union may have anticipated that the withdrawal of colonial regimes would leave a power vacuum they could exploit (as they attempted in the Congo

[18] A view constructively reflected in Soviet initiation of the practice of abstention.

and have successfully achieved in South Yemen), so Soviet support for liberation movements appears to be motivated not only by the desire to stir up trouble between the Western powers and Afro-Asian peoples, but also to create situations which again they could turn to their advantage. But the situation is increasingly complicated by Sino-Soviet rivalries within the national liberation movements themselves. The verbal militancy shown by the Soviet Union may be motivated as much by the need to match up to Chinese pretensions as by any strong commitment to those movements. In the last few years the Soviet Union also seems to have shared the disillusion of the Western powers in closer involvement with much of the Afro-Asian world. Soviet protestations of support for Afro-Asian viewpoints continue, but there are some signs that the Soviet Union gives at least equal precedence to the cultivation of practical arrangements of détente with the United States. In the process "a certain functional division of labour [may have] been devised for the Security Council and the General Assembly. On matters of shared interest and concern with the United States the Soviet Union will turn to the Council; on matters reserved for competition and rivalry Moscow will employ the General Assembly".[19]

### *Afro-Asian Pressures*

There have been marked differences of objective and approach among the Afro-Asian states. Nevertheless, since the early 1960's Afro-Asian pressures have been exerted in three main directions. The first has been to secure the outlawing of all forms of racial discrimination and to declare the interpretation of human rights almost exclusively in terms of the right to national self-determination. The pressure has yielded the Convention on the Elimination of All Forms of Racial Discrimination and also the two Covenants of Human Rights. It is too early to say what impact the 'norms' enshrined in these international instruments will have on the actual practice of states – a framework for action, a goad to backsliders, a smoke-screen for the delinquent? The second has been the attempt to set up within the UN itself counterparts to the Bretton Woods bodies – the rich men's clubs – in which, on the principle of 'one state, one vote' their voting power could be exercised more effectively to secure concessions from the economically powerful. UNCTAD, UNIDO, and the Capital Development Fund are instances of this attempt. It cannot be said that it has yielded much fruit.

The third, and main, pressure in the 1960's, however, has been directed against the last pockets of West European colonialism and more particularly

[19] Vernon V. Aspaturian, "Soviet Foreign Policy at the Crossroads", in Lawrence S. Finkelstein, *op. cit.*, p. 60.

against the white minority regimes in Southern Africa. The Declaration 1514 of December 1960 has been held not only to 'illegitimise' colonialism, but also to legitimise collective enforcement action against recalcitrant colonial powers or white minority regimes. The latter line of argument was reflected in the almost unanimous Afro-Asian support of the use of force by the UN Congo force against the 'neo-colonialist' secessionists in Katanga in 1961–3 and in Indian justifications of their seizure in December 1961 of Goa. "Colonialism", Mr Krishna Menon asserted, "was permanent aggression"; the Indian invasion of Goa was therefore a legitimate mission of liberation. In subsequent resolutions three main propositions have received overwhelming numerical support from the Afro-Asian powers and their sympathisers. The first is that Portuguese attempts to maintain her rule in her African territories constitute a colonial war against the peoples of those territories; similarly, *apartheid* is held to constitute a threat to international peace, as does the continuance in power of the "illegal racist minority regime" in Rhodesia. The second is that force can properly be used to put an end to these situations; it would not be in breach of the prohibitions of Article 2 (4) since it would be fully compatible with the Purposes and Principles of the Charter. In the case of Rhodesia (Zimbabwe) Britain has indeed been repeatedly criticised for her unwillingness to use force. In the case of South Africa the Afro-Asians have argued that action under Chapter VII is essential and that mandatory economic sanctions are necessary to secure an end to *apartheid*. The third point follows logically, namely, the call for assistance for liberation movements in the territories concerned, which might be able to bring about sufficient bloodshed and disorder to justify external intervention, preferably, but not necessarily, through the UN. The same kind of considerations apply to South West Africa (Namibia); in October 1966 the General Assembly asserted that the territory should come under the direct responsibility of the UN and the Security Council has been charged to find means to give effect to this demand.

The difficulty is, of course, that as in the early years of the Cold War the arithmetical majorities which the Afro-Asians can mobilise in the General Assembly do not reflect actual power relationships. As Alan James remarks: "States who are most zealous in identifying and condemning sin do not possess the wherewithal for its eradication."[20] The only states, mainly the Western ones, capable of exercising effective power have not been prepared to do so. Pressure by the UN may have also sometimes had the opposite effect to that intended. For instance, by undermining the position of moderates in Southern Rhodesia or by closing the ranks of 'whites' of

[20] Alan James, *The Politics of Peacekeeping* (London, 1969), p. 404.

almost every political hue in South Africa behind the *apartheid* policies of the Republic's leaders. Moreover, the aim behind majority Afro-Asian pleas for strong enforcement action is now not so much the reform of existing policies as the overthrow of existing regimes. Such an aim may well be justified; but it is at present impracticable.

Given the ignominies many African peoples have had to endure, Lord Caradon was surely right when he once said that it is astonishing that "so many African leaders have so consistently preached and practised not hate and violence, but tolerance and co-operation". But the continuing inability of the UN to assist appreciably in the achievement of any of their objectives is bound to excite acute frustration and a search for instrumentalities other than the UN. In such a situation revolutionary forces, whether emanating from Moscow, Havana or Peking, are bound to prove increasingly attractive.

## A Burgeoning Community?

In the past twenty-five years or so the UN has acted as an instrument of, and an influence upon, both the great powers and the Afro-Asian members. Apart from helping to 'legitimise' Western policies it has provided the Afro-Asian members with an instrument of pressure with which they have been able to secure some minor concessions from the powerful, if only because it has enabled them to "act on the imagination and conscience of a great nation", that is, of the United States, whose public, as Conor Cruise O'Brien rightly remarks, has been brought up to believe that it believes in having a "decent respect for the opinions of mankind". But a similar sensitivity has been shown by others, even occasionally by the Soviet Union, and not only, it would seem, on grounds of diplomatic expediency alone.

How far, however, has the Organization been able to serve as an instrument of collective action on behalf of a burgeoning community of mankind? Experience suggests that here the cementing force is not so much good will as fear – "Man is a creature civilised by fear of death" – and the pressures of technological innovation. Not only has the technological revolution made the co-ordination of states' activities an absolute necessity across a wide range of daily matters, but the widespread awareness of the unparalleled threat to mankind from the continuing nuclear arms race and of the need for a concerted effort to underpin "the delicate balance of terror" if a nuclear holocaust is to be avoided does help to create a sense of a common predicament from which the UN has been a beneficiary.

As Conor Cruise O'Brien writes, "the so-called balance of terror and not the existence of the United Nations remains the primary guarantee against the outbreak of world-wide conflict. That guarantee, however, is not so secure and so perfected that humanity can afford to neglect the use of secondary guarantees, leaving the primary guarantee in the instincts which protect the survival of the species time to do their work. This is the sphere of the United Nations, the ritual at the brink".[21]

Thus in several crisis situations the UN has been influential in securing a cessation of hostilities, as in Indonesia in 1949, in Kashmir in the same year and later in the Indo-Pakistan War in 1965, and in the successive Arab-Israel rounds as well as earlier in 1948–9. It is true that such pressure as the Organization can effectively exercise is primarily a function both of great power diplomacy and of the vulnerability of the contestants, both diplomatically and domestically, to any pressure, individual or collective, they are prepared to exert. Nevertheless by internationalising a crisis the UN can "bring into play . . . certain very ancient responses, tending in Lorenz's terms to 'inhibit' through 'ritualising' those aggressive actions that are injurious to the survival of the species".[22] It is this ritualisation of crisis situations that may help to put a premium on restraint and negotiation.

UN peace-keeping forces, the subject of Dr Bowett's chapter, have constituted a form of executive action on behalf of the international community. The early hopes that their role would steadily develop have, however, been belied by the continuing opposition of the Soviet Union, France and several other countries to making financial contributions to operations of which they do not approve and to endowing the office of the Secretary-General with the kind of executive functions which would enable future operations to be less of a prey to day-to-day political pressures. It is true that a certain psychological receptivity to this kind of UN alternative to unilateral great power intervention has been created. Nevertheless, within the super powers' 'spheres of interest' – of 'responsibility' – the UN is excluded from any such role, practically in the Western hemisphere and categorically within the system of socialist states. Moreover, 'peace-keeping' has so far been applicable to international peace only, whereas both in South-East Asia and in Africa the most disastrous conflicts have taken the form, in effect, of civil wars from which the UN is firmly excluded. Important though UN peace-keeping has been (and still is in Cyprus) its future, at least in its present form, is problematic.

In the field of peace settlement the mediatory resources of the Organization have been plentiful, their use minimal. On matters which touch on their so-called vital interests, states are rarely receptive to disinterested

[21] Conor Cruise O'Brien and Felix Topolski, *The United Nations: Sacred Drama* (London, 1968), p. 287.
[22] *ibid.*, p. 285.

mediation, however skilfully and persistently it is exercised. On the other hand, from the Jessup–Malik exchanges in 1949 during the Berlin crisis to the Johnson and Kosygin meeting during the 1967 Middle East crisis, the Organization has served as an exceptionally valuable point of diplomatic contact. It has become in Dean Rusk's words, "the world's greatest switchboard for bilateral diplomacy". Nearly every General Assembly provides a unique gathering of Foreign Ministers and Heads of States who can discuss in privacy and with little publicity any especially intractable problems, while the presence of the permanent missions has created in effect a continuous diplomatic conference. Such developments do, in a sense, register the concern of the international community that even if problems may not be settled, they should at least be prevented from getting wholly out of control.

The fears that the 'delicate balance of terror' might be upset by the continuing nuclear arms race have also provoked a "cogent awareness of a common peril" – a community of fear reflected in the disarmament debates. However, until the Cuban missile crisis of 1962 Washington's and Moscow's concern for 'nuclear superiority' made a mockery of most UN disarmament discussions. With the subsequent acceptance, at least by Washington, of 'nuclear sufficiency' the UN has played some part in most of the arms control agreements of the 1960's (e.g. the 1963 partial nuclear test ban treaty, the 1967 outer space treaty, and the 1968 non-proliferation treaty), "either in exhorting the nuclear powers to act, in sponsoring the negotiations, or in formally acknowledging and thus in a sense 'codifying an agreement after it was reached'."[23] But it has, of course, been the sense of common peril not the UN which has brought the nuclear powers (other than France and China) to the negotiating table, while it is still a moot point whether the agreements they have reached are not likely to be "more honoured in the breach than in the observance".

It is in the economic realm in particular that the UN is said to be "in the business of building a community, a sense of shared purpose and shared destiny".[24] Yet all the signs at present are that the North/South gulf in the economic field has been growing rather than narrowing. Moreover, "the shape or structure of international society must be materially affected by a pronounced trend towards lop-sided development. That is to say, when the economic system so favours the increasing wealth of a minority of developed national economies over the majority of less developed ones that it produces a list to port, so to speak, in the political system, then this can count as a

[23] Lincoln P. Bloomfield, "Arms Control and International Order", in Lawrence S. Finkelstein, *op. cit.*, p. 80.
[24] Patricia W. Blair, "The Dimension of Poverty", in Lawrence S. Finkelstein, *op. cit.*, p. 125.

political as well as an economic change."[25] In imperial days this 'list to port' could rarely find articulate political expression. This is no longer the case. The sense of growing economic inequality – accentuated by population pressures and often aggravated by racial antagonisms – has already produced a new basis of political alignment in the diplomatic system. It could prove disastrous to the fragile sense of community which programmes like those of the UNDP have done something to cultivate.

The sense of community is also said to be reflected in Assembly resolutions on colonialism and racism which, it is claimed, are indicative of a newly emerging body of customary law or even legal norms to which member states should defer. "Collective judgments are in fact being made as to what is legal and permissible and new, more specific, legal norms are being elaborated to meet felt necessities".[26] Whatever the exact legal status of these norms it is clear that they do at least have very considerable diplomatic and even moral weight behind them. Yet although the law of the Charter (especially Article 2 [4]) and of the practice of the UN may have afforded "general protection to the weak against pressures from the strong that were common in an earlier day",[27] law observance is not encouraged by the inclination to apply a "double standard" or by "a disturbing tendency . . . to disregard constitutional limitations and to disdain established procedures and due process".[28] Indeed, the often cavalier attitude of many Afro-Asian states to legal obligations (even those they themselves have specifically accepted) and their attempts to use "law to solve 'insoluble' political problems – the remnants of colonialism and racism in Africa – and to surmount 'insurmountable' economic problems – the widening chasm between the rich few and the many poor"[29] suggests that one of the main props to any burgeoning community sense is being whittled away.

Finally, the Secretary-General, at least in Dag Hammarskjöld's time, has been in a sense the *persona* of the UN and the symbol of the incipient world community. Claims to be acting on behalf of, or to represent, a 'world community' view do, however, make the Secretary-General and

[25] Susan Strange, "International Economics and International Relations: A Case of Mutual Neglect", in *International Affairs* (April 1970), p. 307.

[26] Oscar Schacter, "The Relation of Law, Politics and Action in the United Nations", *Recueil des Cours, Académie de Droit International*, vol. 109 (Leyden, 1964), p. 184. See also Rosalyn Higgins, *The Development of International Law through the Political Organs of the United Nations* (London, 1963).

[27] Louis Henkin, "International Organization and the Rule of Law", in Lawrence S. Finkelstein, *op. cit.*, p. 108.

[28] *ibid:* 'double standard' in condemning Western interventions, condoning Indian and Soviet occupations, tolerating Arab threats to destroy Israel, and calling for the use of force in South Africa.

[29] *ibid.*, p. 123.

his office very vulnerable to attack, as Dag Hammarskjöld found in the course of the Congo crisis. Despite his outspoken public utterances on Viet-Nam and South Africa, U Thant has otherwise tended to work more within the basis of any consensus that has obtained between the great powers. This may be prudent, but it makes for passivity. Moreover, the demand for more equitable geographical representation on the Secretariat has seriously diluted the concept of international loyalty and reduced its general level of competence. This may be a temporary phase only. Any bureaucracy, however competent, would have found the greatest difficulty in absorbing the inrush of new members consequent upon the expansion of the Organization. There are signs that many of the newer members of the Secretariat are quick 'learners' and that the concept of international loyalty, though unfamiliar, is beginning to strike roots. Ultimately the outcome depends upon member governments in terms both of the tasks they demand of the Secretariat and above all in the degree of respect they show for its "exclusively international character".[30]

## PROSPECTS

Viewed scientifically (e.g. the International Geophysical Year or Problems of the Human Environment) or technologically (e.g. communication satellites) or from outer space ("I saw no political frontiers", Astronaut Armstrong is reported to have said), the world may seem increasingly one. From practically every other point of view – cultural, ideological and political – it remains a patchwork of peoples, races and states, more often than not in "the posture of gladiators". This basic discordance in the international environment in which the UN has to operate is unlikely to become less in the next decade or so. On the contrary, science and technology may develop ecumenically, but the world diplomatically will probably become even more fragmented than at present. Nor, in an increasingly pluralistic world, are aspirations to a 'common law of man' or notions of 'distributive justice', which presuppose a sense of belonging to a community of mankind which transcends the system of state communities, likely to make much headway.

The signs are, indeed, that the international political system is likely to become more complex and loosely structured into, following Stanley Hoffman's categories,[31] three layers of power. The basic layer is the *bipolar layer* of world nuclear powers with, depending on the SALT talks, a possibly less stable 'balance of deterrents' and continuing fundamental

[30] Article 100 (2).
[31] Stanley Hoffman, *Gulliver's Troubles or The Setting of American Foreign Policy* (Atlantic Policy Studies) (New York, 1968).

and deep-seated differences in the way each regards the world outside their respective boundaries. The emerging *multipolar level* of middle powers, several more of which are likely to opt for a nuclear capability, may make for a welcome diplomatic flexibility or by undermining the main bipolar system of the past for greater uncertainty and instability. At the small or mini-power layer *polycentrism* is likely to be more marked than in the past (despite the efforts of regional bodies in Latin America and Africa to cultivate a common front at least towards the external world) with states of questionable viability only too often proving a serious temptation to their neighbours or seedbeds of sanguinary civil wars. In such a world the super powers may be faced, as Hoffman warns, with a choice between costly policing or a retreat that would let the world disintegrate into a series of possibly infectious jungles.

It is a gloomy picture. Yet it is one which could make the existence of the UN more rather than less necessary. Much will turn on the attitudes of the super powers. "Until recently participation in and support of the United Nations by the United States was above all a symbol of America's new internationalism . . . American political leaders today are tending to use the United Nations as a symbol of the possibility of the substantial reduction of the international responsibilities of the United States." Given the Organization's past dependence on active American support, American retrenchment "while creating a need for the United Nations to expand its role in world politics [could] reduce rather than increase the probability that it will and the possibility that it can do so".[32] But it could also make for a welcome sharing of responsibility, especially – though not only – with the Soviet Union.

Preoccupations with Communist China and the achievement of nuclear equality with the United States may make for a greater readiness on the part of the Soviet Union to utilise the UN to negotiate, register, legitimise and occasionally help 'police' arrangements jointly agreed with the United States to dampen down possible threats to a precarious nuclear peace. The Security Council may then become something of a vehicle for a Washington–Moscow nuclear condominium with supporting players. If so, Communist China's absence might for the time being be publicly deplored, but privately welcomed in recognition that unless there is a perceptible shift in Chinese attitudes, her presence would almost certainly bring a reversion to the Security Council's atrophy of the late 1940's.

At the multipolar level one of the major question marks must be the extent of the proliferation of nuclear weapons and the restraints that can

[32] Inis L. Claude, "The United Nations, the United States, and the Maintenance of Peace", in Lawrence S. Finkelstein (ed.), *op. cit.*, pp. 67 and 70.

be built against their use, either overtly or as blackmailing devices. The point to emphasise is that if, as unhappily seems likely, the Non-Proliferation Treaty fails in its purpose, a world of nuclear proliferation will almost certainly be a more dangerous world and the need for some system of restraints greater than ever. The Security Council could at least serve as a vehicle for legitimising such restraints as the super powers might themselves be willing to exert.

In other respects, the contribution of 'middle powers', both in any future UN peace-keeping and in economic mediation between rich and poor would be more than matched by the stake they have as 'consumers of security' in helping to preserve the 'delicate balance of terror' and in assuaging North/South differences.

Finally, the great mass of smaller powers, especially those from Asia and Africa, will no doubt continue to see the UN mainly as a means of extracting economic concessions from the rich and of securing justice for oppressed black African majorities in Southern Africa. Already where racist crises are involved, as Conor Cruise O'Brien remarks, "the tendency for the [Afro-Asian] majority of the United Nations is to pursue justice, at some risk of war". Largely at their behest the Organization's Twenty-Fifth Anniversary called for "Peace, Justice, Progress". But what of '*Order*'? In the almost certainly tumultuous world of the 1970's there can be no prospect of justice unless there is some basis of order. If mankind is to survive, the UN's first task is to ensure at least a modicum of order throughout as much of the world as possible. Power without justice may be tyranny; but justice without order is anarchy.

# 3. THE UNITED NATIONS AND INTERNATIONAL LAW

J. E. S. Fawcett

LE CORBUSIER said that, when he was preparing the headquarters building, he saw the United Nations as a *centre*. This simple, penetrating observation was and remains true, and it is as a centre that the UN has influenced the evolution of international law since 1945.

International law has a place both in the internal structure of international institutions and in the external exercise of their functions. A brief survey of the influence of the UN on international law may then view the UN in turn as an organisation, and as a primitive legislature. But of course only a few examples of this influence can be given here from each of these viewpoints, and those examples will be chosen which appear to be characteristic and so perhaps enduring.

## The United Nations as a legal and political unit

From the viewpoint of the UN as an organisation we may then consider its membership as it has now evolved, and its place as a political unit in the international community, which has in turn two aspects: the UN as principal with many agents, and its impact on the traditional domestic jurisdiction of states.

The increased membership of the UN, now totalling 127, is the *reductio ad absurdum* of the concept of the state as the primary subject of international law. The Security Council has established a committee to determine the criteria of less than full membership of the UN. The task is not easy for the size of population, territory or resources – to take the more obvious criteria – varies much even among small states. However, those with populations of less than 500,000 and correspondingly small resources cannot effectively perform Charter obligations. It is possible that a new international status for small states may be created by the UN, and it may be added that the position of territories, which are still dependent but do not seek independence, should not be overlooked. There appears to be no obstacle in the Charter or in principle to the association of small communities with the UN, which would provide them with a guarantee of territorial integrity and self-government, and also exercise a measure of international supervision over them. The UN took a step in this direction in the arrangements for a Free Territory of Trieste, which though abortive offer a precedent. The Treaty of Peace with Italy envisaged the establishment of a Free Territory under a Permanent Statute to be adopted by the Security Council; and its "integrity and independence shall be assured by the Security Council". This clause was regarded[1] by the Security Council as rendering it competent under Article 24 of the Charter to adopt the Permanent Statute and related provisions in the Peace Treaty Annexes and to accept "the responsibilities devolving upon it under the same". Secretary-General Trygve Lie had given his opinion that Article 24 was sufficiently wide for the Security Council to assume these responsibilities, the only limitations being the principles and purposes set out in Articles 1 and 2 of the Charter. Similar reasoning might be applied to the General Assembly, to which Articles 55 and 60 of the Charter assign the duty of promoting, on the basis of "respect for the principle of equal rights and self-determination of peoples . . . solutions of international economic, social . . . and related problems". Association with the UN on such lines might be politically acceptable and administratively convenient for such territories as the Falkland Islands, Gibraltar, and some Caribbean islands, in place of arid disputes over sovereignty.

The UN came to be recognised as a body politic distinct from its members, as a legal person on the international plane, and as the principal for its servants and agents, in an advisory opinion of the International Court of Justice, handed down in 1949;[2] and Lord McNair has said that that opinion "viewed *sub specie aeternitatis* is probably the most important Opinion that the Court has given". Indeed, there was an element in it of judicial legislation, for it has been argued that the Court need not have gone so far as to attribute legal personality to the UN. But it was the direction in which international organisation was moving, and the Court was careful to point to the limits of advice:

> "It [the UN] is at present the supreme type of international organisation, and it could not carry out the intentions of its founders if it was devoid of international personality. It must be acknowledged that its Members, by entrusting certain functions to it, with the attendant duties and responsibilities, have clothed it with the competence required to enable those functions to be effectively discharged. Accordingly, the Court has come to the conclusion that the Organization is an international person . . . [But] the rights and duties of an entity such as the Organiza-

[1] By 10–0–1, Australia abstaining on the ground that, in its view, such functions of governmental supervision were outside its competence.

[2] *Reparation for Injuries suffered in the service of the UN* (1949), ICJ Rep. 179.

tion must depend upon its purposes and functions as specified or implied in its constituent documents and developed in practice."

This is exactly paralleled by the description of a corporation in English law:

> "a collection of individuals united into one body under a special denomination, having perpetual succession under an artificial form, and vested by the policy of the law with capacity of acting in several respects as an individual . . . according to the design of its institutions or the powers conferred upon it."[3]

The recognition of the UN as a corporate body has a number of consequences, legal and political. So, apart from its capacity under the domestic law of member countries to own property, enter into contracts, institute court proceedings,[4] or protect the use of its name,[5] it has on the international plane its own personal law, composed in part of rules of international law and in part of provisions of the Charter and its internal regulations: thus the contracts of employment which the Secretary-General enters into with staff members are subject to that personal law and not the domestic law of any one country. Further, the UN may protect its servants and agents, through reliance on immunities granted to it in respect of them, and may bring claims for compensation for injury or wrong done to them, as it did successfully for the assassination of Count Bernadotte. Conversely, it will incur responsibility for their acts and their financial consequences.[6]

Politically, the UN acts by majority decisions of its constituent organs, that is to say, a minority of member states have to accept these decisions as authorising action of the UN as such. In other words, the majority decision has to be accepted, as far as the authority of the UN goes, even by those states that have voted against it. This is not to say that the constitutionality of some decisions may not be questioned, as indeed it vigorously was in the very area of financial obligations incurred by the UN,[7] which have just been mentioned. But it is not always realised what a novelty in secular terms majority decisions are in an international body. Lord Robert Cecil, contemplating the formation of the League, said in 1919 that international decisions, otherwise than by unanimity, were inconceivable.

[3] Lord Halsbury, *Laws of England*, 3rd ed., vol. 9 (London, 1954), p. 4.
[4] e.g. *United Nations* v *Canada-Asiatic Lines Ltd.* (1952), Superior Court, Montreal.
[5] *People of New York* v *Wright* (1958), US Court of Special Session, New York.
[6] e.g. *Nissan* v *Attorney-General* (1967) 3 WLR 1044, where Lord Denning MR, described the UN as a "sovereign body corporate".
[7] The issue was liability for the expenses of the UN forces in the Congo (ONUC) and the UAR (UNEF), and was referred to the ICJ for an advisory opinion: *Certain Expenses of the UN* (1962), ICJ Rep. A political settlement of the dispute was reached within the UN.

The recognition of the UN as a distinct political unit in the international community does not make it a super-state. But it has come to be accepted – and this is a useful development in international relations – that the UN and its specialised agencies[8] can each function on the same level as states often taking action in the common interest of which states alone would be incapable.

This leads us to the impact of the UN on the domestic jurisdiction of states. The notion of the domestic jurisdiction of a state is that of its being master in its own house. But state sovereignty cannot be unlimited, if there is more than one state. It is a function of international law to define the limits of state sovereignty in a community of states, and that area, defined by reference to place, person or things, on which a state may exercise its lawful authority to the exclusion of any other, is within its domestic jurisdiction. But this area is not constant, and the Permanent Court of International Justice, when called upon to interpret the expression "solely within the jurisdiction/compétence exclusive"[9] of a state, stated:

> "The words 'solely within the jurisdiction' seem rather to envisage certain matters which, though they may vary closely concern the interests of more than one State, are not in principle regulated by international law. As regards such matters, each State is sole master of its decisions. The question whether a particular matter is or is not solely within the jurisdiction (le domaine exclusif) of a State is an essentially relative question: it depends upon the development of international relations."[10]

As they have developed since 1945, there have been encroachments on the domestic jurisdiction of states in many fields, and Article 2 (7) of the Charter, similar to Article 15 (8) of the Covenant, has not afforded the protection which its drafters anticipated. Indeed it has come to be accepted that, where the political right of self-determination of a people is in issue, or where there is at least a systematic denial of human rights, the UN does not regard Article 2 (7) as a barrier; and the General Assembly has on many occasions debated, and recommended action on, situations of this kind, which would fall traditionally within domestic jurisdiction.

Take the case of Rhodesia. Britain has from the beginning of the UN not treated Rhodesia as being a non-self-governing territory for the purposes of Article 73 of the Charter, and it was not included in the list of

[8] The notion is not limited to them: for example, the EEC negotiated in the 'Kennedy Round', as a single separate unit.

[9] Under the League of Nations Covenant, Article 15 (8) restricted intervention by the League.

[10] *Nationality Decrees in Tunis and Morocco* (1923), PCIJ: B4, pp. 23–4.

such territories contained in the first General Assembly Resolution[11] on that Article. However, eighteen months before the dissolution of the Central African Federation, which was to lead Southern Rhodesia to its unilateral declaration of independence, the UN took a different view and declared that Southern Rhodesia was to be regarded as a non-self-governing territory in the sense of Article 73;[12] and a series of resolutions[13] followed, addressed to Britain as the 'administering power', on constitutional and political developments in the territory. Britain employed the provisions of Article 2 (7) of the Charter in opposing this intervention by the UN, maintaining that, while the relationship between her and Southern Rhodesia was "something halfway between dependence and independence" or as "not executive but primarily of diplomatic character",[14] the political and social situation in that country was essentially within British domestic jurisdiction. In so far as the General Assembly declared Southern Rhodesia to be a non-self-governing territory, and both that body and the Security Council in its subsequent resolutions, consistently addressed Britain as the administering power, the UN appeared to concede that Southern Rhodesia was, at least in the conventional sense, within British domestic jurisdiction. But this did not deflect the UN from treating the systematic denial of political and other rights to the majority as a matter of international concern, overriding Article 2 (7) of the Charter.

## General Assembly Resolutions and the United Nations as a primitive legislature

The UN General Assembly shows the characteristics of a primitive legislature in a number of ways, in its composition of representatives, its procedures, its blocs and caucuses comparable in function to political parties, and in its resolutions. It is with the last that we are here concerned.

General Assembly resolutions, which come into the field of international law, fall into two broad groups: those which elaborate, formulate or declare standards and principles of state conduct, and those which are specifically designed to further the codification of international law.

Resolutions in the first group must be scrutinised with care before their role in the development of international law can be assessed. Among the criteria to be applied are the care with which a resolution has been prepared,

[11] GA Resolution 64 (I), 12 December 1946.
[12] GA Resolution 1747 (XVI), 28 June 1962.
[13] GA Resolutions 1755 (XVII) and 1760 (XVII) in October 1962; 1883 (XVIII), 14 October 1963, 1889 (XVIII), 6 November 1963.
[14] See speech of United Kingdom delegate in the plenary session of the General Assembly which adopted Resolution 1755 (XVII): *Contemporary Survey*, 1962, 11, pp. 248–53.

the size of the majority by which it has been adopted, the clarity of its provisions, and the approximation of the standards or principles declared in it to the consensus that might be expected. To take the Resolution on the uses of outer space as an example: it was the product of a draft, subjected to extensive amendments and to much debate over at least two sessions of the General Assembly; it was adopted unanimously, so that it had in particular the support of the United States and Soviet Union as the principal space-users at the time; its provisions are reasonably explicit and unambiguous, and the principles declared in it are in no way novel or unpredicted, but are rather applications to outer space and celestial bodies of generally recognised principles of law.

Few resolutions of course meet all these criteria even in part. The provisions of a Resolution may reflect so much reservation or disagreement that the final version is obscure or capable of more than one meaning. So a *Declaration on the Inadmissibility of Intervention in the Domestic Affairs of States*[15] contains the clause:

> "2. No State may use or encourage the use of economic, political or any other type of measure to coerce another State in order to obtain from it the subordination of the exercise of its sovereign rights or to secure from it advantages of any kind."

While the general intention is clear, the formulation is so wide that, if observed, it could put in question some legitimate economic relationships, and would actually prevent such punitive measures as, for example, those recommended by the OAU against South Africa.

Again, there can be few matters on which there is a world consensus, and consensus in Assembly Resolutions is essential because, with few exceptions that do not concern us here, they are in terms of the Charter recommendations only, not important obligations on member states to impose, observe or execute them. Therefore, unless and until the General Assembly is to be accorded the authority of a legislature in the conventional sense, the force of a Resolution lies not in its bare adoption by the General Assembly but in the consensus of member states underlying its formulation and adoption. Here in particular the UN functions as a centre, to focus debate and to perfect in universally understood language the inchoate ideas common to its members. Consensus then is indicated by the size of the majority, and a Resolution adopted in face of significant opposition or abstention will not rank as a real development of international law.

A handful of over 2,500 Resolutions adopted by the General Assembly can be regarded as law-making, in that they either extend the UN Charter

[15] GA Resolution 2131 (XX), 21 December 1965.

by interpretation of its provisions, or serve to internationalise general principles of law already recognised by member states, or declare accepted rules of international law to be applicable to new fields or situations. Alternatively a Resolution may embody directive principles, setting a framework for state action.

The Universal Declaration of Human Rights,[16] which will be considered in another context below, can be regarded as interpreting and defining the scope of those provisions of the UN Charter which refer to human rights.[17] Similarly a Resolution on colonialism[18] indicated the Charter basis for the intervention of the UN with governments responsible for the administration of dependent territories, and has been frequently cited.[19]

Among formulations of general principles of law we find the Resolutions on Permanent Sovereignty over Natural Resources,[20] the Prohibition of the Use of Nuclear Weapons,[21] the Nuremberg Charter Principles, Territorial Asylum,[22] and, in a narrower field, Approval of the International Red Cross distinction between Combatants and Non-Combatants. Three points deserve particular notice in these Resolutions. That on Natural Resources, adopted in December 1962, wholly ignores the need for conservation and wise management of natural resources in the common interest. The nationalist approach appears in the first paragraph:

> "The right of peoples and nations to permanent sovereignty over their natural wealth and resources must be exercised in the interest of their national development and of the well-being of the people of the State concerned,"

and it is emphasised in a later Resolution on the same topic,[23] which concerns itself with 'exploitation and marketing' and the 'role of foreign enterprises'. The earlier Resolution on Natural Resources is also significant for its handling of the thorny problem of compensation for expropriation of private property. It declares that:

> "Nationalization, expropriation or requisitioning shall be based on grounds or reasons of public utility, security or the national interest which are recognized as overriding purely individual or private interests, both domestic and foreign. In such cases the owner shall be paid

[16] GA Resolution 217 (III), adopted by 48–0 with 8 abstentions (Byelorussian SSR, Czechoslovakia, Poland, Saudi Arabia, South Africa, Ukrainian SSR, USSR).
[17] Articles 1, 55, 60, 62, 68 and 76.
[18] GA Resolution 1654 (XVI).
[19] See S. A. Bleicher, "Legal Significance of Re-citation of General Assembly Resolutions", 63 AJIL (July 1969), p. 444.
[20] GA Resolution 1803 (XVII).
[21] GA Resolution 1653 (XVI).
[22] GA Resolution 2312 (XXII).
[23] GA Resolution 2158 (XXI).

> appropriate compensation, in accordance with the rules in force in the State taking such measures in the exercise of its sovereignty and in accordance with international law."

Under the second clause, the right to compensation is declared, but with qualifications under which the amount payable is likely to approximate to zero. But the General Assembly is doubtless expressing the present state of the rule, which was once formulated as the requirement that compensation be prompt, adequate and effective.

The principles on which states are called upon "to base themselves in their practices in relation to territorial asylum", contain the exception that no suspected war crimes or crimes against humanity shall be entitled to claim asylum; and the General Assembly has gone further in proposing a convention on the non-applicability of statutory limitations to such crimes, in particular, crimes covered by the Nuremberg Charter; acts of eviction by armed attack or occupation; "inhuman acts resulting from the policy of *apartheid*"; and genocide.

The Declaration on the Granting of Independence to Colonial Countries and Peoples[24] is part interpretation of the Charter, part political manifesto, and part directive principles. The central directive principle is perhaps that on self-determination:

> "All peoples have the right to self-determination; by virtue of that right they freely determine their political status and freely pursue their economic, social and cultural development."

This paragraph now forms Article 1 (1) of each of the UN Covenants on Human Rights, to be considered below, and some argument can be made for saying that the right of self-determination has evolved into a legal right. But the better view of it is as a right of a second order, a right presupposed in any just legal and political order, and standing behind other human rights as a precondition of their exercise. This notion was well expressed in another General Assembly Resolution[25] which declared that:

> "the right of peoples and nations to self-determination is a prerequisite to the full enjoyment of all fundamental human rights."

Other enunciations of directive principles are the Declaration on the Rights of the Child[26] and on the prevention of Discrimination against Women,[27] though the latter contains a number of provisions capable of direct legislative enactment.

Finally, mention must be made of Assembly Resolutions which serve to

[24] GA Resolution 1514 (XV).
[25] GA Resolution 1574 (XVI).
[26] GA Resolution 1386 (XIV).
[27] GA Resolution 2263 (XXII).

extend the Charter and principles of international law to new fields. The exploration and uses of outer space, and of the deep sea-bed, have been dealt with at elaborate length by the General Assembly. The Declaration of Legal Principles,[28] applicable to outer space, was followed by the Outer Space Treaty 1967, which added little of significance. In 1968 the General Assembly established a Committee on Peaceful Uses of the Sea-bed and the Ocean Floor beyond National Jurisdiction, which is struggling to master and lead to some practical international arrangement the innumerable proposals that have been made on the management of the deep sea-bed. The General Assembly on this matter has gone further perhaps than in any previous Resolution in endeavours to control state action by simple directive in declaring that:

> pending the establishment of the aforementioned international regime (for the deep sea-bed),
> (a) states and persons, physical and juridical, are bound to refrain from all activities of exploitation of the resources of the area of the sea-bed and ocean floor and the subsoil thereof, beyond the limits of national jurisdiction;
> (b) no claim to any part of that area or its resources shall be recognised.

The significance of these clauses will be considered with the Continental Shelf Convention below.

It is natural to ask what is the effect of these and like Resolutions, but it is not the right question. Rather should we ask what is their cause. For an understanding of the motivation for a Resolution in the large number of states that have adopted it, makes it possible to judge how far declared standards or principles are a necessary and organic part of the life of national communities, or of relations between them. And to the extent that they are, to assess and even predict their effectiveness. On this approach at least those Resolutions, which meet a felt need to declare agreed principles in concise and comprehensible terms, function as a part of international law, and are likely to be observed as such.

## The Codification of International Law

Article 13 of the Charter provides that "the General Assembly shall initiate studies and make recommendations for the purpose of (a) . . . encouraging the progressive development of international law and its codification". Here it has had some success, though its action has been indirect because of its lack of full legislative powers. It established the International Law

[28] GA Resolution 1962 (XVIII).

Commission as a subsidiary organ, which is composed since 1961 of twenty-five members, each of a different nationality and representing together the principal legal systems of the world. The statute under which the Commission functions makes a working distinction between the progressive development and the codification of international law:[29]

> "In the following articles the expression 'progressive development of international law' is used for convenience as meaning the preparation of draft conventions on subjects which have not yet been regulated by international law or in regard to which the law has not yet been sufficiently developed in the practice of States. Similarly, the expression 'codification of international law' is used for convenience as meaning the more precise formulation and systematization of rules of international law in fields where there already has been extensive State practice, precedent and doctrine."

It is with codification that we are here concerned. The method of work is, in its essentials, as follows: the Commission prepares draft articles on the chosen topic, based on "the texts of laws, decrees, political decisions, treaties, diplomatic correspondence" and other relevant material, obtained on request from member states; the draft articles, supported by a full commentary by the Commission covering in particular points of agreement and disagreement between the draft articles and state practice or accepted doctrine, are then submitted to all governments for comments; the Commission then, on the basis of government comments, submits a final draft with an explanatory report to the General Assembly which, it is recommended, may convoke an international conference to conclude a convention on the chosen topic.

If we omit the conference stage, this process is not unlike that of statute law reform in this country. Here an expert commission is engaged in rationalising and in some degree codifying statute law, cutting out much dead wood. Relying where necessary on outside consultation and advice, it prepares draft bills on particular branches of statute law, which serve to clarify and modernise the law and can be adopted as new statutes by Parliament.

In the UN process the international conference has a role analogous to Parliament, though with the important difference that, when it has concluded a convention which it then recommends to all states by the General Assembly for adoption, the convention must still await a number of ratifications[30] before it comes formally into force. However the rigour of

[29] Article 15 of the Statute of the Commission.
[30] Generally twenty-two ratifications.

this treaty rule is a little relaxed in effect for the following reasons. The Commission draft presented to the conference embodies not only the common view of the widely representative legal experts in the Commission but also extensive comments by many governments. Even at this stage then the draft can be regarded as approaching a consensus of international opinion as to what the law is or should be on the particular topic. The conference procedure fortifies the draft further by the adoption of a rule that each article in the convention must for adoption secure a two-thirds majority of the states participating. The result is that provisions of the international conventions that have emerged from this process are strong, and perhaps almost conclusive, evidence of what is accepted as rules of law by the international community. In short, the UN is moving slowly towards the role of international legislator. But for the present the treaty remains the only recognised legal form in which the codification of international law can be cast; and the critical step, by which a General Assembly Resolution could of its own motion give full legal effect to such conventions, has yet to be taken, and it may well be a long time before it is taken. But, as has been indicated, a stage has already been reached where the legal effect and influence of codifying conventions is no longer wholly dependent upon the treaty process of ratification by states. Of the conventions that have so far been produced, four cover the law of the sea,[31] three deal with diplomatic and consular relations and the role of special missions,[32] and one formulates the law of treaties.[33] Vienna has been the seat of all the conferences which produced these conventions

It is a familiar experience with all codification, whether national or international, that it can seldom be achieved without some modification of the rules of law covered. This is particularly true of the reduction of customary rules to a code. State practice, as regards for example the jurisdiction of the flag state over a ship on the high seas, or the immunity of an accredited diplomat from criminal process, may be so clear and consistent as to be easily formulated in a codified rule. Yet there may be exceptions or variants, not so large as to defeat agreement on a common rule, but large enough to bring subtle changes or even obscurities into the rule as finally accepted. More important is the fact that codification offers an obvious opportunity to alter, improve or modernise, where that is seen and agreed to be necessary. On the other hand, it must be stressed that

[31] Territorial Sea and Contiguous Zone; High Seas; Continental Shelf; Fishing and Conservation of the Living Resources of the High Seas. All four conventions, adopted in 1958, are now formally in force.

[32] Diplomatic Relations (1961), Consular Relations (1963), Special Missions (1969). The first of these is now formally in force and its substantive provisions have been made part of the law of the United Kingdom by the Diplomatic Privileges Act 1964.

[33] Law of Treaties (1969), is not yet formally in force.

codification will be difficult in areas of controversy, where for example there are marked divergencies of state practice or national security is involved, or the field of operation of the law is new and unexplored.

Let us glance at some of the changes in the law that the codification conventions have brought about. The Territorial Sea Convention has radically transformed the rule concerning the base-line from which the territorial sea is measured. Though no precise agreement as to the width of the territorial sea was reached it has established a rule permitting widths of up to twelve miles. The provision concerning entry into and passage through the territorial sea of warships is an instance where divergence of state practice and attitudes made only a partial rule possible, though it was accepted that submarines must navigate on the surface. In the High Seas Convention the opportunity was taken to clarify and in some degree limit the traditional rules concerning piracy, but to extend them also to aircraft: thus wrongful acts do not now constitute piracy in international law unless they are committed against another ship or aircraft, and for private ends.

The Continental Shelf Convention operates in a relatively new field, and it is perhaps not surprising that the limits[34] of the Continental Shelf prescribed in 1958 are already in need of greater precision in face of technological advances and the possibilities of using the deep sea-bed, abyss or ocean floor,[35] and obtaining their resources, and the UN has now addressed itself to this question.

A present assessment of the effectiveness of these codification conventions would have to balance against their authority as evidence of customary international law, already described, the fact that the number of states, which have formally accepted them is still, with one exception, relatively small: up to the end of 1969, the Territorial Sea Convention had gained 37 acceptances, the High Seas Convention 44, the Fisheries Conservation Convention 28 and the Continental Shelf Convention 40. However, the Diplomatic Relations Convention had received 91, and the Consular Relations Convention 38.

It remains to consider the two UN Covenants on Civil and Political Rights, and on Economic, Social and Cultural Rights. They were produced by a different method from the codification conventions, being largely the work of the UN Human Rights Commission and the General Assembly itself, in committee and in plenary session, and were commended to member states by a virtually unanimous vote of 107 in the General Assembly in December 1966. However only 44 states actually signed them and each require 35 ratifications or acceptances by states before they

[34] i.e. a depth of 200 metres or the extent of exploitability.

[35] These terms are used to describe the sea-bed beyond the continental shelf, rise and slope.

formally enter into force, and since, nearly four years later, only six have been recorded their entry into force is likely to be long delayed.

It is not possible in a short space even to summarise these Covenants, which are wider in scope and have more elaborate provisions than any previous international human rights instrument. Three general observations may be made on certain notable features in them, on their relation to the Universal Declaration of Human Rights, and the means proposed for the enforcement of the Civil and Political Rights Covenant. Three features deserve attention. First, the right of self-determination is placed on the same footing as other rights and freedoms, so that it is subject to the same procedure of enforcement, by state application to the proposed Human Rights Committee under Article 41 of the Civil and Political Rights Covenant. It is not hard to imagine the political use that would be made of this provision, nor easy to see how the Committee would handle such applications. Secondly, the right to own property, enshrined as a fundamental freedom in Article 17 of the Universal Declaration has vanished and has no place in either Covenant. Thirdly, a large escape-clause is included in Article 2 (3) of the Economic, Social and Cultural Rights Covenant, which provides:

> "Developing countries, with due regard to human rights and their national economy, may determine to what extent they would guarantee the economic rights recognised in the present Covenant to non-nationals."

It is indeed ironic that a human rights covenant should positively permit discrimination against aliens, subverting a long established rule of international law. The last two features bring out the relationship between the two Covenants and the Universal Declaration. The latter was adopted in 1948 when the UN had 56 members and the tide of independence had hardly begun to flow. The Covenants, whose texts were adopted by 107 countries, including most of those which abstained on the Universal Declaration in 1948, are plainly not only far more elaborate than the Declaration, but represent an evolution in world thinking about these matters, marked particularly in the last two features mentioned. Even if their entry into force is long delayed they must be read as displacing the Universal Declaration as the standard of achievement for human rights.

Lastly, the means proposed for the enforcement of the Civil and Political Rights Covenant are feeble and unrealistic. The prospects for the Optional Protocol providing for individual applications to the Human Rights Committee are not bright: it has so far attracted only six signatures. The method contemplated in the Covenant itself of applications by one state against another, alleging breaches of the Covenant, is likely to be more abused than used, serving political objectives with concern for individual rights and freedom. Further, it may be asked how the Human Rights Committee, a single body of eighteen persons, could possibly cope with individual applications on a global scale, if the Optional Protocol had even moderately wide acceptance. If the experience of the European Convention on Human Rights is any guide, these would come in in their thousands. The problem of language alone would in the direction of the work of the Committee be almost insoluble.

Discussion of the UN and international law cannot close without reference to the International Court of Justice, its principal organ. The part which it has played in the UN system has been slight, certainly less than was hoped or might even have been predicted in 1945. The Security Council has only once successfully directed the parties in a dispute before it[36] to take it to the International Court as the Article 36 (3) of the Charter commends. Requests for advisory opinions from the Court by the UN and its specialised agencies have markedly fallen off. Fourteen requests have been made since 1945, of which only two were from specialised agencies. Since 1962 only one request has been made.

* * * * *

To offer some assessment of this record, we may say:

i. The UN has acted as a centre for a harmonisation of the development of international law, which has been broadly progressive and which, without such a directive centre, would certainly not have taken place;
ii. nevertheless, so long as the treaty or convention is regarded as the only valid means of making modifications or developments of customary international law mandatory for states, further progress is likely to be slow and uncertain;
iii. a marked disadvantage of the UN as a world centre is that it sometimes attempts to introduce on a global scale international rules for national application, which are only workable, if at all, on a regional or more limited basis;
iv. the use of the International Court of Justice in the UN system has plainly fallen below even the minimum that its effectiveness as a UN organ would require, and some reform of the competence and working of the Court is necessary.

[36] In the Corfu Channel case, between the United Kingdom and Albania.

# 4. UNITED NATIONS PEACE-KEEPING

D. W. Bowett

THE past ten years have witnessed a complete transformation in attitudes towards United Nations peace-keeping. It was possible, in the early 'sixties, to contemplate an expansion of UN peace-keeping activities even to the point of proposing an enlarged Headquarters military staff, stand-by agreements with member states, new formulae for financing and so forth.[1] Now, in the early 'seventies, all this has changed and few people place much hope in any development of this sort in the foreseeable future.

The immediate causes of this transformation are known well enough. In brief, the Congo crisis revealed a dispute over the political direction or control of the UN Force, ONUC, which led to Soviet refusal to finance the operations: this aggravated the pre-existing position over the financing of UNEF. Thus a financial crisis resulted which produced a direct challenge to the authority of the General Assembly, a challenge rejected by the International Court of Justice[2] but which the Soviet bloc has nevertheless continued to maintain. All attempts to resolve this problem within the Committee of Thirty-Three established by the Assembly in 1965 have so far failed. True, it remained possible to institute peace-keeping operations on the basis of purely voluntary financing, and the operations in the Yemen (UNYOM) and in Cyprus (UNFICYP) were in fact instituted on this basis. However, confidence in even this limited peace-keeping capacity has been shaken by the abrupt withdrawal of UNEF in May 1967, for if a peace-keeping force can be terminated, simply by the withdrawal of consent to its presence by the host state, it may be doubted how far member states will, in the future, be willing to contribute the human, material and financial resources required by these operations if their prospects of permanence are so slight.

[1] For example, D. W. Bowett, *United Nations Forces* (London, 1964), pp. 561–9; L. M. K. Skern, *Military Staffing at UN Headquarters for Peace-Keeping Operations – A Proposal*, IPKO Monograph No. 3 (Paris, July 1967); William R. Frye, *A United Nations Peace Force* (London, 1957).

[2] In its advisory opinion on *Certain Expenses of the United Nations*, ICJ Reports, 1962, the Court upheld the proposition that the Assembly had authority to authorise a peace-keeping operation, UNEF, and generally to apportion the expenses of any peace-keeping operation amongst the member states.

The *malaise* surrounding UN peace-keeping has certainly diminished the standing and influence of the UN. An attempt was made, notably by Britain, to compensate this setback to military peace-keeping by improving the techniques for pacific settlement of disputes.[3] This, too, has met with little success. In any event, whatever may be the case for improving the techniques of pacific settlement, these techniques supplement and do not replace military peace-keeping. The ideal relationship between the two is that military peace-keeping should be used as a temporary expedient to maintain peace and preserve an atmosphere in which the root causes of the conflict are resolved by peaceful settlement. It has never been contended that military peace-keeping can itself resolve the conflict. What has in fact tended to happen is that military peace-keeping occurred *without* any parallel, effective peaceful settlement procedures so that a military operation originally conceived as one of temporary duration becomes a permanent feature of an unresolved situation: certainly this appeared to be the fate of UNEF until its abrupt departure in 1967.

The assumption that military peace-keeping is an essential part of the role of the UN cannot be made without question. It is certainly true that the Charter did not specifically envisage the kind of military peace-keeping which has developed over the years. The use of military forces for enforcement action under Chapter VII of the Charter is a quite different matter and must be distinguished from peace-keeping as we now use the term.[4] But it is almost because the use of enforcement action under Chapter VII cannot be regarded as politically practicable that military peace-keeping becomes so essential to the UN's responsibilities for maintaining peace. Peace-keeping has become the minimal demonstration of UN authority in certain types of situation which represent a threat to peace. Once this is removed the UN becomes scarcely credible as an instrument for maintaining peace. Evidence of this is to be found in the Middle East. With UNEF removed and UNTSO operating only in the Canal Zone and the Golan Heights, the responsibility for overseeing the 'standstill' agreement negotiated in August 1970 as the result of American initiative has passed

[3] The whole range of techniques of pacific settlement of disputes, including fact-finding, can also be included within the concept of peace-keeping. However, the purpose of this chapter is to concentrate on peace-keeping operations involving military forces.

[4] If one takes the definition accepted by the ICJ in the *Expenses Case*, ICJ Reports, 1962, then the essential distinction is that enforcement action is hostile, coercive action directed *against* a State whereas peace-keeping is a non-coercive operation carried on with the consent of the State and within its territory. A full review of different definitions is given in the Secretary-General's Report, A/AC.121/4 of 31 May 1965, Part I.

from the UN. The 'policing' of the agreement has had to be left to the United States and the Soviet Union, using satellite and high-reconnaissance techniques. Even if the UN could have policed this agreement it is doubtful how far Israel would have agreed to such a role for the UN, so great has been the Israeli loss of confidence in the Organization since the withdrawal of UNEF.

Of course, it may be argued that it would be best for the UN to abandon its military peace-keeping role, at least for a time, and concentrate on its function as a standing political conference and an instrument for co-ordinating technical assistance. This is not an argument which this writer would accept. If, as is believed, military peace-keeping is already a minimal assertion of the proper role of the UN – as conceived in Chapter VII – to remove even this minimal assertion of authority would be to virtually abandon the UN's primary role. The effect of this would be to leave responsibility in the hands of the major powers, principally the United States and the Soviet Union, and in many situations the political antagonisms between the two would mean that the responsibility would not be assumed. It may be that regional organisations could fill the gap, although few of these are in fact capable of acting effectively and, if they do act, it may not be possible to count on their objectivity. It remains a fact of life that all the regional organisations are biassed against one system or another. The NATO, SEATO and OAS complexes are biassed against 'communism'; the OAU is biassed against 'colonialism'; and the Warsaw Pact is biassed against 'capitalism'. It cannot be expected that any of these organisations will act in the interests of world peace as those interests would be perceived by states generally.

In contrast, the clear advantage of UN peace-keeping was that it did tend to represent the majority will and to escape control by any political faction. Moreover, its strength lay in the middle-range powers who provided the contingents and not in the two super powers. This in turn contributed to its acceptability in situations where the assumption of responsibility by the two super powers would not be acceptable to the parties immediately involved.

Here one must concede that the Middle East situation is not typical. In the Middle East it has proved possible for the super powers to assert responsibility because they seem to be in agreement – at least to some extent – on the basic objective of implementing the Security Council Resolution 242 of 22 November 1967, and the parties in the Middle East are apparently prepared to accept their assertion of responsibility. But if a situation requiring military peace-keeping in one form or another were to arise in Africa, Asia or the Americas, it is by no means clear that there would be either basic agreement between the super powers or a willingness by the parties to accept their assertion of responsibility. Thus, great power action cannot be assumed to be an effective substitute for UN peace-keeping in all situations.[5]

For these reasons, therefore, it is felt unwise to accept an abandonment of a UN military peace-keeping role. Efforts to further this role ought not to be relaxed, and paradoxically, the Middle East situation which at present appears to reflect minimal UN influence may yet provide an opportunity for resuscitating UN peace-keeping.[6] If a peace formula does materialise it must involve withdrawal of Israeli forces from territory occupied in June 1967 and it must equally involve the provision of guarantees to Israel concerning her security. It is difficult to see how this can be achieved except through the establishment of neutralised or demilitarised zones and equally difficult to see how any such zones could be made effective without policing by military forces. The possibility of joint American–Soviet military forces is highly remote and President Nixon has publicly stated that such forces are not within his contemplation.[7] There would seem to be no alternative to UN Forces under any such peace-plan.[8] Even in Viet-Nam, the eventual withdrawal of American forces will presumably require supervision and observation by military observers. Conceivably these could again be supplied by the International Control Commission but the numbers required may be very much larger than Poland, India and Canada are prepared to provide so that, here again, there may be a further opportunity for UN peace-keeping.

Given the desirability of planning for a resuscitation of the UN military peace-keeping role, there are a number of basic issues which, in the light of past experience, may need re-thinking and these appear to be the following.

## Constitutional authority to establish a Force

The basic problem remains the Soviet bloc's refusal to accept that the General Assembly has any authority to establish a military peace-keeping

[5] Of course, if UN peace-keeping were monopolised by the Security Council (and subject to the veto) the same lack of basic agreement on aims between the two super powers would serve to frustrate any UN peace-keeping: this is the primary argument for retaining some authority to initiate peace-keeping in the General Assembly.

[6] This view is cogently argued by C. Hanning, "Making a profession of peace-keeping", *The Times*, 1 September 1970.

[7] *The Times*, 1 September 1970, p. 4.

[8] This writer does not regard the suggestion that neutralised zones could be policed by Israeli military settlements situated on the boundary between the zones and the Arab States (i.e. separated from Israel by the neutralised zone itself) as politically realistic.

operation.[9] Such an operation falls into one or other of three broad categories. First, there is the category of military observer groups, normally unarmed and with the limited function of reporting breaches of an armistice agreement or cease-fire resolution of the Security Council or transgressions of a frontier.[10] Second, there is the 'interposition' Force, like UNEF, which is an armed force equipped for self-defence and placed as a form of buffer or trip-wire between opposing forces. And, third, there is the Force equipped with a 'law and order' mandate, that is to say an authority to assist in the maintenance of law and order in a situation of civil strife: ONUC was of this character, as is UNFICYP.

Although there is no real evidence that the Soviet bloc is prepared to concede any authority to the General Assembly, it is likely that its opposition is least with the observer groups and greatest with the 'law and order' type of Force. This suggests that the only practicable policy for the immediate future is to accept as a working premise that the Security Council alone will have power to constitute any peace-keeping forces; but to maintain also the legal position that the General Assembly has a residual or secondary power to do so; and to press the case for such a power where either an observer group or an interposition force is in question and where its establishment is otherwise prevented by a veto in the Security Council.[11]

Coupled with this policy would be that of implementing the Charter to the extent of proceeding with the agreements under Article 43 by which member states agree to contribute military contingents or other facilities to the Security Council for the purpose of action under Chapter VII. It may be added that the Soviet Union has always insisted that this was the proper way to establish UN Forces and there appears to be no convincing argument from the Western side on why this attempt should not be made. Not

[9] The Soviet position has been fully set out in two Memoranda dated 10 July 1964 and 16 March 1967: both are reproduced in IPKO *Documentation*, July 1967, No. 17. What may be described as the Western position is stated in Britain's reply to the Soviet Memorandum of 10 July 1964: this is dated 5 August 1964 and is given *ibid.*, July 1967, No. 16. These same arguments, in more legal form, can be seen in the earlier pleadings before the ICJ in the *Expenses Case*, ICJ Reports, 1962.

[10] Examples are UNTSO which operated under the 1948 Israeli-Arab Armistice Agreements; UNOGIL, established in 1958 to report on any illegal infiltration into the Lebanon; UNYOM, a group established in 1963 with similar functions in the Yemen; and UNMOGIP, a similar group established in Kashmir in 1948.

[11] It may be recalled that the Soviet Union merely abstained, and did not oppose, on the General Assembly resolution to establish UNEF in November 1956. It has also been suggested that, if and when Communist China joins the Security Council, the Soviet Union might then find some virtue in a secondary responsibility for peace-keeping in the General Assembly, in the event that Security Council action is frustrated by a Chinese veto: see "The Role of Force in International Order and U.N. Peace-keeping" by Alan James, *Ditchley Paper No. 20*, published by the Ditchley Foundation, 1969, p. 25.

since 1948 have the five permanent members attempted a discussion of the basic principles which would be embodied in any agreement under Article 43. It must also be remembered that Chapter VII will suffice to enable the Security Council to operate peace-keeping forces as well as to institute enforcement action. So the unlikelihood of agreement on enforcement action under Chapter VII does not mean that peace-keeping operations cannot be taken under that Chapter. Thus, progress with the Article 43 agreements could bring real progress on peace-keeping capacity.

### Finance

This problem has inevitably been coupled with the question of constitutional power to establish the Force. The Soviet position, manifested over UNEF, has been simply that if the Assembly had no authority to establish the Force, no obligation to pay any part of its costs could devolve upon a member state. This means, almost inevitably, that no real solution to the financial question can be reached without first resolving the constitutional issue. Nor is the matter resolved by conceding a Security Council monopoly over the authorisation of peace-keeping so long as the General Assembly retains authority over financing the operation. There would be little point in the Security Council authorising an operation for which the Assembly members as a whole declined to pay the costs – always assuming the operation was not intended to be financed voluntarily.[12]

Whilst the Committee of Thirty-Three has failed to find any solution to this vexed question, it appears that the most likely solution is one which vests financial control in a body which is a General Assembly organ – but an organ so constituted that the permanent members and the states likely to pay the largest shares of the cost have overriding control. This will prevent 'irresponsible' action by the Assembly (in which the vast majority of members will face minimal shares of the cost) and yet preserve the Assembly's overall control over financing. It might also be hoped that a Reserve Fund could be established, constituted by a regular, annual contribution by the entire membership so that the impact of a high-cost operation would be evened out.

[12] It may be noted, in passing, that the French Government has maintained the position that an operation authorised by the Assembly cannot involve a legal obligation for members to pay any part of the costs since the Assembly can only act via recommendations and cannot impose binding obligations. This thesis, that Assembly authorised action must always be financed voluntarily, is perhaps more destructive of the authority of the UN than the Soviet thesis on the limits of the Assembly's authority. For the extreme statement of the French position see President de Gaulle's Press Conference statement of 11 April 1961, reproduced in IPKO, *Documentation*, July 1967, No. 18.

With regard to the actual allocation of shares of the cost, the normal apportionments for the regular budget are already accepted as unrealistic. It may be assumed that the developing states will continue to enjoy virtual exemption from peace-keeping costs and that the permanent members will accept the lion's share which is part of their primary responsibility for maintaining peace. The idea of heavily taxing the 'aggressor', whilst right in principle, is fraught with political hazards. Perhaps a sounder idea is to seek large contributions from states obviously benefiting from the UN peace-keeping presence. In principle, if this saves them heavy outlay on armaments, they could well make generous contributions to the cost of the UN presence.

The final principle which must be maintained is that once it is decided that an operation should be financed by the membership generally (i.e. not to be financed voluntarily), the Assembly's decision on apportionment creates for each member state a legal obligation to pay the amount of its assessment.

## Consent to the presence of a United Nations peace-keeping Force

It is accepted as axiomatic that a Force authorised by the Assembly can only enter a state's territory with its consent. Whether this need be true of a Force authorised by the Security Council is not so clear.[13] In practice, of course, a peace-keeping Force requires the co-operation of the authorities of the state on whose territory it operates and consent is therefore a normal prerequisite. In law, however, the Security Council can take decisions binding on all member states (Article 25 of the Charter) and there may be advantages in retaining the principle that, for Security Council operations, the consent of the state is not legally required. There may be, for example, situations in which the breakdown of law and order is so complete that there really is no government capable of giving consent, and it would be foolhardy for the Council to be hamstrung by its own insistence that a consent must be obtained.

But perhaps the more controversial issue is that of the withdrawal of consent. Admittedly, U Thant's withdrawal of UNEF upon the Egyptian request in May 1967 was a withdrawal of a Force established by the Assembly, not the Security Council: it might be that a different approach would have been taken *vis-à-vis* a Force created by the Security Council. However, the assumption that because the initial presence depended on consent therefore the withdrawal of consent means the termination of the

[13] Dag Hammarskjöld left this point open in his second and final *Report on UNEF*, A/3302, 6 November 1956, para. 9.

Force, is neither necessary nor even logical.[14] All contracts require consent, but once consent has been given it by no means follows that one party may simply withdraw its consent and, unilaterally, bring the contract to an end. The principle to be achieved, and which U Thant has jeopardised, is that, even if consent be initially required for the presence of the Force, once consent has been given and the Force created by resolution of either the Assembly or the Security Council, the mission of the Force can only be terminated by resolution of the parent organ establishing the Force. It will be for that organ alone to decide whether the mission has been completed and circumstances warrant withdrawal of the Force.[15] Unless this principle is established it is difficult to believe that states will be prepared to contribute the men, money, and materials required by a peace-keeping Force. Nothing could be more destructive of the authority of the UN than to allow a single member state to terminate a peace-keeping Force, possibly at the very juncture at which it might be most needed. Thus, in any future agreements between the UN and host states, express provision should be made for establishing this principle.

## The Principle of Non-intervention

Secretary-General Hammarskjöld was emphatic about the need to isolate a UN peace-keeping Force from any internal struggle for power in the sense that the Force should not be used in such a way as to prejudice or influence any such struggle. This principle is clearly right although, as the Congo operations demonstrated,[16] it proves to be an extraordinarily difficult principle to apply in practice. It is, of course, a principle of particular relevance to Forces with a 'law and order' mandate, as in the Congo or Cyprus. But it does have wider application and it relates to the more general principle of objectivity and non-partisanship which demands that a UN Force should carry out its functions *as determined by the parent*

[14] The Secretary-General's justification for his action (also justified on other grounds than the purely legal ground referred to above) can be seen in his *Report on the reasons for UNEF's withdrawal*, S/9906 of 26 May 1967 and A/6730/Add. 3 of 26 June 1967. For criticism of this action see Rosalyn Higgins, *United Nations Peace-Keeping 1946–1967*, Documents and Commentary, 1. The Middle East (London, 1969), pp. 335–67.

[15] It may be expected that the host state's desire to have the Force withdrawn will carry great weight with the parent organ so that, in general, the Force would be withdrawn. But circumstances are conceivable in which the parent organ may feel the need to reject the request for withdrawal or, possibly more likely, in which, after the parent organ has expressed its reluctance to accede to the request for withdrawal, the host state would feel impelled to cancel its request for withdrawal.

[16] See Bowett, *op. cit.*, pp. 196–200. Conor Cruise O'Brien's book *To Katanga and Back* (London, 1962) is a revealing account of the difficulties in practice.

*organ* and should refrain from taking sides in the issues between the parties. Thus, a Force with the task of border control would be in breach of this principle if it allowed arms and supplies to pass to one faction with which it had sympathy.

It must be emphasised, however, that the principle of non-intervention does not operate to limit the powers of the Security Council under Chapter VII.[17] Thus, if the Council expressly authorises the Force to take action which would otherwise be contrary to the rule of non-intervention, the Force is certainly permitted to take the action whether or not it is likely to affect any internal struggle for power: the express authorisation to ONUC to expel mercenaries is a case in point.

## Political direction and control

The discussion of non-intervention leads one directly into the difficult question of how the necessary political direction and control is to be achieved: for, without it, it becomes impossible to translate the broad mandate of the Force into explicit military commands.

In principle, this control ought to lie with the parent organ. There are two difficult sets of circumstances in which this becomes inoperable. The first is where day-to-day control is required in a fast-moving situation. Here, there seems to be little alternative to reliance upon the Secretary-General and his representatives in the field. However, it ought to be possible to organise a rather more effective body in New York than the advisory committee of contributing states used by the Secretary-General for UNEF and ONUC. One would hope to see an executive body, reasonably small and capable of day-to-day consultation, appointed by the parent organ and not limited to the contributing states whose contingents compose the Force.

The second set of circumstances in which the parent organ ceases to be an effective source of political control is where that organ is so split by disagreement as to be incapable of formulating any guidance. This is more likely to occur in the Security Council but, as the Congo operations showed, it can also happen in the General Assembly. It was in such circumstances

[17] It is arguable that this is so only where 'enforcement action' is being taken, but in practice it is believed that any action taken under Chapter VII is not subject to the non-intervention rule. This view is based on the fact that all situations involving action under Chapter VII are, by definition, situations involving a threat to international peace. If this is so, there can scarcely be any argument that the matter is entirely one of domestic jurisdiction in which the UN has no power to interfere. After all, the members have conferred 'primary responsibility' on the Security Council for the maintenance of international peace and security and have agreed to accept and carry out the decisions of the Council.

that Dag Hammarskjöld was forced to assume a responsibility which was unfair to him, as a man, and beyond the true function of his office.

It may be hoped that, with an enlarged Security Council, this impasse will be less likely than hitherto. Alternatively, the executive body envisaged in the preceding paragraph might serve to provide continuing control even where the parent organ is frustrated by disagreement.

## Limitation of force to the exercise of self-defence

The basic assumption has always been that, whatever a Force designed for 'enforcement action' might do, a purely peace-keeping force may use its weapons only in self-defence.[18] In practice this assumption has proved very difficult to fulfil. Certainly in the Congo the express authorisation to apprehend mercenaries[19] meant the use of force beyond what would normally be accepted as necessary self-defence. Also, in the Congo the combination of freedom of movement with self-defence meant that ONUC could initiate hostilities in order to assert its right to freedom of movement where a UN military unit was being encircled.[20] And even in Cyprus, where the Secretary-General established detailed principles governing resort to self-defence, it was stated that these authorised action to prevent a violation by either side of specific arrangements agreed upon where such violation would be likely to lead to a recurrence of fighting between the two communities or endanger law and order.[21] Thus, whilst with an interposition Force like UNEF a reasonably strict interpretation of self-defence has been possible, with a Force entrusted with a 'law and order' mandate such as ONUC or UNFICYP, this interpretation has been impossible.

Perhaps the really crucial issue is the disarming by a UN Force of internal factions. Given both the principle of non-intervention and the restriction to self-defence, the obvious answer (and the one given by Ralph Bunche to General Alexander during the Congo crisis) is that the UN Force has no power to disarm. Yet, both in the Congo and in Cyprus, this has proved operationally to be disastrous to the achievement of the mandate of the Force. The simple truth is that a small UN Force loses in efficiency in more or less direct proportion to the numbers of armed men employed by the rival factions with which the Force has to deal. One solution to this might be for the UN to require from the host state and from other parties

[18] See the Secretary-General's *Summary Study on the experience of UNEF*, A/3943, para. 179.

[19] Security Council Resolution S/5002 of 24 November 1961.

[20] Bowett, *op. cit.*, pp. 203–5. And see the full discussion of the whole problem by K. Goldmann, *Peace-Keeping and Self-Defence*, IPKO Monograph No. 7, March 1968.

[21] *Aide-mémoire* dated 10 April 1964, S/5653.

or factions involved, and at the outset of the operation, some undertaking about the size of their respective forces. The Force might then be authorised to disarm elements newly-created and above those agreed levels. Admittedly, rebel factions might be unwilling to make any such agreement but if, in the absence of agreement, they faced the prospect of a UN Force being authorised to disarm any of their units they might feel it were better to secure, by agreement, acceptance of a certain *status quo* – or balance – between themselves and the governmental forces. Certainly there is no easy answer to this problem but at least the point is manifest that a small peace-keeping force can scarcely stand idly by whilst factions all around it, under varying degrees of control and discipline, acquire weapons with which they can frustrate the whole object of the UN Force.

## Headquarters Military Planning Staff

The customary *ad hoc* improvisation of peace-keeping operations is generally accepted as unsatisfactory and inefficient. If new initiatives are to be taken on peace-keeping it would be highly desirable for some rethinking to be done on the need for a small nucleus of military planners in Headquarters. At one time the staff of the Secretariat included six officers: it is now reduced to one Finnish colonel. At neither level can efficient military planning be carried out.

The need for such a staff will, of course, increase if, as suggested earlier, progress on concluding agreements under Article 43 is made. The existence of agreements committing member states to provide troops and facilities inevitably means that a good deal of continuing liaison will have to occur between these member states and UN Headquarters. Problems of training, equipment, co-ordination of supply and so forth will inevitably arise, and the competent national military authority will expect to be able to liaise with the competent international military authority: this will require more than one Finnish colonel.

One relatively new need suggests itself. The supervision of the Middle East 'standstill' agreement of 7 August 1970 has been undertaken by American satellites and high-level reconnaissance aircraft, using highly sophisticated techniques of photography. This suggests that some forms of future peace-keeping could be undertaken by these means and that, correspondingly, if agreements under Article 43 are to be made they may include the provision to the UN of assistance by such satellites and aircraft. However, it has been evident in the Middle East that the interpretation of the results of these techniques of observation is itself a considerable art, and disputes have arisen over whether Israeli photography and, later, American photography did or did not confirm the Israeli allegations that

Egyptian missiles had been moved forward during the standstill agreement. It may be, therefore, that any future UN military headquarters staff should comprise staff trained in the interpretation of this new form of evidence so that the UN organs could rely not solely on the evidence of the parties but on the evidence provided by the UN's own military staff.

These, then, are some of the important issues upon which re-thinking ought to be taking place. If circumstances are not opportune for serious study of these issues at government level, there is still point in their consideration at the private level. The important thing is that the impetus behind UN peace-keeping ought not to be lost entirely. Circumstances, and government policies, can change very rapidly and the possibilities for a new and important UN peace-keeping role in the foreseeable future are quite real enough to make the effort of re-appraisal worthwhile.

# 5. THE UNITED NATIONS AND COLONIALISM

Rupert Emerson

FROM the time of its birth the United Nations has been involved in one or another aspect of the global sweep of anti-colonialism and decolonisation which reached a high point in 1960 – the UN's African year – and has maintained its full momentum in the succeeding decade. For all of the Organization's intense and unending involvement, however, it is by no means easy to arrive at a balanced assessment of what has been the UN's distinctive contribution to the overturn of the colonial system. Particularly for those who see the UN as the best hope for salvation in an evil world, it is tempting to make the assumption that the Organization's contribution to the attack upon colonialism has been as extensive as the multitude of words and of resolutions on the subject which its different branches have poured forth. This assumption, putting the UN in the centre of the anti-colonial movement, has the merit of recognising that the Organization has indeed been concerned with any number of phases of colonialism for many years. There are, however, legitimate grounds for scepticism that a more sober review of the evidence would sustain the assumption of UN centrality.

At the other extreme the question might be posed as to how much of a difference, if any, it would have made if the UN had never come into existence. To answer that it would have made only an insignificant difference no doubt swings too far in the other direction from that of UN centrality, but it is arguable, if obviously not provable, that the flow of history would have been substantially the same except that the anti-colonialists would have been denied a world forum in which to expound their views and plead their claims.

Before proceeding to a more detailed examination of what the UN role has been, it might be useful at this point to give a single illustration, embracing a number of the new countries, which indicates the slightness of the UN participation in at least some important phases of the drive for decolonisation.

Virtually without any overt UN share in the proceedings, almost the entire French colonial empire has been transformed into an array of independent states, many of which are accused of having succumbed to neo-colonialism and still look to Paris as the co-ordinating centre of their common existence but have achieved full formal sovereignty. The start of the process was in Indo-China in whose tragically embattled career the UN has never had any real share. A greater degree of UN involvement marked the North African transition to independence, but even in relation to Algeria, which for a time made frequent appearance on the UN agenda, it would be difficult to establish that the UN debates and resolutions significantly affected either the conduct of the war or the ultimate peace-making. General de Gaulle, not noted for holding the UN in high esteem, was unlikely to have been diverted from decisions which he was taking on his own by the somewhat hesitant actions of the Assembly. For the rest of French Africa I see not the slightest sign that either the harsh treatment of Guinea or the amicable grant of independence a year or two later to the remaining French colonies in Africa, except French Somaliland, was influenced by any action taken by the UN. The one counter-argument that might be advanced is that Togo as a trust territory moved more speedily to self-government and independence than its neighbours in French West and Equatorial Africa, or Madagascar, but the differences in timing are slight and other influences, such as Ghana's independence, seem more weighty than Togo's example. The most recent manifestation of French colonial policy in the referendum held in French Somaliland in 1967 was similarly a directly French action in which the UN was allotted no share. In brief, it appears to be a justified conclusion that, apart from the trust territories, the French colonies were dealt with by Paris, and notably by President de Gaulle, in French terms and with no particular regard for the UN.

The concern of the UN with the colonial problem as it has evolved since World War II has been varied and extensive. It might, perhaps, be broken down into three major categories, of which the first two have specific Charter reference: the trusteeship system in Chapters XII and XIII, and all other non-self-governing territories in Chapter XI and its far more radical successor, the 1960 Declaration on the Granting of Colonial Independence which marked the culmination of a drastic change in the relation of the UN to colonialism. The third category, dealt with only incidentally in this chapter, is more nearly a grab-bag containing what is left over after the first two are exhausted and consists of those international disputes arising from the process of decolonisation, into which the UN has been drawn.

The first and second of these categories refer to reasonably precisely definable territories although there was for a time an effort, notably the so-called Belgian thesis, to make Chapter XI applicable to all manner of peoples and ethnic groups who might be regarded as not being endowed with self-government or an appropriate share therein in the states in which they lived. American and other Western efforts to use such an interpretation as a stick with which to beat the Soviet Union in Cold War days or as a distraction from the attacks of the anti-colonialists made no headway against the insistence that Chapter XI was aimed only at 'across salt water' dependencies of different race and culture from their alien rulers. Occasional heated controversy also arose as to whether the Assembly majority or the metropolitan power had the authority to determine which territories were to be regarded as non-self-governing under Chapter XI (e.g., the Portuguese colonies portrayed by Lisbon as provinces of a single Portugal and therefore outside the provisions of Chapter XI).

It is a somewhat arbitrary matter how far one wishes to extend the third category. Presumably, among others, the disposition of the Italian colonies would be included as would the UN interventions in the Netherlands–Indonesian conflicts, the Algerian war, and the disputes over Goa and West Irian, but controversies arising after independence, as in the Congo or over Kashmir, are more dubiously included although they are clearly a direct aftermath of the dismantling of colonialism.

## The Trusteeship System

The trusteeship system, now shrunk to a fraction of its original size, may be dealt with somewhat summarily not only because it has lost most of its significance but also because at its height it concerned only a strictly limited group of territories. Furthermore, both the purposes of the system and the nature and extent of the UN role in fulfilling them were relatively explicitly laid out in the Charter and in the individual trusteeship agreements negotiated with "the states directly concerned"[1] and approved by the Assembly, or, in the case of the one so-called strategic area, by the Security Council. The territories involved, whether in the League days as mandates or under the UN as trusteeships, were always a dissimilar and haphazard array, having nothing else in common than that they had had the good or bad fortune to belong to powers which suffered defeat in World War I or II and were therefore taken over by the victors. The heart of the matter was that through bad conscience (an early bow to the growing pressures of anti-colonialism?) or on the basis of some other political calculation, the colonial powers to which the administration of the territories was entrusted – by prior agreement among these powers themselves – for the first time in history agreed to be subjected to international supervision.

The 'A' mandates of the Middle East achieved independence prior to the inauguration of the trusteeship system. The remainder of the mandates

[1] The early flurry over the meaning of this phrase soon subsided and is now no more than an obscure historical oddity.

with the bitterly contested exception of South West Africa were turned into trusteeships by their administering powers, the United States taking over from Japan in the Trust Territory of the Pacific Islands. To this old-established list was added a ten-year trusteeship over Somaliland by Italy; but none of the colonial powers took advantage of the invitation in Article 77 voluntarily to place any of their dependencies under the system, nor was any use made of the interesting provision that the UN itself might become the administering authority of a trust territory. That such an arrangement might have been or might still be used to ease the transition of a colony to independence (e.g., the Congo in the past or the Portuguese colonies in the future) was once conceivable but has since become increasingly improbable. What can be seen as meagre approximations of such a step were the minimal and face-saving taking-over by the UN of West Irian to bridge the gap between Dutch and Indonesian rule and the proposed interim UN control of South West Africa preparatory to the latter's independence in its new guise as Namibia.

Of the original eleven trust territories, nine have come to independence or been merged with independent neighbouring states, seven in Africa and two in the Pacific, leaving only the Pacific Islands (Micronesia) administered by the United States and New Guinea by Australia. The success of the system in bringing the territories embraced within it to independence, thus meeting one of the objectives specified by the Charter, has had the unforeseen consequence of so reducing the number of administering authorities as to make it impossible to meet the Charter's provision (Article 86) that the Trusteeship Council would be "equally divided between those members of the United Nations which administer trust territories and those which do not."[2] Since the permanent members of the Security Council are automatically members of the Trusteeship Council as well, that body is currently composed of the United States and Australia as administering authorities and Britain, China, France, and the Soviet Union as the other statutory members.

The trusteeship system has essentially served its purpose and is no longer of great moment, although trouble might flare up if the future American proposals for the status of the Pacific Islands were not to meet with approval by the UN's anti-colonial majority. The greatest contribution of the system, going back to its League origins, was undoubtedly the introduction of the principle that colonial administration was a matter which might be subject to international control – a control which was significantly strengthened and improved in the Charter as compared with

[2] See Yehuda Z. Blum, "The Composition of the Trusteeship Council", *American Journal of International Law*, vol. 63, no. 4, October 1969, pp. 747–68.

the Covenant. In its substantive results as far as the administration of the trust territories is concerned, it is probable that it made no great difference. The administering authorities were also managing other colonies and appear to have followed much the same lines in both trust and other dependent territories, although they were surely more keenly aware in the former than in the latter that they were being closely watched by an international body and its often suspicious or hostile members. Perhaps the most useful question to ask, and one which is extraordinarily difficult to answer, is as to whether the example set by the mandates and trusteeship systems had a general effect on colonial administration in the sense of raising the level of concern and performance. It may be that it did, if only because of the awareness of international scrutiny. My inclination, however, is to think that while the introduction of such scrutiny was an eminently desirable step, making overt the conception that colonial rule was indeed a "sacred trust of civilisation" for which the colonial powers could be held publicly responsible, in all probability the swing away from old-style colonialism had already gone so far by 1945 as to make new departures inevitable, trusteeship system or no.

It may be a significant measure of the attractions of the trusteeship system that, to the best of my knowledge, no dependency raised a clamour to be transferred from its colonial status to trusteeship. In 1947 India proposed in the Assembly's Fourth Committee that all UN members responsible for non-self-governing territories be requested to submit trusteeship agreements for such of their colonies as were not yet ready for immediate self-government. This move was opposed by the colonial powers and others, and lost in the Assembly by a tie vote of 24–24–1. The contention of India that the trusteeship system offered the quickest and surest access to self-government and independence was challenged by its opponents and appears not to have been taken up by the colonial nationalists who preferred, it seems, to fight their own battles directly with their colonial rulers rather than to get entangled in the more cumbersome multilateral procedures of the UN. In sum, neither the colonial authorities nor their nationalist opponents looked on trusteeship as a desirable substitute for the existing state of affairs.

## Non-Self-Governing Territories

The greater innovation in the Charter was Chapter XI which, extending the trusteeship principle although in somewhat timid fashion, put all non-self-governing territories in the public domain, potentially opening them to attack by the growing anti-colonial forces on an international basis within the framework of the UN. It would be a mistake, however, to read back into the early UN years the anti-colonial assumptions and fervour which have marked the decade since the adoption of the 1960 Declaration. Colonialism had not yet been repudiated as it came to be after, say, the Bandung Conference in 1955. Drastic change was in the offing and the anti-colonial powers still had a strong hold on the UN and the vehemence and speed of the drive to end colonialism were much underestimated. Independence for even the trust territories seemed far enough off to make it unnecessary to worry about how it might be possible to maintain the prescribed balance between administering and non-administering powers in the Trusteeship Council. The colonial powers were still entrusted with the management of their non-self-governing territories, and were asked only to promote self-government, not independence. If they were required in unprecedented fashion to submit to the Secretary-General, "for information purposes", statistical and other technical information on colonial economic, social, and educational conditions, the other side of the coin was that no report on political conditions was called for, nor was any supervisory machinery established by the Charter. There is no need to undertake any detailed account of the skirmishes and battles which were fought in the UN in what now seems a remote time over the interpretation of what could properly be done, withheld, or determined under Chapter XI, since this is a story which has been frequently told[3] and has little relevance to the present day save that Portugal has clung to the old and otherwise largely moribund issues, denying the right of the Assembly to determine what are non-self-governing territories and the consequent obligation to submit reports to the Secretary-General. The pallid Committee on Information from Non-Self-Governing Territories, evenly balanced like the Trusteeship Council between administering and non-administering powers, has left only a slight imprint on the historical record and has been wholly overshadowed by its successor, to be discussed shortly. Most important of all, the attitude towards colonialism has drastically changed, and that, combined with the coming to independence of the overwhelming majority of the colonial peoples, has rendered more or less obsolete the assumptions and procedures which marked the early phases of the era of decolonisation.

For UN purposes a key and much debated issue concerned the relevance to the problems of colonialism of Article 2 (7) of the Charter which denied

[3] See, for example, Emil J. Sady, *The United Nations and Dependent Peoples* (Washington, D.C., 1956). The growing demands and achievements of what he terms the "anti-colonial coalition" in the UN's first decade are concisely set forth and evaluated by Richard J. Kozicki, "The United Nations and Colonialism", in Robert Strausz-Hupé and Henry W. Hazard (eds.), *The Idea of Colonialism* (New York, 1958).

the right of the Organization to intervene in matters essentially within the domestic jurisdiction of any state.[4] According to the older politics and jurisprudence there could be little or no doubt that colonies fell exclusively within the domestic jurisdiction of the administering state unless express treaty or other provisions imposed restrictions, as in the case of the Congo basin. It might be said that this position was further evidenced by the introduction of the mandates system which established a measure of international responsibility for a limited group of territories, thus by implication certifying the non-international status of the remaining dependencies.

For obvious reasons the colonial powers did their best to cling to this older version and to an extensive interpretation of Article 2 (7) while those who wanted international action to clear up the colonial debris turned to other articles. Chapter XI went some fragment of the way which the anti-colonial activists wanted to go, and the Charter's concern with the equal rights and self-determination of peoples was frequently cited in justification of their position as was Article 10's wide-ranging assertion that the Assembly might discuss any questions or matters within the scope of the Charter. But were the grievances against colonialism such a question or matter? Moving on to the Security Council, were disputes between a metropole and its colonies subject to consideration and action by that body, or were they domestic affairs with which outsiders had no legitimate concern? Stark and glaring contrast looms up between the older assumption that colonies are embraced within the domestic jurisdiction of their over-lords, and the accusation supported by the Assembly majority in Resolution 2105 (XX) of 1965 that colonial rule threatens international peace and security and constitutes a crime against humanity.

This issue has never come to full and open determination and the colonial powers continue to deny at least some aspects of the asserted right of international intervention, but the general proposition seems clear that the actual decision as to domestic jurisdiction or no rests with the UN majority which casts its votes on political rather than legal grounds. Overwhelmingly the presumption has grown up that colonial matters are in the international public domain, although it is also true that the colonial powers accept no obligation to obey the UN majority's rulings. The overriding of the claim of domestic colonial jurisdiction dates far back to the beginnings of the UN when a series of interventions in Indonesia were undertaken by the UN despite the protests of the Dutch who were carrying on a colonial war under the guise of a police action. The same problem has come up in a number of

[4] For a full discussion of this issue, see M. S. Rajan, *The United Nations and Domestic Jurisdiction* (Bombay, Calcutta, Madras, 1958), pp. 179–298.

other cases of which one of the most noteworthy was that of Algeria which occupied the Assembly for several crucial years, spanning the watershed of 1960. The French, holding Algeria to be not even as separable as a colony but an integral part of the departmental structure of France, denied the possibility of UN jurisdiction and refused to participate in the Assembly's deliberations. Not until 1960 could the necessary two-thirds majority be found for an Assembly resolution which recognised "the right of the Algerian people to self-determination and independence" and called upon the UN to contribute to the implementation of that right.[5] The widespread doubts which still existed were reflected in the eight negative votes and the twenty-seven abstentions, including Britain and the United States, which countered the sixty-three votes in favour. Two years later independent Algeria became a UN member.

## The 1960 Declaration on the Granting of Colonial Independence

Although effective precedents had already been established, the grounds for the removal of colonial controversies from the protection of Article 2 (7) were much strengthened by the growing conviction in the UN that colonialism, often bracketed with South African *apartheid*, was an intolerable evil, to be done away with as speedily as possible. The outstanding landmark in this movement was Resolution 1514 (XV) of 1960, the Declaration on the Granting of Independence to Colonial Countries and Peoples,[6] which came close to amending the Charter by making the war upon colonialism a major enterprise of the UN, and for many *the* major enterprise, to the dismay of those more concerned with peace and security.[7] Echoing the Bandung Conference of 1955, the necessity of bringing colonialism in all its forms and manifestations to a speedy and unconditional end was solemnly proclaimed, and immediate steps were called for in all non-self-governing territories "to transfer all powers to the peoples of

[5] Resolution 1573 (XV). For an examination of the events up to 1958, see Mohamed Alwan, *Algeria Before the United Nations* (New York, 1959).

[6] See David A. Kay, "The Politics of Decolonization", *International Organization*, vol. XXI, no. 4 (Autumn 1967) for a discussion of this resolution and the uses made of it.

[7] "This resolution was a massive escalation of the obligations accepted by the colonial powers and a reversal of the Charter's priorities with respect to dependent territories. Whereas Article 73 proclaimed that within the system of international peace and security established by the Charter the interests of the inhabitants were to be of paramount importance in administering colonial territories, Resolution 1514 (XV) denies that international peace and security can be achieved as long as there are colonial territories." David A. Kay, "The Impact of African States on the United Nations", *International Organization*, vol. XXIII, no. 1 (Winter 1969), p. 31.

those territories, without any conditions or reservations." Furthermore, the most acceptable justification for colonial rule was outlawed by the provision that "inadequacy of political, economic, social or educational preparedness should never serve as a pretext for delaying independence." In later actions by the Assembly the war on colonialism was pushed several steps further ahead, as in the already cited Resolution 2105 (XX) of 1965. The legitimacy of colonial struggles for self-determination and independence was recognised and all states were invited to provide material and moral assistance to such national liberation movements – i.e., UN members were overtly invited to enlist in armed struggles to overthrow colonial and racially discriminatory regimes. The colonial powers were also requested to dismantle any military bases installed in colonial territories.

One consideration which must be kept in mind in reviewing the Assembly's repeated anti-colonial resolutions is that they often lacked the support of a number of key states. Thus even though the Declaration of 1960 was carried by a formally unanimous vote, nine states, including Britain, France and the United States (it is said, at the direct request of Prime Minister Macmillan to President Eisenhower) in fact abstained. A much larger measure of doubt or opposition was registered in the final vote on Resolution 2105 of 1965 which came out at seventy-four in favour to six against (including Britain and United States) and twenty-seven abstentions, including France, Italy and Japan. The vote on the similar Resolution 2149 (XXI) of 1966 did a little better with a vote of 76–7–20. When so large a number of states, including some whose co-operation is of vital importance, oppose or abstain, it is evident that a decisive gap is likely to divide the ability to secure the passage of an Assembly resolution from the ability to translate it into effective political action.

A test case of absorbing interest, demonstrating the conflicting attitudes, was provided by India's armed attack upon Goa in 1961 when Nehru concluded that further efforts to negotiate with Portugal were fruitless. Portugal immediately brought the matter to the Security Council, charging India with aggression and a violation of Portugal's sovereign rights which dated back some four centuries. Speaking for the United States, Adlai Stevenson predicted the most dire results, including an ignoble death for the UN such as the League had suffered, if this blatant resort to force by India were to escape the Council's censure. India and its supporters took a radically different view of the situation, asserting that since colonialism was permanent aggression and conferred no rights, the use of force against it was *ipso facto* justified. Reversing the earlier standard assumptions as to colonial rule and domestic jurisdiction, Zorin held for the Soviet Union that since Portugal could never have rightfully ruled in Goa, which remained always a part of India, the taking back of the territory and the re-uniting of her people by India was a matter falling exclusively within her domestic jurisdiction and therefore surely not a matter in which the UN might intervene to reprove her. From this standpoint, claimed by India to represent the new international law, it was contended that Portugal was the real sinner, both for its original and continued aggression on the always-Indian soil and people of Goa and for its violation of the injunction of Resolution 1514 which called for the immediate adoption of measures to liquidate colonial empires. In the upshot a resolution calling for a cease-fire, the withdrawal of Indian forces, and negotiations, won a Security Council majority but was defeated by a Soviet veto. The United States and other opponents of India's action made no move to bring the issue to the attention of the Assembly, presumably all too keenly aware that the anti-colonial forces in that body would applaud rather than censure India for its act of national liberation.

## The Committee of Twenty-four

The Assembly's chosen instrument for the prompt and total carrying out of the decolonisation decreed in the 1960 Declaration is a body with the impressive name of the Special Committee on the Situation with Regard to the Implementation of the Declaration on the Granting of Independence to Colonial Countries and Peoples. This body, known variously as the Special Committee or as the Committee of Twenty-four, representing the numbers it achieved in 1962 after a first year with seventeen members, has zealously engaged in activities no less extensive than its title. One observer has rightly remarked that the Committee has tended to become a steering committee for much of the activity of the Assembly, and added, with some exaggeration:

> "Its reports have been of increasing size, outnumbering in length those from any previous subsidiary organ. They have all but crowded every other item except the most urgent from the agenda of both the General Assembly and the Security Council."[8]

As substance and symbol of the change which has come over the world in the colonial sphere, nothing is more striking than the composition of the Committee of Twenty-four. Where both the Trusteeship Council and the Committee on Information from Non-Self-Governing Territories (whose functions were taken over by it) had a membership equally divided between the administering and non-administering powers, the Committee of

[8] Harold S. Johnson, *Self-Determination within the Community of Nations* (Leyden, 1967), p. 42.

Twenty-four has been dominated by a guaranteed majority of confirmed anti-colonialists. This is, of course, wholly in keeping with the task assigned to it as the agency instructed to translate into political reality the sweeping decolonisation injunctions of the Declaration on Colonial Independence. In 1968, for example, in fulfilment of the agreed geographical quotas the Committee was made up of seven African, five Asian, three Latin American, and six European members (Britain, Bulgaria, Finland, Italy, Poland, and Yugoslavia) plus the United States, the Soviet Union, and Australia. Leaving aside Finland and the Latin American countries, this gave the anti-colonialists a virtually unassailable majority of at least sixteen. Who could imagine, prior to 1960, a key League or UN Committee created to preside over the liquidation of the colonies of the imperial powers whose officers would be a Tunisian as chairman, a Venezuelan and an Iraqi as vice-chairmen, and an Indian as *rapporteur*?

The wide scope with which the Committee was endowed was indicated by the fact that in its second *enabling act* of 1962[9] the Assembly invited the Committee "to continue to seek the most suitable ways and means for the speedy and total application of the Declaration to all territories which have not yet attained independence." In general terms the Committee may be said to have sought to apply to all dependencies a more free-wheeling version of the powers allotted to the Trusteeship Council in relation to the trust territories. The Committee, backed by the Assembly majority, appeared to have no doubt that it possessed almost unlimited competence to determine what the powers should do with their remaining colonies – nor any doubt as to the incorrigible untrustworthiness of the imperialists. It asserted the right to gather information from all sources, to hear petitioners and witnesses, including representatives of the liberation movements, to send visiting missions at its discretion, to lay down general lines of policy, and to set target dates for independence. One significant shortcoming, however, was that while the trusteeship system had as a basic element the agreement of the administering powers to UN supervision, the Committee of Twenty-four was endowed with no such agreement. The extensive jurisdiction claimed by the Committee was met by the insistence of the colonial powers that they remained masters in their own colonial domains until such time as independence or some other acceptable status was achieved. Thus the British announced in 1962 that while they would co-operate with the Committee they would not accept any intervention by it in the administration of territories for which Britain was responsible. One of the resulting sore points for the Committee in the conduct of its business has been that the British and others have refused to grant it

[9] Resolution 1810 (XVII), 1962. The first was Resolution 1654 (XVI) of 1961.

permission to send visiting missions to dependencies whose present and future status was under investigation.[10]

In the intervening decade since the adoption of the Declaration a number of colonies have achieved independence, but it would be difficult to establish that the Committee played any significant role in a process which was already well under way although it vigorously publicised the need for prompt action.[11]

It has already been remarked that almost all the French colonies had come to independence or been taken into France as Departments prior to the 1960 Declaration with no reason to assume that the UN was significantly involved. The same is surely true for the impressive array of presently independent former British colonies in Asia, Africa, and elsewhere, with India and Pakistan heading the list, as well as for the ex-American-controlled Philippines and for the once Belgian Congo. Since 1960 a number of other territories, almost all British, and for the most part in east and southern Africa and the West Indies, have come to independence under circumstances which leave little room for an assumption that the Committee's activities had any serious influence. Thus to pick two examples somewhat at random, the UN had no part in either the creation or the break-up of the West Indian Federation and the membership in the UN of its component parts, with some smaller pieces still left over; and it was equally uninvolved in the independence of Malaya and Singapore, the banning of Singapore from the federation, and the formation of Malaysia, save that the Secretary-General was called in at the last moment to certify that the people of Sabah and Sarawak wanted to enter into a union with Malaya.

Inevitably the Committee of Twenty-four has found itself embroiled in the more difficult colonial problems since the relatively simple and straightforward ones were dealt with by the colonial powers without lingering to become subjected to protracted UN scrutiny and criticism. By 1969 the Committee's original list of territories still under colonial rule had been cut well below half of its original size but a substantial workload

[10] See, for example, the resolution adopted by the Committee of Twenty-four on 15 August 1969, regretting that the efforts "to send visiting missions to colonial territories have been persistently frustrated by the administering powers." The vote on this resolution was 17–4 (Britain, Italy, Norway, and the US), *UN Monthly Chronicle*, August–September 1969, pp. 104–7. The Secretary-General in the Introduction to his Annual Report for 1969 gave as an example of what can be achieved through close co-operation between the administering powers and the UN the "fruitful operation" conducted in 1968 at the request of the Spanish government by a UN mission to Equatorial Guinea "which enabled that Territory to accede to independence as a single entity, and later to full membership in the United Nations." *ibid* (October 1969), p. 105.

[11] David W. Wainhouse, *Remnants of Empire: The United Nations and the End of Colonialism* (New York and Evanston, 1964). Appendix I lists the sixty-four non-self-governing, mandated and trust territories on the Committee's books in 1963.

remained. As the British representative analysed the situation in April 1969,[12] the most intractable cases were those located in southern Africa, where the Committee had devoted much attention to the Portuguese colonies, Rhodesia, and Namibia – nominally removed from South African jurisdiction but actually wholly under South African management. It was his suggestion that these southern African issues could best be dealt with by the Assembly and Security Council, already much concerned with them; but it is highly unlikely that the Committee could be persuaded, or that the Assembly would want it, to abandon its involvement with what are after all by far the most grievous colonial issues still extant.

For the rest the British representative pronounced Hong Kong, presumably with little expectation of counter-argument, to be a special case; and Gibraltar might well be put in the same category. This left as the Committee's principal and distinctive concern thirty colonial territories with a total population of some 3,500,000. Britain, the most indefatigable collector of bits and pieces of empire, was responsible for eighteen of these small territories with a population of 1,300,000, ranging from nearly 500,000 in Fiji (independent in October 1970) to less than 100 on Pitcairn Island. The United States, in addition to the Pacific Trust Territory, was responsible for three territories: Guam, American Samoa, and the Virgin Islands, leaving aside Puerto Rico whose anomalous status as a Commonwealth associated with the United States attracted the attention of members of the Committee from time to time.

For these remaining thirty dependencies the one common characteristic is that they all range from small down to mini-size, and therefore in varying degree require special handling. Twenty-five of these little territories, largely in the West Indies, but also scattered around the globe, were dealt with in characteristic fashion in Assembly Resolution 2592 (XXIV) of 1969 which re-affirmed the inalienable right of their peoples to self-determination and independence; denied that questions of size, geographical isolation, and limited resources should delay the implementation of the 1960 Declaration; denounced any attempt at disruption of their national unity and territorial integrity, and the establishment of military bases; asked reconsideration of the question of visiting missions; and called upon the UN to render all help to them in their efforts freely to decide their future status. Also characteristically the vote was 88–1–26 (the latter including Australia, Belgium, Britain, Canada, France, Italy, Netherlands, New Zealand, Singapore, Trinidad, and the United States).[13]

[12] *UN Monthly Chronicle* (May 1969), p. 22.

[13] For what amounts to a virtual compilation of the positions and demands of the Assembly and the Committee of Twenty-four, covering all aspects of the UN attack on colonialism, see Resolution 2548 (XXIV) of 1969.

Neither any investigation of the complex and troublesome problem of mini-states and territories[14] nor any detailed recital of the continuous and unremitting activity of the Committee of Twenty-four and the Assembly can be undertaken here. One point which deserves attention, however, is that the Committee, with Assembly support, has always inclined strongly to the opinion that only full independence can really be regarded as constituting a proper exercise of the right of self-determination, which is undoubtedly generally valid at least for the larger dependencies. It has somewhat grudgingly been conceded, drawing on criteria laid down earlier in relation to the status of non-self-governing territories, that where there is clear evidence of free popular acceptance some alternative outcome of self-determination in the form of association or integration with another independent state can meet UN requirements. Any such decision is not without reason scrutinised with care to guard against imperialist intrigue and neo-colonialism, and a proviso is favoured which allows later reconsideration of any act of self-determination which falls short of independence. In view of the difficulties which small or tiny states face in the world, it might be more advantageous if the Committee were to encourage rather than to discourage freely negotiated arrangements which enable some voluntary pooling of facilities and resources, as in the relations between New Zealand and Samoa or the Cook Islands, the United States and Puerto Rico, Britain and some of the smaller West Indian islands, the Netherlands and Surinam and the Netherlands Antilles, and Malaya and Sabah and Sarawak.

A serious breaking point, as I have already indicated, looms up in the difference between the basic assumptions of the colonial powers and those of the anti-colonial majority as to the powers of the UN in relation to dependencies. If it is an exaggeration to say that the anti-colonialists regard the UN as now endowed with the right to make definitive determinations concerning the destiny of the remaining colonies, it is surely not far amiss to suggest that they see the Organization endowed now with some approximation of such jurisdiction and believe that it rightfully should have the whole of it. The colonial powers, even if in some part only as a series of rearguard actions, cling to their claim of sovereign rights over their dependencies and deny that any UN organ is competent to intervene in, or to strip them of, control over territories for which they claim responsibility. The outcome is that the Committee and the Assembly pass many resolutions which have the appearance of 'laying down the law' for the colonial

[14] This problem is dealt with in *Status and Problems of Very Small States and Territories*, Umtar Series No. 3 (UN Institute for Training and Research, New York, 1969) and Patricia Wohlgemuth Blair, *The Ministate Dilemma* (Carnegie Endowment for International Peace, New York, 1967).

powers, but the latter go on substantially as before making their own decisions as to what reforms they will introduce and how and when they will move to independence or some other arrangement which they find more fitting in the given circumstances. The three most extreme examples are Portugal which continues to deny all UN jurisdiction over or even concern with its extensive colonial holdings, Rhodesia which intransigently clings to its illegal white independence, and South Africa which defies the UN on a number of fronts. For the present purpose in particular South Africa pays no attention to the UN decree that cancelled her mandate to administer South West Africa and effectively recognised the independence of that territory. In my opinion, which is no doubt a minority opinion, the UN debases its currency and its credibility when it blows thunderous trumpets as in the case of South West Africa, which cause no walls to fall down and leave intact what has been destroyed in words.

## Conclusions

It would be pleasant and convenient to be able to conclude this survey with an unambiguous assessment of the role which the UN has played in the historic sweep of decolonisation of the last quarter century, but I fear that the evidence presently available does not lend itself to such a result. The principal point of perplexity derives from uncertainty as to the nature of the relationship between the colonial powers and the UN: to what extent have these powers and their supporters taken significant notice of, and allowed their policies to be shaped by, the anti-colonial speeches and resolutions which have poured forth from the UN organs in a growing flood? An immense measure of decolonisation, unimaginable in its extent and speed only a few decades ago, has been accomplished in response to a variety of different pressures: how significantly has the UN contributed to those pressures?

The Committee of Twenty-four and the Assembly have gone far to strip colonialism of its legitimacy, and yet the colonial powers continue to administer their dependencies and put up at least a bold front of not being afflicted by the sense of guilt which their opponents assert should overwhelm them. But with the exception of Portugal they do acknowledge as never before that colonialism is a basically unacceptable institution which should be brought to an end with reasonable and orderly speed. Although the ethical and political presumptions have turned sharply against colonialism, it would be difficult to conclude that it has in fact become illegal under international law. Colonies in fact go on, even though the Assembly calls for their end, and the multiplicity of transactions carried on under colonial auspices presumably continue to have validity. In the same fashion the right of all peoples to self-determination (with special, if implicit, reference to colonies) has been repeatedly proclaimed and is enshrined in the first article of both International Covenants on Human Rights, but its status as an operative principle of international law is highly dubious.[15]

Inis L. Claude Jr. in 1967 remarked that: "Not everything happens at the United Nations, of course, but the politics of decolonization has been notably concentrated in its jurisdictional funnel," and added that the case of Goa "is a striking example of what the United Nations has done for anti-colonialism or to put it differently what the anti-colonials have managed to do in, and with, the United Nations."[16]

I can only view the first of these statements with considerable scepticism. The UN has not in fact established a working jurisdiction over decolonisation, and the great bulk of the politics of decolonisation has not passed through any UN funnel but has been worked out, whether peacefully or belligerently, by the colonial powers and the peoples whom they ruled. Aside from the trust territories, the UN has only rarely had any share in the proceedings whatsoever. As for Goa, the anti-colonials in the UN had no more to do with it than, with the aid of the Soviet veto in the Security Council, to make it impolitic for the opponents of India's action to lay the matter before the Assembly. India on its own took over Goa and its move neither required nor secured UN blessing.

What the anti-colonials have done in and with the UN is to turn it into an agency a major purpose of which is to agitate against colonialism and to compile the case against it, to bring to public attention the militants who combat it and to urge that aid be provided them in their struggle. The UN in general and the Committee of Twenty-four in particular have furnished the anti-colonials with a meeting place and machinery to co-ordinate their efforts and an invaluable platform from which to broadcast their views to the world at large. The UN has become the major centre for agitation against colonialism, but action to maintain, reform, or end colonialism still remains essentially a matter for the colonial powers and the colonial peoples. I take it to be beyond doubt that the change in the international climate of opinion from acceptance of colonialism to its repudiation is of

[15] See my *Self-Determination Revisited in the Era of Decolonization*, Occasional Paper No. 9, Harvard University Center for International Affairs (Cambridge, Mass., 1964).

[16] Inis L. Claude, Jr., *The Changing United Nations* (New York, 1967), pp. 53 and 61. Professor Claude also develops the challenging theme that the UN has been dominated by two Cold Wars, one between East and West, the other between North and South. The North chose to accommodate the South in order to concentrate on holding the line against the East. "In short, decolonization has triumphed largely because the West has given priority to the containment of Communism over the perpetuation of colonialism." p. 55.

great importance in speeding colonialism's demise. It is less evident that the UN has made a distinctively effective contribution to that change although the anti-colonials have made good and innovatory use of the potentialities of the Organization to multiply the attacks upon colonialism and to appeal to a worldwide audience. The question remains unanswered whether both the climate of opinion and the actual progress of de-colonisation might have been much the same if the UN had never been born.

# 6. THE UNITED NATIONS AND INTERNATIONAL ECONOMIC RELATIONS

Susan Strange

LOOKING back to the early days when the United Nations was beginning to take shape in the mid-forties, most of the ideas then current about the nature and scope of the envisaged post-war international organisation were taken over intact – or sometimes with modification or amplification – from the old League of Nations. Only in two or three respects at most did the concept of what the UN ought to do differ markedly from the League idea. There was the idea that it should be armed with a security force. And there was the idea that it should show some minimal concern for the rights and welfare of the individual as well as for the welfare of states in the international community. And lastly – and as it has turned out, most importantly – there was the idea that an international organisation should be directly concerned not only with political security, progress and stability, but also with international economic conditions – with the prevention of slump, unemployment and dire poverty as much as with the prevention of war. This idea, the expression of collective concern, was the obvious product of the traumatic shared experience of the world economic depression, just as the idea of collective effort to improve international security was the product of the shared experience of war twice in a generation.

What follows is an attempt to examine the content of this idea in a little more detail; to assess in broad outline the consequences in international economic relations from 1945 to the present; and finally to suggest what options and prospects may lie ahead for the UN in its economic activities.

## Concepts, Hopes and Premises

Picking out the predominating themes and ideas from among all those current in the mid-forties about how the UN might express this increased concern for economic conditions and what role it could and should play in international economic relations is not easy. A considerable volume of material was published at the time – probably a disproportionate amount of it in English. Many books and articles were written and speeches made about the economic future of the world and the contribution that international machinery could make to it. Most of the blueprints then outlined now seem decidedly misty at the edges and unduly influenced by the problems of the thirties. This was hardly surprising for the post-war future was clouded with uncertainty; and hopes and fears for it differed widely according to geography, wealth and historical experience. Everyone was united only in the simple hope that it would not – surely, could not – be as bad as the past, and that in improving on the dismal record of the thirties, the UN might be able to help. The UN in short, was to be (so it was hoped) an aid to economic as well as to political progress.

But progress to what ultimate goal? And by what practical means? The underlying issues were, on the whole, avoided. The Preamble of the Charter speaks only of economic 'advancement'. The Purposes mention only the solving of international economic 'problems'. The progressive idea was universal but indeterminate.

Three other coexisting ideas, however, merit attention. None was so universally subscribed to as the progressive idea, but all exerted strong influence on the shaping of the UN in its economic activities; and none was, at the time, directly challenged, though tacit doubts and reservations undoubtedly existed. One was the belief in the interdependence of the political and economic roles of the UN, the belief that economic problems and difficulties were an impediment to peace and economic progress and stability a contribution to peace. As it was succinctly put by one effective publicist for the UN, "We shall not succeed in establishing a secure political world following this war unless we solve our economic problems. High levels of employment and a high degree of economic stability underlie, basically, all programs of international relations. *Unless these economic ends are achieved, any United Nations program along political lines will utterly fail.* It would be suicidal to assume that these economic ends can be reached by letting things take their course."[1] The same thought is to be found in the 1945 report from the Economic and Financial Committee of the League of Nations on post-war commercial policy.[2]

Another influential idea concerned the means to be used to achieve greater economic welfare. This was the multilateralist belief that free trade was the best path to all-round economic progress. It was the ideology of the United States (or, at least, of the Roosevelt Administration) and of the Belgians, the Swedes and some other developed countries. It was the only economic ideology formally incorporated in UN declarations and agreements (e.g. the original Atlantic Charter, the wartime Lend-Lease Agree-

[1] (My italics). Alvin H. Hansen, *America's Role in the World Economy* (London, 1945), p. 27. Hansen was Professor of Political Economy at Harvard and an adviser to the Federal Reserve Board in Washington.

[2] League of Nations, Report of Economic and Financial Committees, *Commercial Policy in the post-war World*, p. 33.

ments, and later the Havana Charter and the General Agreement on Tariffs and Trade). It committed the UN machinery to attempt the elimination of discriminatory barriers to international trade. But, although not directly challenged, it was never really subscribed to by either the Soviet bloc members or by the newer and poorer members of the UN and it was only accepted (as the Havana negotiations showed) by some other important members such as Britain and France with important political reservations.[3]

And thirdly there was the faith in functionalism, in all its variations – the faith, that is, that international organisation and the habits of international co-operation it was supposed to foster could be used to erode and ultimately perhaps to supplant conflicting nationalisms. The influence that this exerted was undoubtedly more internal than external; that is, it encouraged and sustained (and, indeed, inspired) many of those directly involved in operating international organisations as officials or, sometimes, as delegates. And, although it counted few adherents among the top policymakers of the UN's member governments, they did not directly contradict or stamp on it. Meanwhile this faith in a better hereafter possibly accounted for the undismayed perseverance displayed by international officials and participants in the UN and its specialised agencies when their earlier hopes and ambitions were frustrated or disappointed.

No less important in the early days of the UN – and perhaps rather more so – were certain preconceptions or premises then current about the UN's role in the international economy that did at least as much as the three more ideological concepts I have just mentioned to influence the Organization in its choice of goals and aims. I would distinguish three such premises as important. And for convenience would call them the Unitarian idea, the Reformist idea, and the Egalitarian idea. Over the years each of these ideas has undergone a measure of change or modification. And it may be that an examination of how these basic premises have fared will throw more light on the UN's economic work over the last twenty-five years or so than attention either to the formal and ideological concepts present at its inception or to the structural and programmatic changes and innovations it has since undergone.

First, a word of explanation. By Unitarian, I mean simply the 'One World' concept applied to international economic relations. More than interdependence, this is the premise that states in their international economic relations are part of a single system, that broadly speaking the players are engaged in one game, the actors in one drama, rather than

[3] For the political background to the British commitment see Richard Gardner, *Sterling Dollar Diplomacy* (Oxford, 1956. Revised edition, New York, 1969), and Gardner Patterson, *Discrimination in International Trade: The Policy Issues 1945–65* (Princeton, 1966).

in multiple, different and sometimes overlapping systems, games or dramas.

By the Reformist premise I mean the implicit assumption that the UN's role was to work within the international market economy system of the non-Communist world, to try and improve on it – but not to destroy it or even radically to change it. It was to be a reformist agency, not a revolutionary one – though the content of its reformist mission was defined only in the most vague and general terms of producing more welfare and less friction. This vagueness permitted divergent and as it turned out often conflicting interpretations to be harboured within the Organization.

The third premise about the UN's role was the Egalitarian idea. It was taken from principles of liberal political democracy and it supposed that states in the Organization would have an equal voice in matters outside the question of security and that rules decided on any majority decision would be applied equally to all. It was clearly expressed at the founding San Francisco conference when the proposal that seats on the Economic and Social Council should be reserved – as in the Security Council – to the five Permanent Members or else to the 'industrially' important countries was defeated in favour of the more egalitarian rotary arrangement actually adopted.[4]

Summing up, the intentions of the UN towards its new-found role in international economic relations were progressive, but much less precise than its political intentions. It was hoped that it might contribute one of the conditions then thought necessary to peace, and that it might help improve economic conditions for the poorer members. Some of its enthusiasts even thought it would lay the functionalist foundations of eventual world government. But the only firm economic ideology formally adopted by its agencies was the multilateralist policy of non-discriminatory trade liberalisation favoured by the United States. Indeed, its initial ideas were overly influenced in retrospect by the historical experience of the United States and by the intellectual climate of America in the early forties. Even more than in the political arena, this left the UN unprepared for the impact of the Cold War and the non-participation of the Soviet Union and its allies in most of its economic activities. It also made little allowance for the redistributive claims of the developing countries or for the divergent ideas and interests of a revived Europe.

[4] i.e. of staggered elections every three years for one-third of the seats on the ECOSOC. See UNCIO, vol. 10, p. 53. In practice, compromise has triumphed and Britain, France, the Soviet Union and the United States have always been sure of their seats on the ECOSOC. The desire to accommodate Afro-Asian aspirations was, of course, primarily responsible for increasing the Council's membership from 18 to 27.

## The United Nations Factor

We come now to the question of what impact, if any, the UN and its associated agencies have had on the course of international economic relations and the development of the international economy over the past twenty-five years, and by what means this impact has been effected.

To put it in perspective, it seems to me that any serious assessment of these activities – as distinct from a mere chronicle or catalogue of events – must begin by admitting that there has been a very large area of international economic relations over which the UN has had little or no apparent influence. Or, to put it another way, in which the UN factor has been nil. And this in itself is important because it means that the UN has been consequently confined to certain limited areas of concern to its members' foreign economic policy rather than to the whole field.

The Unitarian expectation in fact lasted no longer than the United Nations Relief and Rehabilitation Administration, an organisation brought to a sudden end, it will be remembered, by the unwillingness of the United States Congress to finance political adversaries in Central and Eastern Europe. Until this happened UNRRA had earlier asserted the unitary character of post-war economic problems by providing relief regardless of politics not only to East as well as West Europe, but also to the Far East. The latter venture revealed new depths of political corruption and proved a chastening experience even to Mayor La Guardia of New York City.[5]

From late 1947 or thereabouts there emerged not one world of international economic relations but three. The post-war world was trinitarian, not unitarian; the state-managed economies of the Soviet bloc, the advanced market economies of the 'Atlantic' bloc; and the underdeveloped economies of the poor 'developing' countries. The question then became, not what role the UN would play in international economic relations, but what it might play in relations within each of the three groups and between each group and the other two. A shorthand convenience would be to call the three groups, East, West, and South. This gives six main sets of relationships: East–East, West–West, South–South, East–West, West–South, and East–South.[6]

A rough check on the state of international economic co-operation in 1970, on the main international agencies, their memberships and activities, shows that the UN has played no role at all in East–East relations which

[5] Although a Republican, La Guardia was nominated by the Democratic Administration to head the post-war relief organisation in nationalist China.

[6] One could in fact distinguish at least three other important groupings of states in which economic co-operation and organisation was developed outside the UN, such as the Western Hemisphere, the Sterling Commonwealth and the Franc Zone. But for simplicity and speed I have left them out.

throughout the period were conducted directly by the Soviet Union (and later China) with the East European countries either on a bilateral basis or through Comecon and other exclusive bloc organisations.

In East–West relations, the UN made a valiant but almost totally vain attempt under Gunnar Myrdal at the UN Economic Commission for Europe to act as bridge or go-between between the two alliance systems. So long as the Cold War lasted, ECE had to admit the impenetrability of political barriers – put up by both sides – to East–West trade. Commerce, credit and exchange arrangements were limited to the bare crude minimum. And when the situation did ease it was not the doing of the UN but of individual 'West' countries (especially West Germany) who made special arrangements with the members of the East group.

Similarly, East–South relations between the Soviet Union on one side and its allies and the LDC's on the other were at first minimal sometimes to the point of non-existence. And when in the middle fifties the effort was made to develop a Soviet aid and trade policy, it too was bilaterally managed and highly selective and discriminatory. The UN played no part at all in it.

This leaves, in effect, only three out of the six sets of relationships open to influence from the UN factor. In each of them I would argue that the UN machinery has played only a minority part; in no case and in no sense has its influence been the predominant one. Governments have chosen other instrumentalities to manage their economic relations with one another or they have left them unmanaged or they have dealt with them on an *ad hoc* bilateral basis. The regulatory and redistributive activities of the UN have been marginal in their effect, and their effects have been mixed. This is not to say that the UN has done nothing or that its efforts have been negligible – only that the external constraints on the UN are as important to an understanding of its current mood of frustration and importance as its internal difficulties and shortcomings.

To this point I shall return soon. Meanwhile let us look a little more closely at these other three sets of relationships: West–West, South–South and West–South.

By West–West, I mean the group of developed market-economy countries of North America and Western Europe plus Japan and Australia. These are the core of the international economy and are distinguished by the large areas of national economic activity left to private management by high rates of fixed investment per head and by high rates of capital accumulation and therefore large annual increments of current wealth – a different matter from the percentage rate of growth which can be high but make little difference to current consumption. From 1947, the UN's capacity to influence relations within this group was seriously inhibited mainly as a result of second thoughts on the part of the United States. The multilateralist ideology urged on the UN by the United States had supposed a joint effort by the International Monetary Fund and by a complementary International Trade Organisation to see the principles of free, non-discriminatory trade and payments applied to international commerce. Instead, from 1947 on, the American Congress decided first to claw back from the already drafted ITO its own right to discriminate between domestic and foreign producers, with the result that only an attenuated GATT remained as the basis for UN trade programmes. Secondly, the United States in its foreign economic policy was overtaken by the apparent exigencies of the Cold War. By unilateral decision, it not only set about aiding its European allies through the European Recovery Programme but by unilateral decision allowed them (and their overseas associates in the sterling area and franc zone) to discriminate against dollar imports by means of exchange controls and inconvertible currencies. And though GATT was allowed to begin its intermediary work for the reduction of tariff barriers to trade, it was obliged to submit to a division of labour with the Organisation for European Economic Co-operation which was entrusted with reducing quantitative restrictions on trade. At one point in the Korean War even, both trade-expanding organisations were in part suspended in favour of a temporary trade-restraining body (the International Materials Conference) which tried briefly and with limited success to bring back the wartime planned allocation system for some key raw materials.

Later, when general currency convertibility was restored between members of this group, the pure doctrine of multilateralism was again compromised. The United States gave its approval to establishment of a common market by the European Economic Community, and this meant that again a large area of trade relations within this group was abstracted from UN intervention. And inside four years the strains put on the international monetary system required that the IMF should be supplemented by special arrangements and machinery between what came to be known, from these arrangements, as the Group of Ten.

The Group of Ten in fact became more than an intruder on IMF territory. From the mid-sixties onwards it was used to decide the main outlines of new forms of co-operation such as the Special Drawing Rights arrangements which the IMF was then to administer. Here and in the Organisation for Economic Co-operation and Development (the successor organisation to OEEC) the Western group co-ordinated when they could their policies towards the South group.

This group is of course distinguished by low incomes and consequently lesser involvement in the international economy save as the hosts to foreign private investment and as the producers of primary products for export. Its internal, South–South relationships are therefore, by definition, the least important to it. However, taking their cue from the European countries, 'South' countries have tried at first through the UN and then outside it, to develop international machinery and new discriminatory economic relationships between themselves, usually on a regional basis. Besides the UN Economic Commissions for Latin America, Asia and the Far East, and Africa, there have been a number of attempts, none of them too successful, to develop would-be common markets and free trade areas – all outside the UN.

It is in the sixth and last set of relationships, usually called the North–South relationship (but which I think are more properly described as West–South) that the UN has perforce concentrated its attentions and its activities – which have thus become somewhat skewed or lopsided. As already pointed out, in West–South relations, the prevailing pattern is for the South to sell primary products and act as host to Western investment. The question is therefore whether the UN factor has affected to any marked degree the terms and volume of this pattern of trade or the terms and pattern of this investment.

An early and significant failure to use the UN to regulate West–South trade and to stabilise conditions for primary producers was the defeat of Lord Boyd-Orr's proposals as the first Director-General of the Food and Agriculture Organization for a World Food Board operating international buffer stocks of key commodities. Progress with commodity agreements since that failure has been slow, painful and piecemeal, much of it conducted outside the UN. Market-management of this kind has in fact succeeded best (as in wheat, bacon, dried milk) where a large part of production is in developed countries. Only in 1967 did the IMF start in a tentative fashion to use some of its not inconsiderable funds to finance schemes for commodity stabilisation. (Its compensatory financing scheme to lend money when export earnings fall as a result of falls in world market prices and other circumstances outside the LDC's control was begun slightly earlier, in 1965.)[7]

The major attempt to change the terms of West–South trade through the UN has of course been made through the United Nations Conference on Trade and Development, first in 1964 and again at UNCTAD II in

[7] The only area in which market management has been regularly practised for a long time and is now taken for granted is in transport and communications, where the technological factor tends to exclude the poor countries from participation in the market-managing arrangements. These are often organised not by governments but by the operators, as in the rate-fixing negotiations of the shipping conferences and the International Air Transport Association of airlines.

1968. Through UNCTAD, the South has managed at last to organise a permanent lobby, with a secretariat, to speak for the developing countries. But it is essentially a lobby rather than a pressure group, and the limitations of UNCTAD pressures were demonstrated by the adoption of conciliation procedures before important votes.[8] It is worth noting that the only countries to organise at all effectively for trade negotiation have been the oil states – who are often the least needy of the developing countries.

Apparently much more successful have been the UN efforts to encourage financial and technical assistance in West–South directions. The story is a familiar one, beginning with the World Bank and the Expanded Programme of Technical Assistance and proliferating from these starting points in both directions. The International Finance Corporation, the Special Fund, and the International Development Association have provided new sorts and additional forms of finance, while all the specialised agencies – FAO, UNESCO, ILO, WHO, ICAO, IMF and the Bank as well as the UN itself, have made increasing provision of human capital in the form of technical assistance and training facilities. In 1965, the EPTA and the Special Fund were united to form the United National Development Programme. In the same year, the General Assembly voted to set up the United Nations Industrial Development Organization as a subsidiary agency in which the majority of votes on the Industrial Development Board would be from the South but which would have its administrative expenses met from the regular UN budget.

The concrete results of all this constitutional activity and of the increasing exhortation that has accompanied and preceded it, has been undeniably a substantial increase – some have called it 'immense', but this is a slight exaggeration[9] – in the financial resources channelled through the UN system. The figures are as follows:

*UN Aid Budgets*, 1958 *and* 1967
($ million)

| | | |
|---|---|---|
| 1958 | EPTA budget | 33·8 |
| | UN budget | 10·7 |
| | TOTAL | 44·5 |

[8] See Richard N. Gardner, "The United Nations Conference on Trade and Development", in Richard N. Gardner and Max F. Millikan (eds.), *The Global Partnership: international agencies and economic development* (New York, 1969), pp. 99–130.

[9] Leon Gordenker and Harold Jacobson, "Critical Choices for the UN System", *Orbis* (Spring 1970), p. 48. The budget figures in the table are taken from this source.

| | | |
|---|---|---|
| 1967 | UNDP budget (technical assistance) | 50·6 |
| | UNDP – Special Fund pre-investment aid | 92·9 |
| | UN budget | 45·5 |
| | UN special trust funds | 14·4 |
| | TOTAL | 203·4 |

Large as these increases in UN budgets may seem in isolation, it is important to put them in the context both of other forms of official aid, bilateral and multilateral, and to take into account also the more or less parallel growth, but on a much larger scale, of private credit – direct, indirect and commercial. The tables below attempt to do this for selected years in the last decade or so. (Statistical material for the 1950's is incomplete.)

TABLE I*

GROSS DISBURSEMENTS OF MULTILATERAL AID, 1960, 1964 and 1968
($ *million*)

| | 1960 | 1964 | 1968 |
|---|---|---|---|
| World Bank | 341 | 464 | 605 |
| IDA | — | 148 | 215 |
| IFC | 13 | 16 | 31 |
| Inter-American Development Bank | — | 131 | 233 |
| Asian Development Bank | — | — | 20 |
| African Development Bank | — | — | 2 |
| EEC—European Development Fund | 4 | 85 | 121 |
| —European Investment Bank | — | 6 | 10 |
| UN Institutions | 125 | 263 | 300 |
| TOTAL | 483 | 1,112 | 1,537 |

* *Source:* Lester Pearson *et al., Partners in Development* (London, 1969), Table 25, p. 390.

The first table shows the gross disbursements of multilateral aid through the UN and other agencies. It indicates a steady expansion in World Bank financing, supplemented by IDA lending on concessionary terms – actually 1967 was IDA's peak year, funds later were running low – and by a modest contribution from IFC. UN disboursements have also grown but have been overtaken by the combined disbursements of the various regional funds and banks.

The second table is of net financial flows from all sources, private and official. It shows, firstly, the persistent overshadowing of multilateral aid by bilateral aid. It also shows the steady growth of – mainly bilateral –

TABLE II*

NET FLOWS TO DEVELOPING COUNTRIES IN SELECTED YEARS, 1957–68

(*$ million*)

| | 1957 | 1960 | 1962 | 1964 | 1966 | 1968 |
|---|---|---|---|---|---|---|
| Official aid – bilateral | 3,435 | 4,138 | 4,996 | 5,570 | 5,802 | 5,768 |
| Official aid – multilateral | 421 | 548 | 539 | 382 | 477 | 661 |
| Other official aid[1] | — | 241 | 455 | −63 | 306 | 481 |
| Direct investment[2] | 2,724 | 1,782 | 1,528 | 1,910 | 2,355 | 2,775 |
| Bilateral portfolio | | | 153 | 290 | 282 | 730 |
| Multilateral portfolio[3] | 601 | 691 | 239 | 141 | 15 | 605 |
| Export credit[4] | 454 | 347 | 577 | 851 | 1,189 | 1,734 |
| TOTAL | 7,655 | 8,075 | 8,487 | 9,080 | 10,461 | 12,753 |

[1] Export credits extended by independent government institutions. For 1957, these are included under the last item, 'Export credits'.

[2] Includes British and Italian bilateral portfolio investment.

[3] Investment financed by bonds issued by the World Bank and other international financial institutions.

[4] Figures not complete nor fully comparable.

* *Source:* Lester Pearson *et al.*, *op cit.*, Table 15, p. 378.

official aid from the rich countries to the poor since 1957. The growth of private financial flows (direct, indirect and commercial) has been just as great, but not so steady. The main item, direct investment, actually fell from $2,724 million in 1957 to $1,970 million in 1958 and did not recover until the mid-1960's when it rose, equally precipitately, from $1,910 million in 1964 to $2,702 million in 1965. By 1968, it is clear that commercial credit was becoming an important source of finance for the developing countries, making up more than 9 per cent of the total against under 6 per cent in 1957.

The growth of commercial credit as a form of medium-term finance for development is underlined by the breakdown in Table III of insured credits between those for 1 to 5 years and those for over 5 years. From 1961 onwards (except in 1963) the latter total has been the larger and by 1968 was estimated at $1,272 million against $471 million for the shorter-term credits. The accelerating pace of expansion for the longer-term credits is also suggested in the final table which gives the totals of insured credits extended annually for periods over 5 years. It must be further noted that all these statistics on commercial credit are very incomplete, and if anything, understate its importance. They cover only insured credits, not the uninsured portion of the total credit which may range from 5 to as

Table III*

NET CHANGES IN INSURED COMMERCIAL CREDIT TO DEVELOPING COUNTRIES

($ *million*)

| | 1957 | 1960 | 1962 | 1964 | 1966 | 1968 |
|---|---|---|---|---|---|---|
| Credits for 1–5 years | 173 | 420 | 232 | 400 | 481 | 471 |
| Credits for over 5 years | 318 | 151 | 426 | 542 | 734 | 1,272 |
| Total | 491 | 571 | 658 | 941 | 1,215 | 1,744 |

* *Source:* "Use of Commercial Credit by Developing Countries", *IMF Staff Papers* (March 1970), Table I, p. 37.
All figures are for the net additions to insured credits extended to developing countries by the members of the Development Assistance Committee of OECD.

Table IV*

PUBLIC AND PRIVATE INSURED COMMERCIAL CREDITS EXCEEDING 5 YEARS

($ *million*)

| | 1957 | 1960 | 1962 | 1964 | 1966 | 1968 |
|---|---|---|---|---|---|---|
| Public credits | 80 | 532 | 335 | 532 | 388 | 760 |
| Insured private credits | 14 | 77 | 364 | 953 | 1,291 | 3,200 |
| Total | 94 | 609 | 699 | 1,485 | 1,679 | 3,960 |

* *Source: IMF Staff Papers, op. cit.*, Table 3, p. 40. Figures compiled by OECD Trade Committee, Group on Export Credits and Credit Guarantees, and cover gross credits extended by members of this group to developing countries.

much as 25 per cent of the total. Nor do they include transactions (of which there is surely a growing number) by international companies with their subsidiaries in developing countries. These are often not insured, and nor are those of large commercial enterprises with established local sources of finance in developing countries.

All this may seem to have taken us rather far from the question of the UN's role in West–South relations. But these facts have been stressed for two reasons. One is to emphasise the relative triviality of aid received from the UN.

No one with the above figures in mind can possibly or credibly claim that the UN *per se* has been able to make much significant contribution to whatever growth and development there may have been in the Third World. It is significant that the author of the first major study to be commissioned by a UN Secretary-General on the subject of financing economic development,[10] Professor Arthur Lewis, in a recent review of development problems had some shrewd and trenchant things to say concerning domestic policies and conditions for investment – but in five lectures hardly mentioned the UN.[11]

The second reason follows from it and concerns the political implications of these orders of magnitude. The increasing importance of commercial credit to the developing countries, in effect, introduces a new and possibly rather influential factor into the policy-making of all the UN institutions concerned with development – the UN itself and indeed the World Bank, the Fund and the specialised agencies distributing UNDP funds. The rationale of UN policy, to be sure, has never been too clear – and deliberately so. A rough and ready equality of opportunity was the general aim. And it would have been difficult for a deliberative body, like the General Assembly, or for the UN Secretariat to make a decisive move in either of the alternative directions. It has therefore implicitly refused either to favour the most needy (and how could these anyway be defined?) or those semi-developed countries most likely to benefit and to use foreign aid to most and quickest effect. The policy of rough equality has been feasible so long as bilateral aid-giving more or less balanced itself out. That is to say that when one government – notably, for example, France or Britain – chose to concentrate its bilateral aid on former colonial dependencies, other governments allowed for this in their own aid-giving and chose other beneficiaries. The system, it is true, still allowed some countries to do a lot better than others – notably, South Viet-Nam and other 'strategic protectorates' of the United States. But these were exceptions to the general rule.

The sources of commercial credit, however, are less even-handed than the collectivity of aid donors. The lion's share of longer term commercial credit goes to only about a dozen developing countries – most of them by no means the poorest and most needy, but the largest and those already semi-developed. Many of them are also the main recipients of concessionary lending by the Bank, the Fund and the regional development banks. Argentina, Brazil and Chile are among the dozen and these three are also among the six Fund members who have accounted for as much as two-thirds of all drawings on the Fund by developing countries in the twenty years 1947–67.[12] Mexico and India are also large users of commercial

[10] *Financing Economic Development* (United Nations, 1951).

[11] W. Arthur Lewis, *Some Aspects of Economic Development* (London and Accra, 1969), p. 82.

[12] Edward M. Bernstein, "The International Monetary Fund", in *The Global Partnership: international agencies and economic development*, *op. cit.*, p. 137.

credit – each took over $1,000 million in the five years 1963–8 – and both are also major clients of the World Bank group.

The point I am making is that the international market economy, dominated politically and economically as it is by the West, is growing and expanding very fast, and as it does so it is exerting a strong magnetic pull and influence on the UN aid complex, through trade credits for Western exports now, as well as through direct investment. The choices and priorities of the international market economy are reflected best, among the sources of multilateral development finance, by those closest to and most influenced by it, i.e. the Fund, and to slightly lesser degree the Bank – and these in the UN complex are the most powerful and effective and dynamic. The Fund's basic concern is to preserve, defend and stabilise the international monetary system, which, for all its faults, has provided the necessary media for the international market economy. It is also concerned to extend it by bringing into full participation as much of the developing world as possible – and especially the so-called semi-developed countries. The system must also be preserved as intact and as whole as possible; the Fund's concern with anticipating and preventing drop-outs among its membership is obvious. Meanwhile, the Fund is politically the most oligarchic and the least egalitarian instrument of multilateral development aid. Not only does its constitution and weighted voting system ensure the domination of the West, but since the negotiation of the General Arrangements to Borrow agreement (1962) and the Special Drawing Rights debate (1966–68) it has been very evident that real policy-making for the Fund has been conducted outside it – in the Group of Ten or in Working Party Three of the OECD. In short, there is in the UN system a political continuum which runs from oligarchic, West-controlled decision-making bodies at one end to egalitarian, one-state-one-vote, South-dominated decision-making bodies at the other. And this political continuum parallels an economic continuum between rich, resourceful and growing bodies and agencies and poor, frustrated and static ones. The former are also, and significantly, the aid agencies and donors most influential on others, e.g. through their management of aid consortia for individual countries, and through their not inconsiderable influence on national central banks and finance ministries.

## Conclusions and Prognoses

This leads me directly to some of the main conclusions I would draw about the UN's record in international economic relations and to some of the prognoses that might be made about the future on the basis of them. The first – following on from the above – is that the most effective instruments in the UN system for directing the flow of finance and resources from West to South (and, *faute de mieux*, this has become the prime purpose of its existence) are those which are essentially conservative and system-preserving, rather than those which are essentially radical and system-reforming. Moreover, in these instruments, it is the United States, aided and supported in almost every policy issue by the other rich developed countries of the West, that has the controlling voice. The goal of economic 'advancement' sought by the UN in its economic activities has been and is now increasingly interpreted in conservative rather than radical (still less in revolutionary) terms. And the economic problems to which it directs most energetically its practical efforts and attention are more likely to be those jeopardising the comfort and welfare of the rich West rather than those which oppress the poor South.

The implications of this conclusion for scholars and students concerned with international economics and politics are far-reaching. It suggests, for a start, that two of the three premises I identified as informing the UN in its initial approach to its economic tasks – the Egalitarian premise and the Reformist premise – have been found in practice to be unfounded. The bias of the UN has turned out to be towards preserving rather than towards changing the international economic system. It has also been oligarchic rather than egalitarian and the net effect of its policies is to deal not equally but unequally with its member states. Scholars are not justified therefore in writing as though there was any real equality in these matters. Words like 'partners' and 'partnerships' (as in the title of Pearson Report and that of the otherwise sober and valuable Millikan and Gardner collection quoted above) are just as pure humbug as when they are used by paternalistic commercial corporations about their junior employees. The developing countries in the UN – so far as it is an active influence on financial flows – are subordinates and economic protectorates, not partners. This is not to say that their position is quite helpless, or that debtors have no power over creditors or that they do not have to be treated with respect and courtesy. It is merely to assert that the essential quality of reciprocal obligation essential to the concept of partnership does not in reality exist.

As far as the future of the UN itself goes it would seem to follow that the net flow of finance for development (official bilateral and multilateral aid + private investment capital + trade credit – debt servicing and repatriated profits) will therefore be decided by the demands of the international market economy and not on the basis of political justice or welfare needs as conceived by a majority in the General Assembly. Exhortations to provide the UN with more aid funds, like the Pearson Report, however powerful, will be fruitless. The second Development Decade seen as a UN operation will most likely be as big a disappointment as the First.

Similarly, efforts at internal constitutional reform, shifting the balance of power within the Organization or trying to raise the calibre of its work are likely to be just as vain. It seems plain enough that the donor countries, who are also the major contributors to the regular UN budget and to UNDP, have decided that they want to channel through UNDP only a token amount out of the fiscal burden they impose on their taxpayers for international redistribution and welfare. Nothing that is done in response to the Jackson Report[13] – and it seems likely to be little enough when all is said and done – is going to change this. The flow of funds will merely shift to more conservative channels.

None of this is necessarily a disaster for the developing countries. Their chief concern is first, to overcome domestic obstacles which are the most constraining and, secondly, to ensure that national economic development should somehow be propelled forward on an ever-inflating cushion of foreign credit. This is in fact happening in many countries, but as a result of trends beyond the political control even of the rich governments of the West. It is no more true to imply that the standstill in UNDP aid is arresting the course of economic development than it is to suggest that the funds are making material difference to the pace of development.

So much for the Egalitarian and Reformist premises of 1945. As for the Unitarian premise, we have already seen that this was quite unfounded so far as the UN's capacity to influence international economic relations was concerned. The UN has provided a forum for a continuing debate on West–South economic relations and has been an instrument in a very limited way for directing financial and technical assistance in that direction. But in the other five areas or directions it has been largely bypassed or ignored. Even its capacity to direct effective economic sanctions against individual states has proved extremely limited, whether one thinks of Communist China or independent Rhodesia.

The future prospect for the UN as a significant factor in international economic relations in areas and directions outside the West–South axis is not particularly hopeful. Within the South group, the tendency now is towards smaller regional groupings for co-operation and co-ordination and the impact of the UN on relations between states diminishes as its impact on national politics and government increases.[14]

In the other groups and directions there is little sign of a reverse in existing trends. There has, it is true, been some talk recently of the possibility of East European participation in the SDR scheme. But if

[13] Sir Robert Jackson, *A Study of the Capacity of the United Nations Development System*, 2 vols. (United Nations, Geneva, 1969).

[14] Notably through the part played by the UN resident representative, now to be dignified as 'resident director'. On this point see Gordenker and Jacobson, *op. cit.*

anything should ever come of it, it is likely that the important initiatives will have taken place outside the Fund and that the latter will be – in this as in other matters – a mirror for what takes place outside.

The ideological concepts about the UN in its economic role which were fashionable in the mid-forties have not worn very well either. The high hopes of functionalism have been sadly disappointed and what is left of it is only a mild and watered down version with much more deferred objectives. It is true that functionalist international organisations have grown in size and in number – and the problem of reducing the elephantiasis afflicting international bureaucracies was sharply noted in the Jackson Report. But they have not been able to filch power by stealth – and there have been cases of backward sliding as well as forward creeping. Not only have international organisations sometimes been summarily overlooked, bypassed or put into temporary cold storage, they have even been deserted (as instanced by the recent withdrawal of United States support from the ILO) by their former champions. The working of almost every organisation was affected by the tide of new members from developing continents – the fashionable ideology replacing functionalism and justifying the continued effort put into international organisation was developmentalism. The reason for the current *malaise* and world-weariness in the UN is precisely because no third contender has appeared to take the ideological lead and to give inspiration for effort now that the Development Decade has proved such a disappointment and doubt has been thrown on the credibility of developmentalism.

Nor is it any longer seriously believed that the UN in its attention to economic matters is serving the cause of peace in any significant sense. The idea that economic co-operation will improve the chances of peace by defusing the causes of war or that economic conflicts quickly escalate into military conflict has been disproven by post-war history. Members of the UN have conducted declared and open economic warfare against each other for years without firing a shot – for example, India and Pakistan, or Israel and the Arab states, or even the Russian and American alliance systems. Conversely, war has sometimes broken out between members just when new heights of economic co-operation with each other have been scaled; e.g. the Indus Waters agreement and the Central American Common Market arrangements. Similarly, if trade relations between the United States and the Soviet Union were to develop tenfold and General Motors instead of Fiat were entrusted with manufacturing a people's car, no one would now assume that the two powers would start to discard their armouries of missiles and anti-missile systems.

International economic organisation, we have now come increasingly to see, has to justify itself by economic results, not by its political by-products.

Unfortunately, as I have said, the fruits of developmentalism have been disappointing. And in the member states, the pure milk of multilateralism as conceived by Cordell Hull *et al*, has been adulterated by state practice – and not least by that of the United States. Informed commentators are unanimous that the Kennedy Round of tariff-cutting negotiations conducted in GATT will be the last of its kind and there is even some doubt regarding how many of the cuts then agreed will ever, after all, materialise. Non-tariff barriers are now seen to be the enemy of true multilateralism - but no one has any confidence in the capacity of international organisation to reduce them.

The one practical direction in which the economic policies of the developed countries may be said to have shifted somewhat as a consequence of pressure applied through the UN system is on the matter of trade preferences to developing countries. The pressure began long ago in ECOSOC and increased sharply at UNCTAD I and UNCTAD II. However, it is significant that when the developed countries at last decided in September 1970 that it was time to reconcile the differences between American and Western European policies and to agree on the offer of a single generalised preference for developing countries, they did so by negotiations in OECD and in private and not at the UN or UNCTAD. Moreover a word of caution is perhaps in order. Although the offer is important ideologically and symbolically, its practical significance as an aid to development is open to grave doubt. How many developing countries, it has to be asked, really can produce goods of competitive quality at costs low enough to invade American and European markets in large quantities. Nothing less will suffice. Meanwhile, the significance of international trade in the world economy is paling beside the phenomenal growth in the last decade of international production. This is a matter on which the UN has no coherent policy, although many governments of developing countries are well aware that the economic welfare of their peoples and their national economic health is not necessarily improved when they are hosts to this industrial overspill: many of the highly-capitalised foreign enterprises use advanced technology but little local labour, and therefore make little contribution to local economic welfare.

What then, it may be asked, is there left to hope for from the UN as a factor in international economic relations? The answer to that question follows, I believe, from my final conclusion. This is that the UN's essential role has been, is now, and is likely to remain symbolic. That is to say, it is important primarily (and also almost exclusively) as the vehicle for symbolic actions expressing ideas of collective international concern, moral responsibility and so forth. These ideas are undoubtedly gaining ground slowly throughout international society. But the international polity – the system of separate nation-states entrusted with responsibility for national security and welfare – is too static to allow these ideas more than symbolic expression. For this symbolic role the UN is in many ways ideally suited and has no close rival. It is *not* suited for direct action on the fast-changing and expanding international economy which requires various kinds of highly specialised, sophisticated and specific gearing or adjustment-mechanisms and organisations, enabling the advanced states to have their cake of national responsibility while eating the benefits of an expanding international economy: or so they hope. These adjustment or gearing-mechanisms mostly exist outside the UN. The impact of the UN on the international economy therefore is only indirect, through the effect of its symbolic acts on the foreign economic policies of individual governments – for instance, as in the matter of preferences for developing countries. It acts via the international society on the units of the international polity, not on the coexisting international economy.

As Walter Kotschnig observed in connection with the UN Development Decade:

> "The United Nations Development Decade is not designed to produce a blueprint for the millennium. It has not produced and is not expected to bring forth a definitive plan to end poverty . . . the UNDD concept does, however, provide an ordering principle."[15]

Kotschnig quotes Philippe de Seynes, UN Assistant Secretary-General for Economic Affairs, to the same purpose:

> "The concept is alive and enduring. . . . It has become a symbol of the collective responsibility of the international community for the development of the Third World."[16]

The point has been made more sharply in a brief but shrewd reassessment of the UN made recently by Robert Wilson, in which he concludes that the Organization is "much more a symbol than an instrument". It is a "symbol of international community" and stands for internationally acknowledged ideals of peace, tolerance, compassion and concern for the social welfare and economic betterment of all mankind.[17]

A similar thought seems to be behind the summing-up by Robert Burton, a veteran internationalist, on the occasion of the UN's twenty-fifth anniversary celebrations:

[15] W. Kotschnig, "The United Nations as an Instrument of Economic and Social Development", *International Organization,* vol. XXII (Winter 1968), p. 23.
[16] *ibid.*
[17] Robert Wilson, "The United Nations as Symbol and Instrument", *American Journal of International Law* (January 1970), pp. 139–43.

"Son mérite principale reste aujourd'hui d'avoir donné en un quart de siècle son sens plein à la notion de la développement, en faisant prendre conscience aux peuples, voire même aux gouvernments, des pays riches de leurs responsabilités dans l'état de famine, de misère, d'ignorance où se trouve les trois-quarts de l'humanité."[18]

Even the UN Secretary-General, U Thant, though putting a braver face on it did not really differ when he said, in connection with the Development Decade idea: "The adoption of a target . . . showed that the concept of shared resources is beginning to enter the philosophy of states . . . in their relations to other states".[19]

Where I would differ from the implications of U Thant's phrasing is that a 'beginning' always implies the prospect of further growth, and of this I am not at all convinced. The reason, it seems to me, why the UN is likely to remain primarily a symbolic institution is that, in economic, just as much as in other matters, progress beyond a symbolic role is barred by real political conflicts and controversies (concerning the redistribution of wealth and the redrawing of international rules concerning trade and investment, for example) which cannot be resolved in the absence of an ultimate political authority to decide them. Conor Cruise O'Brien has written of the UN as a 'sacred drama' mainly in connection with its peace-keeping and conciliatory roles.[20] It seems to me that perhaps the description also fits in large measure a good deal of its activities in the economic and social field.

[18] *Le Monde Diplomatique* (October 1970).
[19] Quoted in Kotschnig, *op. cit.*, p. 23.
[20] Conor Cruise O'Brien and Feliks Topolski, *The United Nations: Sacred drama* (London, 1968).

# 7. THE UNITED NATIONS AND REGIONALISM

Ernest B. Haas

## The Phenomenon of Regionalism

After twenty-five years or so of experience with the United Nations system it hardly entails much risk to assert that regionalism is the tail that wags the global dog. Of 127 members of the UN, 109 belong to at least one regional organisation not affiliated to the UN; 72 of them belong to several. 54 of the members self-consciously associate themselves with a regionally-defined military bloc; 67 members equally self-consciously proclaim their non-alignment, even though this stance in effect commits them to act as a bloc when they seek to constrain the behaviour of one or more of the organised blocs. If one were to add up the financial and personnel resources poured into NATO, the EEC, the OAS and even SEATO and contrast them with similar efforts devoted to the UN system, the balance would be lopsidedly regional. It is true that the African and Asian states have been less willing to earmark resources and energy to their regional organisations. Yet of the 50 major inter-governmental regional organisations created since 1945, 19 are made up of African and Asian states, respectively.

I am using the notion of regionalism in its broadest sense. Regional organisations provide merely the most obvious piece of evidence of a trend. The phenomenon also includes the practice of bloc-formation through the medium of formal alliances and less formal military understandings of some staying power. Moreover, blocs also take the form of long-lived diplomatic constellations professing overlapping conceptions of national interest and ideological commitment. When the work of the UN is examined in the overall context of world politics one must come to the conclusion that during the bipolar phases of the modern international system the two major blocs were the prime actors in the world drama, each using the UN simply as an instrument to advance – with varying degrees of success – the interests of its bloc. In short, participation in the UN for the major blocs was instrumental, one of the many means available to advance and protect national and regional interests. Furthermore, the United States and the Soviet Union both used their regional machinery equally instrumentally. But the net effect during the bipolar phase was the subordination of the global machinery to the regionally defined confrontation. On the other hand, the loosening of the bipolar world that occurred after 1956 also complicated the earlier picture of the UN's subordination to regional politics. Not that universalism triumphed over regionalism; regionalism itself grew more complicated as more blocs and organisations came forward and as the two bloc leaders were compelled or persuaded to relax control over their respective allies and clients. In short, the very atrophy of the bipolar system confirmed the dependence of the UN on the dynamics of regionalised world politics.

Everyone knows that this development was not anticipated by the framers of the UN Charter. Moreover, the evolution of regionalism for years provided the material for many learned laments that the provisions of the Charter were effectively being sidestepped. What are these provisions?

The structure which came into existence at the end of the Second World War made very few concessions to any principle of organisation and order short of a global one. The preservation of international peace and security was entrusted to the Security Council; more accurately, peace and security were to depend on the agreement of the world's major powers united in the Security Council. The General Assembly was given only a secondary jurisdiction devoid of the competence to enact binding decisions. What about regional security arrangements? Regional arrangements were given the competence to maintain peace and provide for the pacific settlement of local disputes; in fact, the UN was under an obligation to encourage their use for this purpose. However, regional organisations were forbidden to use enforcement measures without authorisation from the Security Council and were enjoined to keep the Council informed at all times of their plans and activities.

Two exceptions from the primacy of UN jurisdiction are part of the global legal and institutional system: measures against former enemy states of World War II can be taken without authorisation; and since "nothing shall impair the inherent right of individual or collective self-defence if an armed attack occurs" members are free, singly and in alliance, to resist aggression until the Security Council has intervened, provided they report their activity to the Council and do "not in any way affect the authority and responsibility of the Security Council".[1] The Soviet Union has based some of its regional military pacts on the first of these exceptions and the Warsaw Pact on Article 51; the United States has justified NATO, SEATO and the Rio Pact by virtue of Article 51 exclusively.

World trade and monetary issues, similarly, were seen in 1945 in almost exclusively global institutional terms. By virtue of the Bretton Woods agreements, a world monetary system was created which was designed to avoid a repetition of the currency policies followed by the major trading

[1] Both quotations are from Article 51 of the UN Charter.

states during the Great Depression. The International Monetary Fund made no concessions to the needs of late developing regions; it created rules expected to be universally valid even though their administration was effectively lodged in the hands of a few large industrial states. The World Bank, similarly, was devoted to rules of sound finance which were assumed to be universally valid and acceptable. An International Trade Organisation was to be added to these institutions. While its draft rules recognised the special needs of state-trading nations and paid some attention to the position of poorer countries dependent on single commodities suffering from price fluctuations, the basic rules of trade remained non-discrimination based on the most-favoured-nation clause and full reciprocity – thus dealing a blow to such regionally-defined preference systems as the Commonwealth.

Hence it is necessary to sketch briefly the facets of regionalism and of regional political dynamics which quickly overwhelmed many of these rules and in fact disintegrated the global system into a network of competing regional clusters of power and interest. The Cold War was recognised as a basic fact of international life by 1948, though its beginnings were felt in the very negotiations which resulted in the acceptance of the UN Charter. This gave rise to the alliances and treaty organisations which persist to this day, and to the subordination of the Security Council to the bloc diplomacy of its leading members. It also gave rise to a world trade-and-finance system geared to the reconstruction and stability of the industrial West, to a compartmentalisation of world trade and investment. By 1955 the poor 'southern half' of the globe was in revolt against that system, on occasion in alliance with the socialist bloc which had never accepted the Bretton Woods system. And the economic revolt of the Third World introduced the next major regionally-based challenge to the system erected in 1945.

Hence some impressive institutional features confirming the role of regionalism found their way into the very functioning of the UN, in seeming contradiction to the philosophy of the Charter. The economic realm was the first claimant. The General Assembly created the Economic Commission for Europe in response to early demands (not fulfilled, of course) that the UN take an active hand in the economic reconstruction of devastated Europe. This step was followed almost immediately by the creation – on the basis of Latin American demands opposed by the United States – of the subsequently very influential UN Economic Commission for Latin America. Soon thereafter, the Economic Commission for Asia and the Far East emerged and much later the Economic Commission for Africa. The World Health Organization, similarly, began its work with an overt recognition of the principle of regionalism as its basis. Other specialised agencies found it useful to institute standing regional conferences, centres or working parties by 1950. Each of these developments – though not of equal importance and influence with respect to later events – reflected a concession to the demands of regionally defined interests with respect to economic development, commodity prices, investment or trade policy, or to regionally perceived needs in the social welfare field. When Third World needs in Latin America, Africa and Asia began to coalesce and overlap the pressure for a new UN approach to economic development was born, to find fruition in UNCTAD, an agency whose very being is based on the most intricate of inter-regional balancing acts.

The UN became a victim of opposing military blocs soon after the outbreak of the Korean War, though the trend was plainly visible in the General Assembly's handling of the Greek civil war complaint. That trend was institutionalised and confirmed in the Uniting for Peace Resolution. By giving the General Assembly the right to deal with breaches of the peace and acts of aggression in the event of a Security Council deadlock, to authorise the marshalling of UN military forces and to engage in active mediation and conciliation, the resolution in fact gave any two-thirds majority the right to take over key military and diplomatic tasks. But not all states voting for such activities were obligated to join in. Thus the political meaning and effect of the resolution was to give one bloc (NATO) the ability to use UN resolutions and symbols to legitimise bloc policies which would in all likelihood have been carried out in any case. To do so, only a dozen or so Latin American votes would have to be picked up. The UN security system became the appendage of a dominant bloc – until members of that bloc and a number of neutrals whose votes were necessary to make the bloc prevail began to have second thoughts, as in the later phases of the Korean conflict. In that event, the institutional logic of dependence on UN resolutions had the unintended consequence of restraining bloc leaders – a lesson the United States had to relearn when the Uniting for Peace Resolution was invoked at its expense in the Lebanese crisis of 1958, while Britain and France experienced the same sting during the Suez crisis of 1956.

This paradox is easily explained if one simply keeps in mind the dynamics of negotiation and voting: the cylinders which make the UN engine run are regionally-defined caucussing groups and regional voting blocs. In order to obtain passage of any resolution which is salient with respect to the issues under discussion, inter-bloc diplomacy is necessary to assemble the necessary two-thirds; if a state wishes to block passage of a resolution it must seek to disrupt a given bloc or prevent it from joining another. In either event, the logic of bloc voting is confirmed and enshrined as the basic principle of UN decision-making.

If bloc voting is central to an understanding of the Organization two other concessions to regionalism follow naturally. Election to membership of most UN organs (including the non-permanent members of the Security Council) is based on regionalism. Tacit and overt agreements exist, some gentlemanly and some less so, governing the rotation of member Blocs nominate their candidates each year and governments cannot hope to be elected without the endorsement of their caucussing group. Once 'legitimately' nominated, the prior agreement on inter-regional rotation assures election in most cases. Finally, the principle of equitable regional distribution governs the selection of members of the Secretariat, even if the extreme of that formula – the famous 'Troika' – is encountered only intermittently inside the tall building along the East River.

These are the facts of the penetration of the global structure by the forces of regionalism. What are their significance for world peace, for world economic welfare and for the integration of our planet into a less divided whole? It is one thing to identify and describe a trend; it is quite another to assess the possible damage caused by the trend to the basic values of peace, plenty and world cohesiveness.

## The United Nations, Regionalism and the Maintenance of Peace

It used to be thought that the advent of regionally-based alliances and treaty organisations – ANZUS, NATO, SEATO and CENTO – by definition hindered the preservation of world peace. Instead of the UN's pivotal role being consistently demonstrated in the discussion of threats to the peace, the identification of the aggressor, and the implementation of measures designed to deter or restrain him, the major treaty organisations based on Article 51 of the Charter took upon themselves the task of deterring (and threatening) each other while their leading members merely made use of the UN to buttress their activities outside the Organization. Regional security organisations – the OAS, the Arab League, and later the OAU – did not legally challenge the supremacy of the global structure because they were anchored in Articles 52 and 53 of the Charter.[2] But did they not in practice hinder the achievement of world peace under universal standards when they were used to prevent the airing of disputes in the UN?

[2] Several other multi-purpose regional organisations which are *not* primarily economic or military in function must be mentioned here. The Council of Europe and the Organization of Central American States represent cultural and political interests of their members; they also claim a competence in the peaceful settlement of regional disputes. Neither has been very active or effective in that capacity, with the exception of the Council of Europe's role in helping settle the Saar question. The Organisation Commune Africaine et Malgache and its predecessor, UAM, seek to speak for most francophone African states on a variety of topics but have played no strong role in the maintenance of peace or the settlement of disputes. The Association of South-East Asia attempted very rarely and with indifferent success to mediate regional disputes.

Was their existence not inconsistent with global standards when they were used in practice as if they were alliances? The insurgents in Santo Domingo in 1965, shouted "UN sí, OEA no!" when confronted with the intervention of both organisations. They thought there was such an inconsistency.

In the euphoric world of 1945 these practices would have been considered destructive. Since then, they have become simple facts of international life, facts which largely determine the operating rules of the international system: states seek to protect their interests through the pooling of influence represented by regional organisations, regional caucusses and regionally determined voting. Hence the question cannot be approached by simply noting the inconsistency and going on to deplore it. A more complicated question must be posed: *in what circumstances* have important regional organisations helped or hindered in the preservation of peace? Only when this question is answered can one then consider whether these circumstances are sufficiently general to enable an overall judgement to be made and to prescribe the utility of regional peace-keeping efforts in the future.

A few figures on the quarrels among states will help in this quest. Since 1945, 130 international 'disputes' have occurred which I consider serious enough to have been capable of triggering some fighting. All inter-state wars are included; so are internal wars which involved the significant participation of outside states. Moreover, all disputes not involving hostilities but based on serious claims and counterclaims have been included. I excluded incidents which do not go beyond the exchange of diplomatic notes and the voluntary recourse to judicial settlement. Of these 130 disputes, 72 per cent were referred to some international organisation; the UN received 73 per cent of the disputes over which it could have had jurisdiction; regional organisations received 80 per cent of the disputes which arose among their membership and which could have been referred. Clearly, both the UN and regional organisations are considered highly 'legitimate' forums for the consideration of major disputes. These disputes were distributed as follows:

| *Referred to* | *UN* | *OAS* | *OAU/UAM* | *Arab League* | *Council of Europe/NATO* |
|---|---|---|---|---|---|
| UN only | 65 | — | — | — | — |
| Regional organisation only | — | 10* | 6 | 0 | 1 |
| UN and regional organisation | 15 | 8 | 1 | 3 | 3 |
| None | 29 | 3 | 3 | 4 | 0 |

* Does not include disputes handled by the Inter-American Peace Committee alone.

Despite the flowering of regional organisations the UN receives the majority of disputes which occur; moreover almost half of the disputes referred to regional organisations also appear on the agenda of the UN. Finally, only the OAS and OAU seem to possess an independent legitimacy as organs for the preservation of peace. Only they seem capable of attracting the preference of their members in certain types of disputes as contrasted with the appeal of the UN; the Arab League is appealed to only in the context of concurrent or prior activity in the global forum.

In seeking to assess the interplay between regional and UN efforts in the maintenance of peace one should note, first of all, the massive fact that of 97 disputes referred to all kinds of international organisations since 1945, only 36 involved some degree of choice as to whether they would go to the UN or to regional organisations, or if the UN would be enabled to exercise a mediatory role above and beyond the pressure of regional blocs within it. In other words, 63 per cent of all disputes submitted to multilateral settlement escaped the rivalry between the competing principles of universal or regional action. Either appropriate regional mechanisms did not exist or the governments involved did not wish to use the ones that did exist. The question of whether regionalism helped or hindered the maintenance of peace in conformity with UN Charter principles, therefore, must be answered by looking at the 37 per cent which did evoke the possibility of rivalry.

The interplay between regional and universal peace-keeping efforts can be summarised in the form of four recurrent patterns or 'roles' assigned to them by the governments initiating action. (1) Regional action may simply be used by states so as to compensate for the inability of the UN to serve the long-range interests of the states initiating the action; I shall call this pattern the 'hegemonic substitute role' of regional action because it is being used to bolster permanent bloc hegemony at the expense of UN action. (2) Regional organisations may also be used on an *ad hoc* basis to sidestep the UN in a specific situation in which the initiating state feels it will not get its way in the UN, a pattern I call the 'rival role'. (3) A 'complementary role' is played by regional organisations when the UN deliberately engages the help of a regional grouping in the settlement of a dispute, thus recognising *de facto* the function which the Charter establishes *de jure*. (4) Finally, regional organisations may play a 'willing substitute role' in situations in which the UN membership is unwilling to have the universal organisation enter the fray and prefer to abdicate to regional action or not to challenge it when it occurs.

*Hegemonic Substitute Role.* Whenever the bloc leaders themselves are in direct confrontation UN mediatory action is often impossible by definition. Hence the bloc leaders seek to obtain a UN-provided mantle of legitimacy for regional action decided upon independently of UN deliberation. The objective is to *prevent* independent UN action and to permit a regional grouping under the bloc leader's control to engage in military and/or diplomatic action. NATO and ANZUS were used in this fashion in the Korean case by the United States. The OAS was used in the same way during the Cuban Missile Crisis. SEATO was so used for some years in order to make it more difficult for the UN to be seized of the Viet-Nam war, even though the United States after 1963 was not always able to keep that conflict off the UN agenda. The Soviet Union, for its part, invoked the Warsaw Pact to ward off any attempt at UN intervention regarding the invasion of Czechoslovakia. The efficacy of this method of sidestepping the UN depends on the cohesion of the regional grouping in question; it may be supposed that as the international system moves away from bipolarity and towards a multi-bloc pattern it will decline in importance. In its heyday this pattern certainly undercut the UN's capability of becoming an autonomous front of legitimacy and authority.

*Rival Role.* The objectives of the key states in this pattern are more modest than in the first case. They tend to feel that the intervention of the UN in the dispute would result in an outcome less favourable to the key state's preferences than intervention by a regional organisation in which most members share the leader's objectives and/or prove amenable to the leader's power. However, the key features of this pattern is the fact that it involves disputes *within* a bloc which the leader wishes to isolate from the concern of extra-bloc states, whereas the first pattern involves inter-bloc crises and conflicts. In point of fact, only the OAS has consistently played the part of the rival to the UN, a part increasingly challenged since 1960 by the Soviet Union, some African and Asian states, and by Latin American countries restive under United States leadership (if not in actual conflict with it, as Cuba is).

Prior to 1960 only one significant case arose which exposed this pattern to public view – the American-organised intervention in Guatemala which obtained eventual symbolic approval from the OAS; the attempt made by the Arbenz regime to invoke UN protection against the OAS-sanctioned invasion proved futile. In the many other instances of very minor threats to the peace which arose in the western hemisphere, the parties turned to the OAS as a matter of course and no voices of criticism were then heard in the UN. In fact, during those fifteen years the disputes in question did not involve ideological questions, communism, the Cold War or the decolonisation struggle. And as long as such salient issues were lacking the

OAS in effect played a willing substitute role to the UN challenged by no government.

After 1960 all this changed as Cuba became an outcast communist state in the hemisphere, revolutionary activity elsewhere increased and the United States sought to use the OAS to organise collective anti-communist measures in the hemisphere. The United States and some Latin American countries sought to exclude the UN and use the OAS in its place before and during the Bay of Pigs Invasion, in the attempt by the Dominican Republic's Juan Bosch to topple the Duvalier regime in Haiti, during the military and economic sanctions ordered against the Trujillo regime in 1960 (without prior authorisation from the Security Council) and in the massive United States/OAS intervention in the Dominican Republic in 1965. Despite Soviet objections to the non-observance of the provisions of Articles 52 and 53 of the Charter on the part of the OAS, the United States had its way until 1965, when she was forced to tolerate a UN mission in the Dominican Republic and had to fend off efforts in the Security Council to remove the OAS Inter-American Peace Force. It seems probable that as international conflict in the western hemisphere becomes increasingly part of global ideological struggles, the Soviet position favouring more UN and less OAS involvement will attract more support from among such OAS members as Mexico, Ecuador, Uruguay, Chile and Peru. The rival role played by the OAS with considerable success until now may thus be undermined, implying the possibility of a proportional increase in UN authority – unless the result will be a return bilateral or unilateral display of force.

*Complementary Role.* Explicit co-operation and co-ordination among regional and UN agencies is what the Charter calls for. In almost all cases of action by the OAS mentioned above co-operation was at best tacit and overt co-ordination was absent. In the disputes now offered the reverse was the case: regional action took place simultaneously with UN consideration and with UN blessing. Thus the Arab League was used to negotiate among Arab states the formula for ending the civil war in Lebanon and Jordan in 1958, in order to make possible the withdrawal of American forces and UN observers from Lebanon. The Arab League with UN blessing organised an inter-Arab peace force designed to protect newly independent Kuwait against threats from Iraq, even though the UN was unable to adopt a meaningful resolution of its own. These instances, however, should not lead us to forget that throughout the various phases of the Palestine conflict the Arab League functioned as an *antagonist* of UN measures: regional organisation was used to defeat the implementation of explicit UN resolutions. Furthermore, the Arab League (as the Yemen civil war, the Algerian–Moroccan war and the fighting in Oman show) has been a singularly unsuccessful agency for dealing with disputes among its own members, *unless* the dispute had already succeeded in triggering wide interest among states outside the region.[3] The only other case of successful complementary action between the UN and a regional organisation is the solution of the intra-African mêlée caused by Moise Tshombe's appeal to Belgium and the United States during the Congo civil war of 1964, a dispute which was referred to the OAU for settlement by the Security Council.

*Willing Substitute Role.* That leaves us with the largest number of cases of joint concern to the UN and regional organisations, cases in which the Organization's membership was grateful that it was not compelled to deal with the dispute and happy to defer to a regional agency. This category, however, includes two variants: situations in which the dispute had been brought to the UN and the global forum defers to the parties or to regional agencies without serious debate; cases which never went to the UN in the first place, without causing the least protest or anguish in New York and without giving rise to charges that Chapter VIII of the Charter has been violated. Ten cases went to the OAS without referral to the UN, eight before 1960 and only two after that date, for reasons discussed above. Thus, in the case of the United States–Panamanian dispute over the Canal, the UN gladly deferred to the OAS after Panama had seized the Security Council of the issue. Of seven disputes referred to the OAU and UAM, only one also found its way to the UN though the parties were persuaded in several other situations to "try OAU first" before seeking to commit the major powers through the UN. Two disputes were referred both to the Council of Europe and to the UN at different times, and neither organisation was able significantly to effect the outcome.

It is clear that formal co-ordination and informal co-operation between the universal and regional forums is minimal, inconsistent, and possessed of a very uncertain future. But to discover whether this weak formal relationship actually inhibits the maintenance of peace according to universal standards we must evaluate each of the 36 disputes. The tabulation shows these results.[4]

[3] The Yemen civil war was unsuccessfully debated by the Arab League. Referral to the UN, therefore, involved the invocation of the global forum as a complement to the unsuccessful regional one rather than the reverse. The Arab League has not dealt with the current war between Saudi Arabia and South Yemen; nor did it deal with the dispute between the Trucial States and Saudi Arabia.

[4] See Table at the end of the chapter for the list of cases and the coding, pp. 139 to 140. I wish to express my gratitude to my collaborator in a comparative study of conflict resolution by international organisations, Joseph S. Nye, for enabling me to use his data on conflicts submitted to regional organisations.

| Role Accorded to Regional Organisation | Total | Regional Action | | |
|---|---|---|---|---|
| | | *Helped* | *Hindered* | *Neither* |
| Hegemonic Substitute | 6 | 2 | 3 | 1 |
| Rival | 5 | 0 | 2 | 3 |
| Complementary | 6 | 4 | 0 | 2 |
| Willing Substitute | 19 | 15 | 0 | 4 |
| TOTAL | 36 | 21 | 5 | 10 |

Regional action *helped* in the restoration or maintenance of peace in conformity with the principles of the UN Charter in almost two-thirds of these cases; it *hindered* the attainment of these global objectives in less than 14 per cent. But that number includes the Viet-Nam war, the Cyprus civil war, and the Soviet invasion of Czechoslovakia. Moreover, while the western-orchestrated UN action in the Korean and Greek conflicts has been scored as helpful in the restoration of peace, these judgements may not be free from debate. Finally, such ideologically intense, though militarily less dangerous, disputes as the American interventions in Guatemala, in Cuba and in the Dominican Republic, were also the victims of regional attention at the expense of Charter principles. Put differently, the United States has been most often the culprit who sacrifices global principles to regional expediency. Whenever regional action was taken with the specific objective of preventing UN action the results have never been fruitful in terms of universal standards of peaceful conduct among states. On the other hand, in the large number of situations in which regional action was deliberately encouraged by the UN or accepted without demur, the results proved overwhelmingly positive. With respect to the maintenance of international peace, therefore, it cannot be validly argued that the advent of regionalism has seriously handicapped the work of the UN.

## Regionalism and Economic Development

Does the advent of regionalism help or hinder the attainment of higher standards of living, more striking growth rates, or the redistribution of the world's wealth from the industrial north to the south? The great dissatisfaction of most poor countries with the universalistic rules of Bretton Woods and of GATT has been described. This dissatisfaction was hardly allayed by the tolerance which the United States showed towards Western Europe until the mid-1950's in permitting a discriminatory trade and payments system to evolve there while denying the same leeway to Latin America.

Regionalism in Western Europe was encouraged by the United States because it was considered an instrument for strengthening the continental countries against Soviet aggression and internal communist dissent. Moreover, economic regionalism was expected to lead to political unification, an outcome actively promoted by the United States until the early 1960's. Economically, the most important development in world trade and finance was the arrival of the European Common Market as an independent force. That arrival was made concrete to the United States in the Kennedy Round tariff negotiations. It created an urgent need in African countries to conclude long-range trade and investment agreements with the EEC for fear of losing traditional markets and sources of aid. Britain and Scandinavia, having failed to prevent the success of EEC, sought to protect their collective economic interests by creating the European Free Trade Association as a parallel force.

The EEC, however, was perceived not only as a threat but also as an example. Moreover, the example was stressed and overtly advocated by ECLA which argued that economic development demands industrialisation, and industrialisation, after the import-substitution phase has been passed, demands the creation of larger markets for the industries to be created. Larger markets and increasing investment opportunities, finally, call for regional economic integration. Hence ECLA made itself the architect and protagonist of a series of schemes designed to lead to the economic integration of continental Latin America and Central America, respectively; the Latin American Free Trade Association emerged in 1960 and the Central American Common Market in 1963. The failure of LAFTA materially to advance industrialisation or regional integration, in turn, has led to the contradictory demands for the creation of an Andean Common Market as well as for a comprehensive pan-Latin American Common Market. Regional integration and the emergence of regional economic blocs continues to be regarded as a very important step in speeding the economic development and modernsiation of the Latin American countries; in the minds of many Latin American politicians and economic planners, the programme plays the role of a panacea for their troubles. Whether integration would, in fact, advance economic development and mass welfare is far from demonstrated.

In the absence of proof to the contrary, however, the ECLA argument has found echoes elsewhere. Common markets and free trade zones in East and Central Africa have emerged. The ECA advocates the creation of such 'sub-regional' economic blocs as instruments of economic development. Discussions designed to lead towards such blocs are under way in the

Maghreb and in South-East Asia. The Caribbean islands and Guyana have set up their own free trade association. Moreover, regional development banks have emerged in Africa, Asia, the Caribbean, Central America and for the western hemisphere in general. The latter three have as one of their basic purposes the financing of projects of interest to more than one country; in short, they are to serve industrialisation with a regional focus.

What are the implications of these developments? Clearly, they involve a massive retreat from any global or universalistic free trade rules. These arrangements – if successful – would give each bloc additional negotiating power *vis-à-vis* third countries because of their ability to influence the price of regional exports and manipulate the demand for imports. To the extent that regional investment schemes are successful these blocs would also attain a measure of autonomy from the world money market, a trend actually supported by several industrial countries which have agreed to contribute to the coffers of the regional development banks *even though* some implications of a successful regional development policy might be considered damaging in the short run to developed countries. In short, it can only be said that the earlier universalistic trade and payments rules were *not* perceived by developing countries as contributing to their welfare. Whether the regionalised pattern will contribute more is not yet clear; but as long as the developing countries believe that it will, one cannot yet argue that the advent of regionalism hinders the achievement of the welfare aims enshrined in UN objectives. In fact, the Central American and East African experiences suggest that it may actually help.

In addition, there is a more indirect impact of regionalism on world economic policies which is expressed in the work of the UN and its associated agencies. This impact can best be described as 'regional pressure group' activity. Moreover, the result of its work has unambiguously been helpful to economic welfare in the Third World as compared to earlier ways of approaching world trade and financial questions. It is beyond dispute that the grudging recognition on the part of the industrialised states that massive redistributive policies are in order would not have developed in the absence of this regional pressure group activity.

What is this pressure group? In a broad sense, it is the majority of underdeveloped nations in the General Assembly and the conferences of the specialised agencies. In a more specific and organisational sense it is the 'Group of 77' in UNCTAD, a permanent caucus of most developing countries in Africa, Asia and Latin America, serviced by the UN Secretariat. This permanent caucus, in turn, is made up of three regional groups: one each identified with Latin America, Africa and Asia. There is considerable disagreement between the regional groups on such issues as preferences for exports in manufactured items, certain commodity agreements and the desirability of special commercial ties with the EEC or the United States. Moreover, cohesion and agreement within each group is not easily achieved. While the 77 are usually unanimous in pressing for redistributive world policies in general, they are often far from united on specific items within this global programme. Nevertheless, it bears repeating that the underdeveloped countries now possess standing institutions to press their claims within the overall UN framework, institutions which are likely to grow in strength rather than fade away. Put differently, the economic policies of the UN system and to a growing extent of single states now evolve strictly in response to the pattern of inter-regional bargaining set in motion by the regional groups.

What has the pressure achieved? Several new global programmes have been established, contrary to the wishes of the more industrialised countries, as a result of the pressure. Moreover, new institutions were created to implement the programmes, sometimes over the opposition of the industrialised countries. One such is the UN Industrial Development Organization; another is the still-to-be-financed UN Capital Development Fund. The most important is UNCTAD itself. The standing machinery created in Geneva in 1964 was responsible for developing the idea of tariff preferences to be accorded to developing countries' manufactured exports by the wealthier countries. The West had long rejected this idea as incompatible with the twin pillars of GATT: non-discrimination and reciprocity. The confrontation in UNCTAD was the medium for bringing about western agreement. Long hostile to commodity agreements, the United States agreed to negotiate several under UNCTAD pressure, and also agreed to the principle of compensating poorer countries for losses incurred as a result of deteriorating terms of trade. Finally, it was partly the pressure exerted at UNCTAD which caused the United States to drop its opposition to the formation of regional common markets and free trade areas in Third World areas. Finally, it should be noted that the planning effort which accompanied the launching of the Second Development Decade (1970–1980) represents a major recognition on the part of the West that the future of international trade and aid are increasingly intertwined and should be approached so that the separate programmes of various UN agencies proceed in tandem.

In addition to creating new institutions capable of generating pressure for new policies and programmes aiming at redistribution, the Third World blocs have also succeeded in forcing changes in the older global trade and financial institutions. GATT abandoned its insistence on reciprocity in the negotiation of trade concessions, as well as relaxing several other rules in favour of the interests of the developing countries. When the structure of the International Monetary Fund was revised by the creation of special drawing rights it was recognised for the first time that the Fund's policies should give recognition to the special balance of payments problems of the developing countries. The World Bank not only took the initiative in persuading the United States to permit the relaxation of rigid banking principles in loan operations, through the creation of the International Development Association; it also altered its lending policies to give special attention to non-profit producing infrastructure projects in agriculture and education. Since the launching of the Second Development Decade the Bank has taken a leading role in the rational allocation of loans in terms of global trade and growth objectives.

If regionally organised pressure has produced these changes in UN institutions and programmes, the developed countries themselves have not remained unaffected either. First of all, in defending themselves against the claims of the developing countries they have upgraded the role of two regional organisations of their own: the West and Japan use the Organisation for Economic Co-operation and Development as their planning agency for countering and negotiating the demands of the Third World; the East European countries have begun to use Comecon for the same purpose in their dealing with the Group of 77. Regionally-based pressure begets regionally-based resistance. In more positive terms, OECD has also been employed as the institution in which the western countries review each other's aid policies and seek to persuade each other to offer more aid on easier terms. While the total volume of aid has increased only very gradually in recent years, the terms under which the aid is offered have been eased consistently.

Have regional pressure activities successfully influenced aid policy as well as policies towards trade and finance? Probably not. It cannot be argued that UNCTAD has brought with it an increase in western-financed aid. UN aid coffers have not been overflowing. Bilateral foreign aid has declined in many western budgets. The OECD review of western aid antedates the creation of UNCTAD and owes nothing to regional pressure. In short, regionalism has helped in the creation of new global institutions and programmes in the trade and financial fields, but its impact on foreign aid has been neutral. The volume of aid has not risen but the advent of regional pressures can hardly be blamed for it.

## Regionalism and Global Integration

The vision of the spontaneous wholeness of mankind united in the attainment of the principles of the UN Charter is not a realistic yardstick against which to measure the impact of regionalism. It must be recognised that the fact of regional activity and organisation – if not its dominance – explains *how* the international system actually works. More important, it can be shown to have produced positive results in terms of major Charter objectives. Peace has been promoted and preserved more frequently than would otherwise have been the case. Economic welfare has been advanced more rapidly than would have occurred in the absence of regionally-orchestrated pressure. The question to consider now is whether this state of affairs can be expected to continue or whether the practices of regional politics will in the future undermine the further integration of the globe under universal practices, norms and institutions.

There are those who argue that regional integration aids global unity because it results in a reduced number of sovereign units. Regional blocs, perhaps eight or ten of them, will make up the international system in place of the present 130 or so sovereign states. The mere reduction in the number of actors is thought by many to be conducive to peace because fewer potential disturbers remain and because the sharing of values and norms among ten is simpler than among 130. This reasoning is acceptable only under certain conditions. The mere transformation of nation-states into larger units still possessed of the characteristics of nationhood will change little except provide more powerful actors. Regional entities with a 'regional' spirit can go to war just as effectively against one another as can nation-states, a possibility developed quite graphically in Orwell's *1984*. Regionalism conduces to peace and value sharing *only* if the regional entities are *not* like nation-states. One might imagine regional entities organised for a variety of very specific tasks: economic development, conservation of marine life, air safety, smog control and the peaceful solution of territorial disputes. Each activity would have its own 'government', in which not all states in the region might participate. Each activity would have its own clientele of cities, pressure groups, provinces and professional associations. The amalgam would not resemble a nation-state so much as the administrative/political structure of the modern welfare states which lack a single strong executive. Under such circumstances the traditional state might really wither away, and not spawn an equally passionate successor in a regional entity which is really just a bigger nation-state. Only the 'non-state' regional amalgam can be expected to aid global integration via regionalism, and then only if the same trend appears at roughly the same time everywhere – a most unlikely prospect.

It must be admitted that one major reason why the penetration by regional forces of the UN system has not prevented the evolution of a modicum of world order is the extremely low degree of integration which characterised the international system to start with. Indefinitely continuing regionalisation cannot be assumed to contribute to increasing world order in all policy domains and under all circumstances. What can be said about the practices that should *not* continue if one wishes to make sure that regionalisation does not hinder global integration in the future? What practices should be actively fostered in order to contribute to a higher degree of global integration? Apart from practices one might sketch in pure or ideal terms, what is the likelihood of their being adopted? To deal with these questions demands a brief scenario describing the probable evolution of the international system in the next decade. Since I assume this system to be launched already, I am suggesting in fact that even if the practices to be discussed were adopted it is too late to stop the trends which describe the system; it is the system *after* the next which might be headed off.

The era into which the world is moving appears to be characterised by these features. Military blocs are losing in cohesion. The two bloc leaders can no longer count on the obedience of their allies and will therefore resort to more direct contacts and to more unilateral behaviour. Economic blocs will gain in cohesion. Western Europe will move towards unity on matters of defence and foreign policy. The global stalemate with respect to nuclear weapons will continue whether or not there is a comprehensive arms control agreement. The proliferation of nuclear capability will also continue, though the qualitative differences between nuclear latecomers and the two super powers will not disappear. More effort will go into redistributive policies designed to make the Third World catch up economically and socially. A consciousness towards safeguarding world ecological and environmental values will grow. The two super powers will show less willingness towards military and ideological self-assertion and other groupings will show more. Nationalism in the West will wane; but it will intensify in the Third World. With the completion of the decolonisation process there will be less global consensus on basic political and human rights and values. The world will be divided into many untidy and overlapping blocs lacking clearly defined leaders and military/diplomatic power will be distributed in a way in which some groups will have disproportionate shares in some domains, and other groups in other domains. In short, the ensemble will be a multi-bloc asymmetric system.

If such a system is to be kept from disintegration at the expense of autonomous regional groupings certain practices ought to be avoided. Peace-maintaining functions entrusted to the UN should not be deflected through the patterns summed up under the 'hegemonic substitute' and 'rival' roles. The chances are good, in any case, that these practices will decline in popularity, as the military blocs on which they depend continue to erode. Bilateralism in the dispensing of foreign aid should be curtailed. On the other hand, the burgeoning practice of *ad hoc* inter-regional bargaining on trade and monetary questions (mostly outside the UN system) must be discouraged unless one wishes the economic scene to be shaped by a series of mutually inconsistent inter-regional pacts. The present trend away from conterminous economic-military-diplomatic blocs should be encouraged in order to decouple issues and foster the likelihood of multiplying ties and interdependence across regions. And we should train ourselves *not* to think of the UNCTAD pattern of institutionalised inter-regional negotiation as approaching an international political party system. The members of the negotiating groups are states, not individuals. They are ruled by dictators, kings, revolutionary cliques, and tutelary parties more often than by freely elected leaders. While the negotiating pattern is certainly more egalitarian than was true in the past, it is hardly more democratic in the sense in which political parties are normally thought to institutionalise democracy. The chances are, however, that the inter-regional pattern with states as the main units will be institutionalised.

What practices should be positively fostered if one wishes to contribute to the kind of global integration under which regional forces will be held in check? UN peace-making should continue to rely on the 'complementary' and 'willing substitute' rules. In Africa this trend may be expected to continue anyway, but the case for the western hemisphere is far less clear, as the attachment of the Latin Americans for the OAS erodes. The complete multilateralisation of foreign aid under UN auspices should be pursued, as should be the centralisation of world policy-making with respect to basic trade and monetary questions. This requires far more institutionalisation than the familiar UNCTAD process now permits, and demands that the kind of planning that goes into the Second Development Decade be broadened in terms of the issues and variables considered. The chances of this happening at a global scale in the near future are far from bright, though in the European regional context it may occur soon. The UN machinery should be enabled to engage in social and technological forecasting, to link economic possibilities and desiderata to their social consequences and technological prerequisites. The UN should be more active in determining when the diffusion of science and technology contributes to welfare and when it creates more new problems than can be solved. World ecological problems should be stressed in a global rather than a regional perspective, whether the issue is the climate, marine resources, air pollution or population pressure.

Finally, certain global institutions ought to be devised to help in keeping the regional dynamic from disintegrating the UN system. Instead of relying primarily on instructed government delegates as the actors in the world drama, more reliance should be placed on individual experts and on working parties made up of such experts, especially in the areas of planning and forecasting. Similarly, more attention might be given to the involvement of non-governmental groups, including political parties, in the making of UN policy relating to economic, social and technological change.

The likelihood of any of this occurring varies enormously from point to point. Realistically, one cannot expect all of the positive suggestions to be enacted and all of the negative practices to be avoided. Realistically, I believe that peace-making and peace-keeping under the auspices of the United Nations is decaying and will be used less in the immediate future as the West turns inward and the Third World engages in hostilities that are unlikely to threaten world peace at large. Moreover, I also believe that regional peace-keeping activities are likely to decline. In short, the character of the international system is apt to make irrelevant the type of analysis I have employed for evaluating the last twenty-five years or so. The opposite, however, appears to be shaping up in the world economic drama. UN institutions are likely to continue to benefit from the intensified inter-regional bargaining pattern dealing with aid, trade and money. Since there is good reason to suppose that regional economic units – common markets, free trade areas – will continue to flourish and grow more internally coherent, it follows that these units will become major participants in any global confrontation. However, it *cannot* be assumed that economic bargaining will proportionately or symmetrically infect other issue areas or domains. Hence the globalisation of the economic bargaining process, based on regional units as actors, *cannot* be expected to yield an overall pattern of global integration unless the analysis is based on the crudest Marxism. Conversely, the fragmentation of issues and bargains cannot be expected to make federations and political unions of regional common markets, development banks and pollution control districts. And so mankind is condemned to tolerate simultaneously integration and disintegration at the global level, a united front in economics and a divided one on matters relating to the maintenance of peace. If Utopia did not arrive in 1945 neither will the tensions between globalism and regionalism make life resemble that depicted in *1984*.

TABLE

LIST OF DISPUTES INVOLVING REGIONAL ACTION

| *ole* | *Dispute* | *Date* | *Organisation eventually seized of dispute* | *Outcome* | *Regional action helped/hindered peace in conformity with Charter principles* |
|---|---|---|---|---|---|
| *Iegemonic ubstitute* | Greek Civil War | 1944–49 | UN-sanctioned pro-Greek action under western control | Greek government wins | helped |
| | Korea | 1950–53 | UN-sanctioned action under western control | *status quo ante* restored | helped |
| | Cuban Missile Crisis | 1962 | OAS for blockade; UN for inspection | settled bilaterally | neither |
| | Viet-Nam | 1963– | UN discussion leads to nothing | unsettled | hindered |
| | Cyprus Civil War | 1964– | UN; after failure of NATO | peace restored, issue unsettled | hindered |
| | Czechoslovakia | 1968 | UN discussion leads to nothing | USSR intervention succeeds | hindered |
| *ival* | Guatemala | 1954 | OAS; UN defers | US intervention succeeds | hindered |
| | US/Cuba | 1960–61 | OAS; UN defers | none | neither |
| | Dominican sanctions | 1960 | OAS; UN defers | Trujillo overthrown | neither |
| | Bay of Pigs | 1961 | OAS; UN unable to act | US intervention fails | neither |
| | Dominican Republic | 1965 | OAS; UN action marginal | left-wing coup stopped | hindered |
| *omple- entary* | Lebanon | 1958 | Arab League and UN | UN and Arab League action end civil war | helped |
| | Kuwait | 1961 | Arab League | independence protected | helped |
| | Yemen | 1962 | Arab League and UN | both failed to affect outcome | neither |
| | Haiti/ Dominican Republic | 1963 | OAS | restoration of peace | helped |
| | Panama Canal | 1964 | OAS | bilateral settlement | helped |
| | Congo Civil War | 1964 | OAU | Congo government wins | neither |

| *Role* | *Dispute* | *Date* | *Organisation eventually seized of dispute* | *Outcome* | *Regional action helped/hindered peace in conformity with Charter principles* |
|---|---|---|---|---|---|
| *Willing Substitute* | South Tyrol | 1960 | Council of Europe and UN | bilateral settlement | helped |
| | Cyprus independence | 1954–60 | Council of Europe and UN | bilateral settlement | helped |
| | Saar | 1954 | Council of Europe | bilateral settlement | helped |
| | Costa Rica/ Nicaragua | 1948 | OAS | restored peace | helped |
| | Costa Rica/ Nicaragua | 1955 | OAS | restored peace | helped |
| | Honduras/ Nicaragua | 1957 | OAS and ICJ | restored peace | helped |
| | Panama/Cuba | 1959 | OAS | restored peace | helped |
| | Nicaragua/ Costa Rica | 1959 | OAS | died down | neither |
| | Honduras/El Salvador | 1969 | OAS | restored peace | helped |
| | Haiti/ Dominican Republic | 1949 | OAS | restored peace | helped |
| | Ecuador/Peru | 1955 | OAS | restored peace | helped |
| | Dominican Republic | 1959 | OAS | none | neither |
| | Bolivia/Chile | 1962 | OAS | calmed parties | helped |
| | Algeria/ Morocco | 1963 | OAU | stopped fighting | helped |
| | Somalia/ Ethiopia | 1964 | OAU | stopped fighting | helped |
| | Biafra | 1967–70 | OAU | Nigeria wins | neither |
| | Upper Volta/ Ghana | 1964 | OAU | bilateral settlement | helped |
| | Rwanda/ Burundi | 1967 | OAU | bilateral settlement | helped |
| | Gabon/Congo (Brazzaville) | 1962 | UAM | died down | neither |

# 8. BRITAIN AND THE UNITED NATIONS

F. S. Northedge

BRITAIN, like France but unlike the United States, the Soviet Union or any other major power, has been a leading member of the two universal organisations for the maintenance of peace in the twentieth century, the League of Nations and the United Nations, throughout its history in the case of the former and from its foundation in 1945 until the present moment in the case of the latter. There never has been any serious question of her withdrawal from either organisation through dissatisfaction with its effectiveness or disapproval of its collective attitude towards her foreign policy. Prime Minister Edward Heath was putting no more than the slightest of glosses on the British position when he ended his speech at the twenty-fifth session of the UN General Assembly on 23 October 1970 by saying that the UN "can rely on the full support of Her Majesty's Government and of the British people".[1]

It is true that among the public at large and in the political parties British support for the League, among those who did support it, was probably more fervent and intense than support for the UN has been among the latter's enthusiasts in Britain since the Second World War. One reason for this no doubt is that Britain played a much more important role in the League than it has ever done in the UN. It is many years since a British Foreign Secretary, Sir Austen Chamberlain, could say, in 1925, that "it is in the hands of the British Empire and if they will that there shall be no war there will be no war".[2] That role of predominance has been lost for ever. But another reason was that by 1945 international organisations for peace had become an accepted part of the established landscape of international life. None of the three major victorious belligerents, Britain, the Soviet Union and the United States, doubted during their negotiations in the course of the Second World War that a new beginning must be made on a world organisation to keep the peace when the war in Europe ended. That much the League had done for the cause of peace-keeping by universal international efforts. At the same time, the mere fact that a new world organisation was felt to be essential in all quarters during the 1939–45 War meant that the excitement of controversy had been taken out of the

[1] *The Times*, 24 October 1970.
[2] 182 H.C. Deb. 5s. Col. 322, 24 March 1925.

question. The fate of all political causes is to be enveloped in a kind of apathy once they have achieved their object; for then only one thing is worse than failure, and that is success. This has happened to British public opinion in regard to international organisations for peace.

Nor is it surprising that Britain should have been a persistent and active member of both world organisations. As a *status quo* power, during both the imperial and post-imperial periods, Britain has stood to gain from any international machinery which exists to inhibit violent change within states or between states. "We are determined to work for peace and for harmony between peoples", said Mr. Heath in the speech just referred to, "because it is only in such conditions that Britain, as part of the international community, can prosper". It is significant that when majorities at the UN have called for radical change, as during certain phases of the decolonisation process, official British attitudes have been reserved, if not positively hostile. Moreover, as a country with world-wide international interests and commitments, especially commercial, even with Britain's shrunken international status of the present day, she benefits from the peaceful settlement of international disputes which threaten world order. The latter theme has in fact become the standard refrain with all British spokesmen at the UN in recent years. And, as a highly industrialised state with an exceptional degree of dependence upon international trade, Britain's support must be afforded to world organisations such as the UN which include within their programmes the improvement of world economic conditions and increases in the purchasing power of all members of the international community.

## British diplomatic style and the United Nations

There is therefore a logical basis to British membership of such organisations as the League and the UN, whatever government rules in Westminster, and this has served to keep that membership always beyond the sphere of doubt. Nevertheless, it would be a mistake to ignore certain features in the British style of foreign policy, and the British outlook on world affairs, which have sometimes placed a strain on the country's participation in such organisations. In the first place, the makers of British foreign policy have never traditionally placed much faith in the 'forensic' type of diplomacy – if indeed it is diplomacy – which is normally carried on in UN organs and which was carried on, though to a somewhat less extent, in the Council and Assembly of the old League of Nations. British diplomats, with their long-established habits of quiet and discreet negotiations and of understated language, were shocked in the early years of the UN Security Council by the unrestrained stream of passionate vilification aimed at them by Soviet or Soviet-supported delegates; they were unused to being called 'raging war hyenas' and the 'running dogs of murderous capitalist imperialism'. In the event, British delegates, notably Sir Gladwyn Jebb (now Lord Gladwyn) and, on one memorable occasion, Prime Minister Harold Macmillan, in exchanges at the General Assembly with Mr Khrushchev, gave as good as they got in televised wrangling matches with Communist orators. But nobody in Britain seriously believed that these departures from the traditional usages of self-restraint carried matters much further in our dealings with the Communist world.

More recently, the determination of the now numerous African delegations at the UN to damn utterly South Africa and Portugal for their racial policies in Southern Africa and to pass resolutions committing the UN, for instance, to take over from South Africa the administration of South West Africa without indicating the practical means of doing so, have earned the rebukes even of such a sympathiser as Lord Caradon, the principal British delegate at the UN during the Wilson administration. Such behaviour, in the official British view, risks converting the world organisation into a loquacious and impotent talking shop. Linked with this, of course, is another British diplomatic trait: the pragmatic feeling that in international affairs,

> "Sticks and stones may break my bones
> But words will never hurt me."

Since 1945 British governments have by no means always respected and applied the good old rule that in framing one's foreign policy, commitments must be rigorously matched with capabilities. But they have equally rarely failed to reflect that rule in judging the collective verbal efforts of states – especially new states – at the UN.

Closely allied with these British attitudes is the sense that in the last resort it is the mutual relations between the greatest powers of the day, not speech-making or the votes of a host of small and weak countries, which have in the past determined the outcome of the supreme issues in world affairs, and will continue to do so in the foreseeable future. Just as British Ministers (though not intellectuals or publicists) looked with apprehension on the emergence of the successor states in Eastern Europe at the close of the First World War for fear that they might interfere with the reconciliation of Germany and Soviet Russia to the new post-war international order, so too, after the Second World War, Sir Winston Churchill on a celebrated occasion in May 1953 and Mr Harold Macmillan repeatedly throughout his premiership of 1957 to 1963 called for quiet talks between the paramount powers, away from the clamour of UN General Assembly gatherings and intended as part of a process of feeling one's way back to firmer ground in the Cold War.

Hence it is strange to read in Mr Harold Wilson's address to the United Nations Association in April 1967, when he was still Prime Minister, that the first of the six principles, as he saw them, governing British policy towards the UN was that "the status of the General Assembly should not be diminished as compared with that of the Security Council".[3] True, the British shared the American sense of disappointment over the repeated deadlock in the Security Council over the Cold War; the British government accordingly continues to insist that the veto of the great powers in the Council should not be used to prevent that body investigating international disputes. True, too, the British were foremost in proposing the admission of new and often decolonised states into the UN in the first decade of the Cold War at a time when the Soviet Union was vetoing the membership of such countries, presumably in order not to increase the non-Communist vote in the General Assembly. But Britain's heart was not with the United States when the latter sought, as early as 1947 and through the so-called 'Little Assembly', to secure the kind of resolutions condemning acts of Soviet policy which she could not obtain in the Security Council owing to the Soviet veto. Hence Britain did, as a matter of history, support the United States in her efforts to engineer a partial transfer of security functions from the Council to the Assembly; but this was always done with distinct mental reservations.

This was evident in the aftermath of the American-sponsored 'Uniting for Peace' resolution adopted by the General Assembly in November 1950, which made it possible for the Assembly to organise resistance to threats to or breaches of the peace, though purely on a recommendatory basis, if the Security Council was too deadlocked to act. During the Suez crisis in 1956 Britain found herself in the dock, along with the Soviet Union, which at the same time was engaged in suppressing the Hungarian revolution, at special emergency sessions of the General Assembly summoned under the 'Uniting for Peace' resolution. As it happened, and thanks to Mr Lester Pearson's efforts, these meetings had an outcome in the shape of the UN emergency force sent to the Middle East in 1956–57 which gave the British government the opportunity to extricate itself from an acutely embarrassing situation. But the fact that, in the minds of many British people, Britain was classified along with the Soviet Union as a lawbreaker by a host of Afro-Asian countries, when in reality, according to her Prime Minister, Sir Anthony Eden, she was defending the rule of law governing the Suez Canal in the face of the UN's inability to do so, did not endear the General Assembly to the British public. The General Assembly, so stated no less a person than Sir Winston Churchill, acted "on grounds of enmity,

[3] *Britain and the UN by Rt. Hon. Harold Wilson, M.P.*, a UNA publication, 1967.

opportunism or merely jealousy and petulance". Lord Glyn, speaking in the House of Lords, echoed the feelings of many when he described the General Assembly in the immediate aftermath of the Suez crisis as "a seething mass of corruption".[4]

When Britain joined with the United States in the early 1960's in demanding the application of the sanctions provided for in Article 19 of the UN Charter against countries such as the Soviet Union and France which refused to pay their share of the expenses of UN peace-keeping forces sent to the Middle East and the Congo, she did so in a half-hearted manner and with much soul-searching. Certainly, according to the opinion of the International Court of Justice at The Hague, the defaulters were legally in the wrong and sanctions against them would presumably have been in order, if a consensus could have been obtained in the UN to impose them. But it was well recognised in Britain that if undue pressure were applied by the UN against a great power, the risk was run that that power might quit the Organization, and Britain had had too much experience of great powers quitting the League in the 1930's to wish to see it repeated. It was also realised that it would not be wise for the great powers utterly to rule out the occasional use of force by themselves in defence of vital national interests by making it possible for the General Assembly to step in and take the situation out of the great powers' hands.

Time was to show the validity of the latter argument. When the United States suddenly decided in September 1965 no longer to press for the application of the sanctions of Article 19 against the financial defaulters, she did so no doubt because by that time she had become deeply immersed in the Viet-Nam war, and the last thing the American government wanted was a weak UN force, manned and staffed by neutral states, vainly attempting to hold the line between North and South Viet-Nam and, even more important, between the Vietcong and the regime in Saigon. Some British apologists might be inclined to argue that they themselves favoured the application of Article 19 at the time because they believed in the principle of General Assembly action to maintain the peace on the ground that that body was somehow more 'democratic' than, say, the Security Council. But the greater probability is that British Ministers and officials gave a sigh of relief when the United States decided to abandon the attempt to have Article 19 applied against the defaulters. No British policy maker could ever agree that a UN, denuded of some of its great-power members and full of small countries which pass endless resolutions without having the capacity to implement them, can be an effective guardian of the peace. Britain has tended always to favour the 'Concert of the Powers' conception

[4] House of Lords, *Official Report*, 25 July 1957, col. 132.

of the UN rather than the 'town meeting of the world' conception promulgated by the late John Foster Dulles.

Again, British sensitivity to the realities of power as distinct from the 'one-state one-vote' principle for the UN has caused British governments consistently to favour the admission of Communist China into the world organisation, either in substitution for or alongside the existing Nationalist Chinese delegation. Few in Britain, it seems, are under any illusion that Communist Chinese representation in the UN would at once convert the Peking regime into the kind of 'peace-loving' entity which qualifies for UN membership in the terminology of the Charter. None the less, it is a sound British instinct to accept and recognise a foreign government once it is firmly established in power, and also to regard the 'threatfulness' of another state as a strong reason for being in diplomatic communication with it rather than for ostracising it. The point was made by the present British Foreign and Commonwealth Secretary, Sir Alec Douglas-Home, when he said at the General Assembly on 24 September 1970 that,

> "If the representatives of Peking were seated here their influence would be greatly felt. I cannot forecast what it would mean. They could well, by the rigidity of their political doctrine, make our tasks more difficult. But they have, more than many, to gain from expanding trade, from prosperity and from inter-dependence. They could add immensely, if they chose, among the rest of us, to real co-existence. Their intentions, in the opinion of the British Government, should be put to the proof here in this Assembly of Nations."[5]

Yet Britain has patiently acquiesced in the United States' stubborn refusal to deal with the Peking government in the UN context, so much so as to be placed in the absurd situation in 1955 of recognising that government's legal right to establish its rule over the offshore islands of Quemoy and Matsu while arguing that any Communist attempt to recover the islands must be resisted because it would "give rise to a situation endangering peace and security, which is properly a matter of international concern". By making this statement in the House of Commons Sir Anthony Eden could only have meant that the United States would forcibly resist what the British government considered as Peking's right to recover its own property.[6]

This British support, or tolerance of, United States policy towards the UN has often been criticised as evidence of Britain's allegedly 'satellite'

[5] *Speech by the Secretary of State for Foreign and Commonwealth Affairs in the General Assembly of the United Nations, New York, September* 24, 1970, the Central Office of Information, 1970.

[6] 536 H.C. Deb. 5s. cols. 159–60.

status in relation to Washington. But it is firmly and sensibly grounded in the strong British belief since and before 1945 that any world organisation for peace is most effective when it enjoys the active support of all the greatest powers of the day. It is also a reflection of the nightmarish experience of the 1930's which British politicians almost unanimously never wish to see recur: the spectacle of a predominantly European organisation, namely the League of Nations, attempting to dissuade and deter aggression while one of its chairs, labelled 'The United States', remained vacant. Hence the British agreed, with some reservations, to the siting of UN headquarters in New York, in order to pin American loyalty to the new world organisation, and, as we have noted, with the efforts of John Foster Dulles and other American statesmen to shift authority to the General Assembly when the Security Council was deadlocked.

Finally, there is yet another element in Britain's diplomatic style which sometimes militates against her enthusiastic participation in such highly organised instruments as the UN. One has only to glance at the UN Charter and compare it with the old League Covenant, or some such purely British political document as the Statute of Westminster of 1931, to realise the essentially trans-Atlantic character of the former. The looseness and frequent infelicity of wording; the verbosity, coupled with imprecisions, which compares so unfavourably with the austere stylistic economy and clarity of the Covenant; and above all, its rules of procedure, committees, sub-committees, commissions and sub-commissions: all these are at one and the same time alien to the European diplomatic tradition and expressive of American love of resounding abstract ideals framed in lofty language, and the American addiction to complex machinery. Again, British deference towards America goes some way towards explaining the conflict between European and trans-Atlantic forms here. No doubt influential, too, was the wish to get as far away as possible from the defunct and luckless League of Nations, and also perhaps that period of organisational day-dreaming which seems to have gone on at the Dumbarton Oaks Conference in 1944, which drew up the first draft of the Charter. The Dumbarton Oaks conference appeared to issue a draft Charter which looked almost like a blueprint for a world government, with the Security Council as the Cabinet; and then unhappily the Yalta Conference met in February 1945, and ruined the scheme by inserting the veto into decisions of the Council.

There are, of course, advantages in the complex structure of the UN which we have today, with its so-called 'goldfish-bowl' diplomacy; it means considerable economies for the smaller countries whose delegates can meet in New York the spokesmen of all the countries of the world without the necessity for an expensive global network of diplomatic missions. Nevertheless, the British political instinct has always tended to favour the more informal and intimate gathering, such as under favourable conditions takes place within the Commonwealth system, in which it is argued that bargains can be struck and agreements reached as though in the sedate calm of a Pall Mall Club. This takes us back to that first trait of British foreign policy which is at variance with much in existing UN practice, namely the essentially British concept of 'quiet diplomacy'.

## Party attitudes to the Organization

We have so far considered features in the general style of British foreign policy and the extent to which they suit or jar upon the mechanics and spirit of the UN. This is proper in so far as the permanent machinery of British foreign policy, the Foreign and Commonwealth Office and the diplomatic service, no doubt bestow on that policy more continuity and sameness than, say, the home civil service does on domestic policy. Moreover, it is widely acknowledged that in foreign affairs the political parties, when in office, tend for a variety of reasons to follow roughly similar courses; especially has this been the case since 1945 when the options confronting successive British governments have been so limited in number. The Labour government's unwillingness to share in the implementation of the UN plan for Palestine of November 1947, unless it was accepted by both Jews and Arabs, is matched by Sir Anthony Eden's seeming indifference to majority opinion expressed in the General Assembly during the Suez crisis in 1956; and numerous other parallels could be cited. All the same, a strong case can be made out for saying that on the whole the British Labour party has shown somewhat greater sensitivity to UN opinion and Charter obligations than the Conservatives. It is hard to think of a Labour leader describing Assembly decisions in the terms used by Sir Winston Churchill in the passage already quoted.[7] And it was a Conservative, not a Labour, Foreign Secretary, Lord Home (now Sir Alec Douglas-Home), who, in a famous speech at Berwick-on-Tweed in December 1961, said that in the UN there was "one rule for the Communist countries and another for the democracies, one rule for the bully, who deals in fear, and another for the democracy, because their stock in trade is reason and compromise", even though the Minister at the end of that speech came "down decidedly on the side of hope" for the world organisation.[8]

On the other hand, it was a Labour government which first sent a Minister, Lord Caradon, to head the permanent British delegation to the

[7] See above, pp. 144-5.
[8] Kenneth Young, *Sir Alec Douglas-Home* (London, 1970), pp. 138–9.

UN. It was a Labour administration, too, which adhered to the UN resolution of 1963 recommending a ban on the sale of arms to South Africa, whereas it was a Conservative government, returned to office as a result of the general election in June 1970, which at once called the Labour decision into question and made known its readiness, in principle, to reverse it.

The reasons for these differences between Conservative and Labour (with whom we must include Liberal) attitudes to the UN are not far to seek. Traditionally in Britain the Labour party has been the party of internationalism, however vaguely or sentimentally conceived; of third-party settlement of international disputes; of disarmament effected through an international agency such as the UN. During the League of Nations period the Conservatives provided no outstanding exponent of the League cause apart from Viscount Cecil. When Winston Churchill called for 'arms and the Covenant', he was thinking of arms first; the Covenant represented in his mind all those countries, whether members of the League or not, which were willing and able to enter into a defensive pact against the Fascist dictators. On the Labour side, leaders from Ramsay MacDonald to Harold Wilson have ostensibly placed the world organisation pre-eminently in their thoughts.

Doctrinally, too, a party of the Left which attributes human conflict to international social circumstances, such as poverty or the accumulation of armaments, rather than the 'old Adam' in the human make-up, and believes that there is nothing inherent or inevitable in the present ubiquitous conflict between different national interests, might be expected to be somewhat more loyal to an institution dedicated to the resolution of such conflicts than a party of the Right.

Latent in the latter's thinking is the notion that international conflict, like all human conflict, springs from a basic will to power and acquisitiveness in man against which there is no alternative but to defend oneself by one's own strong right arm rather than through the essentially artificial and idealistic machinery of international institutions. Thus, whereas in the late 1930's under Clement Attlee and in the 1950's under Hugh Gaitskell, the Labour party seemed in its declarations to be renouncing the right of any state to decide the supreme issues of war and peace on its own and by itself, the principle laid down by both Prime Minister Heath and Foreign and Commonwealth Secretary Douglas-Home at the Conservative party conference in October 1970 was that on all basic issues, British foreign policy will continue to be determined by a British government consulting primarily British national interests. Mr Heath added at his speech to the General Assembly on 23 October 1970 that "I speak today for a newly elected British Government committed to vigorous policies in the interests of the security and prosperity of the British people:

> "I make no apology for defining so plainly our objectives before this assembly. For I am satisfied that the policies which we propose are fully in accord with our commitments under the Charter and our record as a member of this Organization."[9]

But Mr Heath left no doubt that, as far as he was concerned, he did not propose to allow anyone except the British Government to decide whether the final sentence in that declaration was true or false. All this needs to be said about the nuances of opinion among the two major British parties on the subject of the UN against the background of the assumption that in practice, as distinct from words, the two principal parties are far more at one in their international policy than their public declarations might seem to indicate.

## Britain's record at the United Nations

Turning now to the actual record of Britain as a UN member it may be stated without exaggerated national pride that this compares favourably with that of any other member state, and certainly with that of any of the other major powers. Britain has by no means been the readiest of countries to resort to force or the threat of force when other means for the settlement of international disputes have failed. In the Norwegian Fisheries case in 1951, for instance, the British government loyally and without hesitation abided by a judgement of the International Court of Justice at The Hague which was decidedly unfavourable to this country. The same could be said of the legal proceedings in the Anglo-Iranian oil dispute in the same year; there was hardly a suggestion in Parliament, much less among government circles, that force should be used against Iran. Even in the notorious Suez case in 1956, so often quoted as a 'clear' example of the violation of the UN Charter, it cannot be said that Britain did not practically exhaust all the conventional means for the settlement of international disputes before force was used. Before force was actually resorted to in that crisis the matter was referred by Britain and France to the UN Security Council, in which Britain eventually exercised one of her rare vetoes, which she had every right under the Charter to do. Moreover, one of the most significant features of the Suez crisis was the protests voiced by large sections of British public and Parliamentary opinion against the use of force without UN approval. There are few other countries in the world today in which the government can be conceivably embarrassed by powerful sections of its own public opinion loudly proclaiming that in the final resort the state can

[9] *The Times*, 24 October 1970.

only legitimately use force when it is acceptable to majorities in the General Assembly.

It is true that in many of the major and most dangerous disputes in the post-war world, those arising in East–West relations, Britain has not been at the forefront in urging recourse to settlement through the UN. But this has been based upon the wise and proper assumption that issues which the great powers themselves cannot solve, to say nothing of the UN, such as the long East–West debate over the status of Berlin, serve only to weaken the world Organization if they are referred to it. On the whole, British governments have been loath to refer Cold War problems to the UN (though in the early years they joined with the United States in the futile exercise of getting the General Assembly to back Western disarmament proposals as against those of the Soviet Union) merely for the empty satisfaction of scoring verbal points off the other side which serve to exacerbate the opponent rather than conciliate him. At the same time, long before the United States, under President Kennedy and later President Johnson, recognised the need for peaceful co-existence with the Communist world, a British Prime Minister, Mr Macmillan, at the UN and elsewhere, was pleading the same argument in season and out of season, to the chagrin very often of his NATO allies. When eventually in his American University address in June 1963, Mr Kennedy agreed that the old United States notion of the Communist world, including China, as a single monolithic bloc controlled by Moscow was an illusion, Mr Macmillan had been arguing much the same point almost from the moment he became Prime Minister in January 1957.

Again, Britain has been in the forefront in the last few years in calling for a review, for the purpose of improvement, of the existing machinery for the settlement of international disputes as listed, for instance, in Article 33 of the Charter. The British delegation to the UN in a letter to the Secretary-General of 20 August 1965 argued that "the subject of peaceful settlement is of such importance that it merits a separate study directed not simply to elaborating general principles but also to examining existing and new methods and machinery for peaceful settlement."[10] In December 1965 the chief British delegate to the UN, Lord Caradon, introduced a motion into the Special Political Committee proposing that the Assembly should institute "a penetrating survey of the means and methods leading to the adoption of recommendations and measures which would enable states to have greater recourse to the means of peaceful settlement".[11]

This resolution failed to gain the support of the majority of African

[10] General Assembly Document A/5964 of 20 August 1965.
[11] G.A., Twentieth Session, Official Records, Special Political Committee, 489th Meeting, p. 2.

states. These, under the leadership of the Ghanaian delegation, suspected that Lord Caradon's resolution might be a Machiavellian British device for ruling out the use of force, in preference to peaceful means of settling disputes, in the case of the Smith regime in Rhodesia, which had illegally declared its independence from Britain only a month previously. When the British delegation introduced their resolution once more at the following session of the General Assembly, much the same suspicions were in evidence and debate on the resolution was suspended *sine die*. One after-effect of the British initiative, however, was that the Board of Trustees of the United Nations Institute for Training and Research authorised the Executive Director to report to the twenty-third session of the General Assembly in 1968 that UNITAR hoped "to examine and assess methods (including new methods) of peaceful settlement and machinery for reconciliation of differences among States".[12] The idea behind this move seemed to be to call in aid not merely practical diplomatic experience, but all the resources of social and political science, to the study of the resolution of international conflict. But it is to be hoped that this will not discourage the British government in its own efforts to make the question of the peaceful settlement of disputes a matter of prime concern to the UN as a whole.

But it is with respect to decolonisation and the general racial problem that Britain has come under the strongest fire at UN meetings, and it is important to examine how justified these strictures are. First, it is worth pointing out that Chapter XI of the UN Charter, dealing with non-self-governing territories, commits member states which possess such territories to facilitate their progress towards self-government – which, incidentally, would be interpreted by many, if not most, international lawyers as implying something less than complete independence. But this commitment, moreover, is wholly recommendatory. No metropolitan state is bound to accept any time-table laid down by a UN committee for the attainment of self-government by its colonies, as Afro-Asian anti-colonialist and Communist representatives at the UN have vociferously contended. Nor is any metropolitan state committed by Article 73 (e) of the Charter to submit *constitutional* as well as other relevant information concerning the advancement of its dependent territories. Nevertheless, Britain has always been a leader in accepting successive broadenings of the implications of Chapter XI of the Charter, often in the teeth of stubborn resistance by other colonial states, notably Portugal.

First, Britain acceded to the anti-colonialist demand that the information gathered under Article 73 (e) should be submitted, not to the UN Secretary-

[12] G.A., Twenty-third Session, Document A/7263, 14 October 1968.

General, as the wording would seem to imply, but to a committee representing member states and responsible to the General Assembly in this particular matter. Secondly, Britain conceded the demand, which again was not authorised by the UN Charter, that she could be questioned on the information submitted, and later that the information presented to the committee should include facts about constitutional as well as other forms of progress. This again was another gloss on the Charter. Lastly, Britain made the far-reaching concession that members of the Committee on Information from Non-Self-Governing Territories, should be empowered to visit certain of her dependent territories in order to see things for themselves and put questions to the local subjects of British rule. No other colonial power ever went as far as this; yet over the years Britain has won less praise for these policies at the UN than countries which firmly resisted a much less far-reaching policy of accountability for colonial policy to an international organisation.

The fact was, of course, that by 1961, when the UN Special Committee on Colonialism was created, decolonisation had become accepted policy among all important sections of British political thought. 'The wind of change', Mr Macmillan's phrase, in Africa and elsewhere had been recognised as inevitable. In these circumstances, when Britain had nothing further to gain from retaining its dependent territories, it is extraordinary that a campaign arose in the UN charging Britain with imperialism because she was at first in doubt whether such countries as Fiji, with its half-a-million people, could properly figure at the UN General Assembly on a par with such gigantic powers as the United States and the Soviet Union. Britain then earned further disapproval among the new anti-colonialist states at the UN by digging in her toes and refusing to move in the matter of Gibraltar. In her favour it may be said that it seems a curiously inhuman conception of decolonisation which has persuaded the Spanish Republic, as well as the Afro-Asian and Latin American states which support her at the UN, that Gibraltar, with its 20,000 inhabitants, should become a separate state or join with Spain despite an explicit expression of their will to the contrary. Britain has no economic and hardly any strategic benefit to gain from clinging on to Gibraltar; but she can surely not abandon a people who have voted almost unanimously for staying British. And yet the Special Committee has gone on repeating over and again the refrain that such people as the Gibraltarians must be 'decolonised' whether they like it or not. This is assuredly an instance in which the voice of the UN cannot be the voice of reason or humanity.

Even more important, however, are the tempestuous clashes at the UN over Rhodesia and the race problem in southern Africa generally. As for Rhodesia, there is certainly nothing in the UN Charter which obliges a member state to apply force against one of its colonies, as the African states seem to demand, even in defence of the fundamental human rights and freedoms which the Charter lays down, however politically or morally correct it might have been to use such force at the time of Rhodesia's illegal declaration of independence in November 1965. Moreover, Britain acted as a loyal UN member state when she applied to the Security Council for mandatory sanctions against Rhodesia in December 1966. She has herself since that time operated such sanctions as effectively as any UN member state and more effectively than some. What can be said in criticism of Britain's Rhodesia policy is that this country, in refusing to use force against the Smith regime, could legitimately be described as acting in a racially discriminatory manner, since it was the fact that the dominant community in Rhodesia was made up of white men which was the principal factor in ruling out the use of force. But, again, there is nothing in the Charter which obliges a state to use force without discrimination against white *and* coloured; on the contrary, it is the injunction *not* to use force or the threat of force in Article 2 (4) which has to be applied without discrimination. Britain, on behalf of a moral principle and at no little cost to herself, has done all she could, short of the use of force, to bring the Smith regime to heel. Possibly she might have been more successful if only all other UN member states had done the same.

The case of South Africa and Portuguese Angola and Mozambique, however, is on quite a different footing. While the British Labour governments of 1964–70 verbally expressed their abhorrence of *apartheid* and, though to a less extent, the Portuguese regimes in Southern Africa, and, in addition, voluntarily applied the non-mandatory ban on arms sales to South Africa recommended by the Security Council in 1963, they never supported the motion of mandatory economic or military sanctions against either South Africa or Portugal. According to the memoirs of Mr George Brown, then at the Department of Economic Affairs, there were times during the economic crisis in the summer of 1966 when the Labour Cabinet was by no means united on the policy of maintaining the voluntary ban on arms to South Africa.[13] To have supported mandatory sanctions against the two offending regimes, or either of them, would have meant agreeing that the situation in southern Africa was a threat to peace within the meaning of Article 39 of the UN Charter. Although Britain argued that this was the case when applying to the Security Council for mandatory economic sanctions against Rhodesia in December 1966, it is hard to see how a country like South Africa, which is strong enough to resist almost any attack from the independent African states and has herself no obvious

[13] George Brown, *In My Way* (London, 1971).

wish to attack them, could be regarded as an immediate threat to peace and hence a subject for mandatory sanctions.

But this does not mean that a decision to resume the sale of arms to South Africa, which the Conservative government seems to have reached when they returned to office in June 1970, would be wise even if, by the terms of the Charter, it would apparently be legal.[14] Its probable effects in seeming to place Britain on the side of the white ruling minorities in southern Africa, could not but weaken Britain's comparatively good standing in the UN. An even graver consequence might be that of driving the independent African states into the arms of Russia or China or both, just as Egypt, followed by other Arab states, was thrown into Russia's arms when the United States and Britain tried to pressurise President Nasser into joining a Middle East defence organisation in 1954–5 and when in the summer of 1956 they withdrew their promise of financial assistance for the building of the Aswan Dam.

All in all, then, it would seem that the United Kingdom has little to be ashamed of in her UN record, bearing in mind, as we argued at the beginning of this Chapter, that the British style of foreign policy does not at all points suit membership of world organisations for peace and security such as the UN, and bearing in mind, too, that all states, Britain included, must in the final resort act in their national interests and as their constituted governments see those interests, not as fortuitous two-thirds majorities in the General Assembly of the UN prescribe. Certainly Britain might have done, and could still do, more. It was odd, for instance, to hear Mr Harold Wilson, when Prime Minister in 1967, urging fellow member states to train and earmark units of their armed forces for service under UN command; so far as is known, Britain has never done so, though the Wilson government did agree to make available in advance the logistic support for six battalions of UN forces.[15] Also it would certainly pay Britain in the long run to assist in shaping the UN into a more effective agency for reducing the gap between the rich and poor peoples of the world. It was depressing to hear Mr Heath say as Prime Minister at the twenty-fifth session of the General Assembly that Britain would 'do its best' to reach by 1975 the one per cent target of national income agreed to at the second UNCTAD as long ago as 1968 as a contribution towards the economic development of the new states.[16] This is not a matter of humanitarianism or charity; it is a hard-headed insurance policy for the future. No international order is secure unless it commands the moral approval of the round bulk of the people who have to live under it. The present international order does not command the

[14] Written in October 1970.
[15] See above, p. 144, n. 3.
[16] *The Times*, 24 October 1970.

moral approval of the round bulk of the poor states. They are no doubt too weak at present seriously to jeopardise the international order. But we must not assume that they will always remain so.

## British responsibilities

If the UN is to survive it must be seen to be working in the interests of most of its member states most of the time. In the last resort every state will pursue what it considers to be its national interest and if this, conceived in however enlightened terms, leads it into courses at variance with the UN Charter or the views of the majority of the General Assembly, so much the worse for the latter. Britain has a peculiarly heavy stake in the kind of world which those who framed the UN Charter had in mind: a world free from war and massive armaments, free, too, from racial or international violence and tensions, a world more prosperous than the present one, with its wealth more equally distributed, and above all a world which so commands the moral approval of its peoples most of the time that they have no desire or incentive to reduce it to chaos or to stand idly by while others reduce it to chaos. At the same time, British governments have a responsibility to ensure, through UN machinery where appropriate, that their dilemmas and difficulties are well enough understood abroad that UN member states do not ask Britain, through their resolutions in that Organization, to undertake tasks which exceed her capacity to fulfil. But if Britain is to live and prosper in the world she has an obligation, under whatever government, to be as good and loyal a member of the UN as effort and sensitivity to the interests and outlooks of other countries can make her.

# 9. THE UNITED NATIONS IN HISTORICAL PERSPECTIVE

David Mitrany

## The Nature of the Organization

The United Nations might well claim "I struggle, therefore I live"; even if its state of crisis may appear to have become endemic. To get some sense of whence the crisis springs, and so possibly of what lies ahead, the political analyst has to try to distinguish between two separate sources: between difficulties arising from the constitution and consequent working of the Organization itself, and difficulties brought upon it by events in the world outside. Not only are the two distinct from each other but, as in all political systems, there is a continuous inner stress between them – between the fixed institution and a social life that is never at rest. In the case of the UN both the fixity of the instrument and the fluidity of the life it has to serve are much greater, and therefore under greater stress than any national or federal or other established polity. Like all political institutions, the UN has to fit the needs it is meant to serve, and that means a capacity to adapt itself to conditions that are endlessly changing. For the UN that is a very hard test: as for an association of independent members, any substantial change virtually needs the consent of them all. In one sense the Charter is more like a federal constitution, with provisions for preventing change more conspicuous than those for enabling change – but only in that formal sense. In the years since the Second World War, in fact, even the old federations have experienced the strains of adjustment. Yet no matter how rigid, a federal constitution is subject to interpretation by the courts, and the judicial history of the US Supreme Court provides evidence enough that it can be as much an instrument for speeding change as for delaying it. The International Court of Justice has no such standing in the evolution of the UN; it functions only when the parties are willing to make use of it, and even then its decisions have merely the force of an advisory opinion. The UN indeed has no executive with authority and means to enforce the Court's decisions if the situation were otherwise.

In the second place, even the power of revision of a federal court is not and cannot be the wilful act of a majority of its bench. Their decisions reflect, a little slower or a little faster, a change that has already found its way into general opinion–as that arch-realist 'Mr Dooley' once put it, "the Supreme

Court merely follows the election returns". In a federation as in any organised society adaptive changes are generated through the daily working of the life of the community; and it is natural that the process should work especially strongly in times of national crisis. The UN is no such organic community. Its members engage in a large variety of economic and social and cultural exchanges, but they do so on a contractual basis, as separate units, not as interlocked parts of a whole. Those exchanges would go on just the same if the UN did not exist; and as things are, each participant can and does interrupt or alter them at will without any reference to their common membership in the UN. Indeed, they do so now more freely than before and with greater disregard of customary rules and even of mutual obligations under the self-judged imperatives of 'national planning' and 'social security' – with little sense that the international community also has some claims in all that. And, lastly, unlike the binding effect of a crisis on national societies, an international crisis would be likely to bring the UN not greater unity but rather confusion and division, as it did to the League of Nations.

On a broad view of the historical lines, this century has seen three positive efforts towards that most difficult step in political advance that has faced modern society – an international system resting on the voluntary acceptance of a common law and authority. Compared with the utopian or largely diplomatic schemes of former times, the advance in outlook and purpose within only two generations represented by those three attempts was immense – from the Hague Conferences at the turn of the century, to the League of Nations in 1919 and the UN in 1945. The change in outlook is itself witness to a growing sense of the need to complete the pyramid of political organisation that would enable the peoples of the world to live at peace within a common rule of law and order. Yet in spite of that rapid progress in intent, all three attempts were overtaken by political and social changes before they could take root and grow. Of the first two it could be said that it was so because the international soil in which they were planted was too shallow; the sense of international community had hardly spread beyond the limited circle of idealistic pleaders. The Hague Conferences did not venture beyond general plans for the arbitration of disputes, and some valuable humanitarian regulations on the manner of conducting war. The League of Nations went a good deal further, seeking above all ways for the prevention of war; but President Wilson's devotion to the idea of a common international society had to face President Harding's more generally representative wish for a "return to normalcy", to independent national decision and action.

In our own time, after a second World War, the third attempt was more determined and more promising. The UN was the expression of an almost universal acceptance of the need to stop war altogether and thus of a conscious attempt to create an organised international system invested with some real authority. It has the advantage over the League of Nations in that its membership includes almost all independent states (with West Germany outside but sharing its purpose, and Communist China rashly ostracised). Yet even more than the first two experiments the UN has been overtaken by the march of events, to the point where it looks on almost helplessly at the changes of our time. If the weakness of the League of Nations was largely inherent, restricted as it was in membership, scope and powers, the weakness of the UN stems largely from the force of events. The great leap in outlook and conception the UN represents has been outleapt by a three-fold revolution – political, social and technological:

(i) The UN's stronger working constitution compared with the League has gradually been faced with a majority of new and unprepared states; states which struggling to achieve a 'national' personality tend to assert their separate independence. Can they be welded together into a communal system with sufficient authority to act for the whole, which the UN needs if it is to serve the historical situation?

(ii) The UN's arrangements for international economic and social action have to contend with the search for 'social security' through national planning which leads to a hardening of the state. The social revolution is universal in old states and in the new, but inevitably sharper in the latter, making them more assertive still. For as the Soviet jurist, Levin, has argued, to justify Russia's insistence on untrammelled sovereignty, a country in a state of revolutionary gestation cannot accept external obligations that might interfere with that process. Can the UN guide that powerful and restless social current towards a common purpose and partnership?

(iii) It is obvious that, organically speaking, these two currents – international sub-division and national centralisation – acutally flow against the proclaimed purpose of the UN. In complete contrast is the third current, the scientific-technological revolution, which is moving fast beyond the scope and authority of the national state. It is marked indeed by the emergence for the first time of true global issues that are outside the range of traditional international politics. With satellites and space travel we have reached the no-man's land of sovereignty. It is no longer a confrontation of 'national interests' but the appearance of imperative universal interests. That is a true historical turning point, and as such bound to prove also a turning point for the UN – perhaps an ultimate test. Can the UN secure control over such global issues, issues that now threaten to run away beyond man's foresight and control?

## The United Nations and the Three-fold Revolution

Historically our experience is unique also in the sense that the political and social upheaval is universal. Earlier commotions may have affected a particular country or at most a region; but now both substance and communications are such that they reverberate quickly throughout the political world. Moreover, our society appears to be in a state of permanent revolution – not that of Marx, but in its own nature. It is a total social, political and technological revolution, without a visible end, without a set purpose – such as the reform of a political system, or the displacement of a power group, or the abolition of the institution of property – and therefore with no clear horizon or predictable spectrum. The only constant in the situation is change itself. That must seem a brittle foundation and environment in which to set up the edifice of a cohesive international system; but the looseness of material and conditions also offers opportunities, and the task cannot wait. What omens can be drawn from its brief experience as to whether the UN can find the capacity to live up to its historical task?

We may gain some insight into that by looking in turn at the three currents just mentioned as they appear reflected in the mirror of the UN:

(i) First, the great increase in the number of states. It was the intention of its creators that the UN should be a universal association, and on a formal level all newcomers have to be absorbed. But other circumstances besides numbers were bound to create problems at the working level. Within the nominal principle of sovereign equality, the unorganised international system before 1914 was in effect a directorate of the great powers, which at the same time controlled much of the overseas world in Africa and South-East Asia. New states were made rarely, often with some probationary limitation, and with little if any say in the bargainings that went into great power policy. The dominance of the powers was still undiminished after the First World War, at the Paris Conference, in form as well as in fact; and special impositions, like the Minorities Treaties, could still be laid upon new or renewed states as the price of recognition. Under the UN all that has virtually been wiped away. New states have been made with the greatest of ease without regard to size or experience or viability. Membership of the UN is virtually automatic, and outside the Security Council their equal legal status is effective at once, so that it has actually given them a majority in the General Assembly.

The immediate impact was all the greater because the sheer range and speed of that political fertility were unexpected and took the UN as an institution by surprise. The "de-colonisation of Africa has altered the balance of political forces and has . . . therefore fundamentally altered the nature and role of international organisations".[1] In the second place, the new states did "not bring to the Organization the perspective of those older nations which either as participants or as onlookers shared the experience on which the Organization was founded", "a common history of political involvement at the international level".[2] That lack of continuity had not been felt with the few new states created since the middle of the nineteenth century; now it came in a mass. Yet even so it might not have affected so greatly the working of the UN were it not for two ideological factors: many of the new states brought with them strong attitudes against 'colonialism' and 'imperialism', though their very presence and position were proof that both were vanishing fast; and they also tended to conjure up without respite the potent issue of colour and racialism. And the effect was made worse by infiltration with the general ideological division between East and West.

That ideological partnership was the more ironical as Stalin at first wanted merely a union of the great powers, and it was the West which stood for a democratic universality. And while the USSR can look after itself, and so can the Western states, it is the poor and weak new-comers who must be the losers through any debility in the UN. As the African proverb says, "when two elephants fight, it is the grass that suffers". The new Balkan states had earlier experienced that when the Slav and Germanic groups of powers were competing in the *Drang nach Osten* policy. In matters of defence and national security they are wellnigh helpless. Under the former pedestrian type of warfare even small states could put up some kind of defence and were welcomed as allies in the groupings of the balance of power; but in the nuclear confrontation they can have little part and are both helpless and useless without some system of international security. And they are almost as helpless to ensure their own social security in this technological age and in competition with advanced countries without the mutuality of an international economic and social system of co-operation. In their present state they themselves have little to contribute towards it, and their factory-fresh independence will serve them poorly without the superior and fortified emancipation through a collective system. Hence their very existence, let alone the hope of a good life, is bound to the prospect of the UN; and every weakness in the UN is a threat to their statehood. If there be no virtue in being big and strong, neither is there virtue in being small and weak. One of the remarkable experiences of the

[1] Harold Jacobson, "New States and Functional Organisations", in Robert Cox (ed.), *International Organization: World Politics* (London, 1969), p. 74.

[2] Lawrence Finkelstein, "The U.N. Then and Now", *International Organization* (Summer 1965), p. 7; and David Kay, "The Politics of Decolonization", *International Organization* (Summer 1965), p. 28.

League of Nations was the exceptional influence, against the temper of the Covenant, which a few small states gained in its deliberations and decisions – simply because through delegates like Nansen and a few like him they made themselves spokesmen for a new international spirit. Historically it is admittedly an unhappy dilemma for these newly enfranchised peoples that they have to practise nationalism when their prospects lie almost wholly in a unifying internationalism.

(ii) Historically that is made evident by the policy which serves them as instrument for that nationalist consolidation. It has to be remembered that during the great economic depression of the early 1930's all the governments involved claimed that it was due to extraneous circumstances beyond their control. We have yet to discover all the harm that was done when the West, just as the world was in need of a broad international advance, plunged back into national planning with its massive and jealous state controls. That led to an intractable opposition of two elements: the aspiration for social change is universal and pressing, and the aspiration for international peace is universal and pressing; yet at present there can be no unity of view on the part which the national state should have in meeting them. The states with the strongest revolutionary impulse dive headlong into the deepest nationalist pool. Unless national planning can be geared to international planning it must bring about a more hard-set division between states than ever before. How could any scheme for international security survive in such a welter of competing national plans?

We cannot live in two different worlds at the same time. The issue is the more perplexing because the very elements who formerly were committed to the ideal and practice of internationalism are now in the vanguard of national planners. 'Total war' had already given the state a lien on economic life; 'total social security' will spread it in every country also over social life and outlook. A state organised within its own limits to fulfil with its own ways and by itself the new vision of social security need not be a National-Socialist state, but it could not help being a social-nationalist one. In the debate on the ECSC in the House of Commons even the moderate Labour Prime Minister, the late Lord Attlee, came down hard against British membership with the argument that "we could not allow a vital sector of our economic life to be controlled by a foreign committee".

Historically, the issue of national planning is full of traps and paradoxes. To begin with, a semantic fallacy is hidden in the very name. Planning implies by customary definition something sensibly organised, stable and foreseeable. In fact national planning is unpredictable even within the state: internationally it is wholly wilful. Economic policy and transactions are apt to be changed suddenly and one-sidedly in the name of the needs of the particular plan; and such changes in one plan in turn upset in varying ways and degrees the plans of all the other states involved. A planned state is an uncertain state; and as large economic issues and transactions now come under state controls and decisions, that means that every point of economic contact now is also a point of political contact, and therefore a point of potential conflict between countries.

One of the great developments since the Second World War has been the ideal and policy of technical assistance; it has extended the idea of the welfare state into something akin to a welfare world. Yet little thought has been given to the risk that foreign aid and technical assistance, as largely practised hitherto, may actually distort the purpose and prospect of the UN. A generation ago I had occasion to point out that the whole generous scheme of League loans – using international expertise and international means and international controls – worked for the consolidation of the separate national economy of the receiving regimes, and at no point was used to restore lines of economic co-operation torn asunder, as in the Danubian region, by the Versailles peace settlement. Is not that in a large measure also the effect of technical assistance? A real dilemma springs from the conflict between national and international planning; and the resulting paradox is that the more socialistic the policy of a country, the less does it contribute to international progress – the more revolutionary, the more reactionary! A strange perversion of the original Marxist creed. And in relation to our subject it has to be noted that ways and means for mitigating that nationalist trend have had to be found through arrangements like GATT, OECD, etc., outside the purview of the UN (though the UN's own Economic Commission for Europe has done some fine service in co-operation). The general conclusion therefore has to be that national planning has made and is making unreliable partners in the intended community of the UN; and that in this regard also groups of states are seeking more reliable bonds in regional groupings outside the UN.

(iii) Historically, the most crucial problems lie in the new global issues – nuclear power, space exploration, the exploitation of the deep sea-bed, and others yet to come. They are new not only in themselves but also in the kind of twist they bring into international relations. It is a central characteristic of these global problems that they are essentially technical in character and therefore cannot be settled politically, like economic or territorial issues, by bargaining and adjustment leading to a compromise. They demand comprehensive solutions under some continuous arrangement. For a second characteristic is that those technical conditions are eternally changing. The issues they raise cannot be settled by rigid clauses valid for the time-limit of a pact, rather it is the duration of the technical conditions in which it was born that limit the validity of the pact. The original atomic conditions were outstripped by nuclear development, and so are the ICBM's being outstripped by missiles launched from submarines, and possibly from the sea-bed and satellites and other inventions yet to come. As with national decisions relating to them, such matters are determined on a technical basis by technical experts, not by public debate and consensus. They are very much more difficult to determine and to decide when no common authority is established and respected.

A debate in the UN Assembly would be meaningless: the main powers would not disclose their resources and know-how and the bulk of the other states would not dispose of experts capable of taking an informed part; besides the risk of wilful obstruction for irrelevant reasons which could only once again strain relations within the UN. It is indeed significant that these global problems, even more than the economic matters mentioned above, are apt to be negotiated and settled outside the UN, as was the case with the nuclear non-proliferation Treaty. And it is equally striking that the weight of Soviet policy, which in general has tended to support political obstruction by the phalanx of new states, on these global issues falls on the other side, and shows a strong interest in the wide acceptance of global rules and controls – as seen in Soviet pressure on Western Germany to sign the non-proliferation treaty. That Soviet position has also shown, finally, that in such issues the UN and the world cannot afford to ostracise countries with a potential interest and power, such as Communist China and even South Africa; rather that it is vital to bring them into the orbit of a common scheme, whether they are members or not. Historically, therefore, the question is once more: can the UN find the authority and the means for controlling such global issues, issues which cannot be made safe by partial agreements between a particular group of states?

## Charter Revision and Political Division

This brief summary suggests some preliminary conclusions: (i) that in a political sense the partnership of the UN is not supported fairly and reliably by many of its members; (ii) that in the essential and beneficial purpose of furthering economic co-operation in the place of economic competition the partnership is widely violated by its members, in conception and in practice, while taking advantage of the resources of the partnership: hence a tendency to seek relief in regional alternatives which end by using much the same ways of discriminating between the local group and the rest; (iii) that the crucial new global issues, above all the nuclear issue, are apt to deploy themselves outside the bounds of the UN. What can its prospect be, beyond an indifferent and lagging existence, unless these trends are altered fundamentally? And what are the possible ways and means for doing that? Broadly speaking, there are two possible roads for helping to bring about these changes: one is the constitutional road, through formal changes in the structure and relationship of authority within the UN itself; the other is through changes developing gradually through common activities and working relations among the members.

To look first at possible constitutional changes. To placate the distrust of many states at San Francisco for the dominant position given to the five great powers – permanent places on the Security Council, with the right of veto – a liberal formula for its eventual revision was included in Article 109 of the Charter. Under that article a reviewing conference could be called together at any time by a two-thirds vote of the members, if it included one of the great powers; and if not called before, a proposal for such a conference was to be placed automatically on the agenda of the General Assembly after ten years and could be approved by a simple majority of its members with the support of one of the five powers. (The ten-year period was apt to bring to mind, not without some relevance, that the same period was set down for the renewal of the ill-fated Austro-Hungarian *Ausgleich*, which at every renewal produced a crisis that led the Viennese wits to speak of the arrangement as *Monarchie auf Kündigung*.) Be that as it may, the Tenth General Assembly came and went without taking up the exceptional facility provided for it alone for a review of the Charter.

That episode has significant lessons for the prospect that is facing the UN and its members now. In anticipation of a reviewing conference in 1955 there was naturally a great deal of discussion of the issues, numerous and varied, which might be brought before it, and to what purport – and mention will be made of some of these later. Private contributions to that discussion would fill volumes and, being private, their temper, as one might expect, did not fail at times to reach the extreme at one end or the other. But on the central preliminary question of whether to call a reviewing conference at all, the US supported by the Latin American states took the lead among those in favour, and therefore took some pains to prepare the ground. The Secretary of State, Mr John Foster Dulles, had launched the subject already in 1953 when he addressed the American Bar Association in Boston, and in the following year a special sub-committee of the Foreign Affairs Committee of the Senate held prolonged hearings to the same purpose. As the US had been largely responsible for the concession embodied in Article 109 (3), Mr Dulles had insisted at the Senate hearings that for them it was a matter of good faith towards the smaller states to convene a reviewing conference. Yet these states themselves were not so sure of it. When the matter came up at the Eighth General Assembly, on proposals that arrangements should be put in hand for the necessary preparatory work, many delegations – not least those from Western

Europe and the British Commonwealth – were reluctant to commit themselves to the idea of a conference, much less to disclose their eventual position on particular issues. At the other end of the scale, Soviet Russia and her supporters were utterly opposed to the idea. A year later at the Ninth General Assembly, the last preparatory opportunity, the matter was not even discussed; and at the moment of decision, at the Tenth General Assembly, it was allowed to lapse.

The main reason for that apparent self-denial was of course the division between the great powers. No doubt there would have been differences on what changes were desirable and in what sense, but it never came near any argument on details. It must be remembered that at that time the USA had the leading influence in the General Assembly and probably could have mustered the necessary simple majority for the calling of a reviewing conference. Some extreme voices urged that the opportunity be used to expel the Soviet bloc altogether; but wellnigh all opinion, public and private, agreed that a forced conference could do no good and might do much harm. There was the risk that Soviet Russia might simply refuse to participate, as she had done on other occasions. And in any case, the arrangements for ratification were such as to make it impossible to bring about substantial changes against her opposition – changes such as easing the veto power or shifting authority from the Security Council to the General Assembly. Many commentators feared that the only likely upshot would be a sense of futility and frustration, and inevitably a display of the gap that divided the Western and the Eastern blocs on all major issues. The general conclusion was that at the time it was not possible to strengthen the working of the UN through Charter revisions, whatever their merit. It had all been summed up in a blunt speech at a plenary session of the Eighth General Assembly (24 September 1953) by the Swedish Foreign Minister, M. Osten Unden:

> "The demands for revision . . . would render the contents of the Charter even more Utopian; they would remove its provisions still further from reality. The general public should not, however, have the illusion that such proposals would constitute a short cut to a more stable peace. The prospects for a lasting peace depend on the international policies pursued by states, particularly by the great powers, and not on the drawing up of perfect provisions in the Charter of the United Nations."

What guidance does that experience give us for possible progress, fifteen years later? The prospect of infusing fresh strength into the UN through Charter revision is, if anything, worse – and that for two reasons. In spite of some easing of the Cold War, general relations between the two ideological blocs are now certainly no better, and no common approach could be charted because those relations are also unpredictable. The dilemma with the foreign policy of dictatorial regimes is that it provides no steady bearings. Domestic policy can be arbitrary only within the recognisable risks of the country's needs; but foreign policy need not be anchored in tradition or harnessed to public opinion, and is apt to be little bound by international rules and considerations. There was a good illustration of this difficulty in an elaborate American study of Soviet foreign policy which appeared two years ago. The penultimate chapter, entitled "The Perils of Khrushchev", ended with the fall of "the man who had dominated the Soviet Union for ten years and who had shaken the world with his threats and designs". The passage was followed by one which opened the next chapter: "Caution was the most obvious characteristic of the new team which took over the reins of power from Nikita Khrushchev"; and, in any case, in her difficulties with her "junior partners" – which the writer thought since 1964 a more appropriate description than 'satellites' – "military intervention of the order of 1956 was out of the question in view of the vastly changed conditions".[3]

The Soviet invasion of Czechoslovakia must have taken place about the time when this expert historical assessment was being bound in hard covers; and its true meaning was made plain a few months later in the statement which has become known as 'the Brezhnev Doctrine'. Having over the years claimed absolute sovereignty for its own revolutionary regime, Mr Brezhnev then pronounced that Communist satellites must accept a restricted sovereignty – under an implied Soviet protectorate. It so happens that about the same time Mr Henry Kissinger, now President Nixon's principal adviser, committed himself to a similar, if private, pronouncement, that the right to absolute sovereignty could no longer be tolerated in this nuclear age.[4] These seemingly identical views revealed the conceptual gulf between them in relation to the prospect of a corporate international system. The first was linked in the name of a partisan ideology, a sectional creed, to Russia's claim to a private right of inquisition. The second was moved by fear of some wild use of nuclear means, a risk for humanity at large, and so propounded a right of general supervision by and for the world as a whole.

Neither Article 2 of the Charter nor the Declaration of Human Rights was invoked at the UN in protest against the invasion of Czechoslovakia or, especially, against Mr Brezhnev's gubernatorial claim. And that reveals a second reason why any strengthening of the UN's authority through constitutional reform is not possible at present. Since 1955 the line of

[3] Adam B. Ulam, *Expansion and Coexistence, The History of Soviet Foreign Policy, 1917–57* (New York, 1968), pp. 694, 695 and 713.
[4] *The New York Times*, 3 December 1968.

influence in the General Assembly has been reversed: most of the seventy or so new Asian and African members have inclined to line up behind the Communist bloc and its generally unco-operative mood; though some American studies suggest that more often it is rather Soviet Russia that lines up her support behind the captious politics of these newly enfranchised states.[5] Their fragile and unproved independence needs more than that of older states the support of an organised international system – they have done little towards it so far. At the UN, with a few exceptions, they have tended to use their new position for quixotic skirmishes with 'colonial' and 'imperialist' ghosts of the past rather than in the pursuit of a communal life for the future. In such a mood and with such a change in the balance of power in the Assembly any formal increase in the UN's authority is more unlikely now than it was at the tenth anniversary. The one formal reform has been the increase in the size of the Security Council from nine to fifteen to reflect the increase in membership – though the class division with the obstructive power of veto has been left unchanged; and the increase in the size of ECOSOC. The same circumstances have affected the other possible channel of change, i.e. changes in the standing and effectiveness of the UN's several organs through the development of their work.

One reason given for the failure of the Tenth General Assembly to make use of the opportunity for a reviewing conference was that in the meantime the smaller states had got a deal of what they wanted through the gradual shifting of influence from the Security Council to the General Assembly and its subsidiary committees – through changes in procedure rather than through formal revision, through majority decisions, through interpretations and recommendations, and so on. A conspicuous example was the 'Uniting for Peace Resolution', of 1950. One might also mention the use by the Security Council of the instrument of 'recommendation' in the Korean case though it is not provided in the Charter; but the accidental circumstances of that occasion also showed by its very success the limits of the role of the UN in any conflict between great powers. For many reasons such working evolution is the healthiest process of change in all political societies, a natural response to 'a clear and visible need'. But at the UN the mood of the majority referred to before has too often silted the channel for such evolutionary reform. It was at work in the use and abuse by a majority in debates on colonial issues falling within the range of domestic jurisdiction, in disregard of both custom and legal rules (Art. 2 (7) ). They have been apt to obtrude the same mood occasionally into the work of Specialised

[5] Hayward Alcker, Jr., "Dimensions of Conflict in the General Assembly", *American Political Science Review* (September 1964).

Agencies whose constitutions are, and whose beneficial work must be, strictly non-political.

There was natural concern in 1965 when at the Twentieth General Assembly the group of mainly Asian and African members voted that resolutions on decolonisation could be adopted by a simple majority. One might see some merit in that attitude if its intent had been to widen and strengthen the authority of the UN in the service of human rights everywhere. But how many states from that majority would allow similar inquisitions within their own domain? Colour is not the only illiberal division, not the only distinction used for keeping individuals and groups in political and administrative subjection. It is not so long since the Nazis used the method of violently denouncing the treatment of German minorities elsewhere to muddy and confuse international life – as they used very effectively the Sudeten of Czechoslovakia – and so cover up their own ruthless politics. The purpose of the UN is to advance a liberal internationalist policy: that cannot be done unless its rules and principles apply to all members and to all kinds of sectarian discrimination alike in stern equality. As in other matters, it is doubtful whether the abuse of inquisitorial debates could be checked by any revision of the Charter, as "it is hardly likely that the majority would relinquish the right to be indiscreet".[6] But it could be done, as I have urged in regard to minorities long ago, by a procedural rule of *tu quoque*: a rule that no state should be allowed to table a complaint against another state and claim for its own or other minorities greater or wider rights than it allows itself within its own jurisdiction. Any complaint would thus serve to mirror that state's own conduct; and the true picture would then appear in all its colours, not merely in black and white. Such a procedure would help both to check the misuse of human rights incidents for unrighteous political ends and in the process reveal the whole range of the problem facing the would-be makers of a tolerant international society.

M. Unden's insight into the dilemma of the UN at its tenth anniversary is even more valid now. Even if Charter revision were possible, it would not help to give the UN more formal functions and powers. One does not strengthen a weak arm by giving it a heavier weapon to wield. The shortcomings in its achievement and the uncertain prospects stem largely from the choking of the Security Council through the misuse of the veto, and the clogging of the potentially greater part that could be played by the General Assembly through the misuse of its debates and voting rights. The Assembly is the only organ of the UN which enjoys full equality in voting. After twenty-five years of widening experience, from a considerable

[6] Lawrence Finkelstein, "Revising the UN Charter", *International Organization* (May 1955), p. 223.

expansion of its activities and opportunities, one might have expected also a ripening maturity. Together with the great increase in membership that would have made the Assembly something of a real world forum. Instead there are growing and almost despairing calls for revising the Assembly's working arrangements upon some basis of 'weighted' voting. Some such arrangement would seem inevitable, but much more difficult now than if it had been made part of the original Charter, and almost sure to be opposed by Soviet Russia if attempted as a direct change. But the point to note is that the calls for some such change come especially from devotees of the international idea; even from the present liberal and non-western Secretary General[7]; just because they know from their anxious insight into the world of international relations that the heart of the UN's problem is not the play of power but the freedom to act – the place and the part allowed to the UN in the new world that is fast engulfing us. Few disputed in 1954, and few would dispute now Mr Dulles's statement at the Senate hearings that "the UN as it is, is better than no UN at all". The difference between then and now is that there is an inflationary risk for the UN, as there is for money, as its value is being steadily outstripped by the flood of new problems and situations. Apart from partisan obstruction and the problematic of constitutional changes, there is now as in all government an excess of pressures and burdens at the centre. Instead of increasing the Organization's responsibilities – favoured by some over-devoted quarters – the better prospect may lie rather in the second alternative, in finding ways to relieve the UN of some of its burdens. For anything that helps to reduce barren partisan debates and sets it free to get on with positive work must enhance its general standing and prospect.

[7] It was echoed by the equally liberal and experienced Mr Lester Pearson (responsible for the recent report on international aid) in his final Reith lecture, in November 1968. Mr Foster Dulles had said already at the American Senate hearings of 1954, at a time when the composition of the General Assembly was less volatile, that "in the light of the growing responsibility" of that body a change was needed, and he suggested a 'combination vote' which would require majorities both on a one-vote basis and on some weighted basis (reflecting perhaps the combination of voting in the US Congress). There have been many variations on the theme. One idea that would avoid a new 'class' division was offered by the Commission for the Study of the Organisation of Peace in its Seventeenth Report, *New Dimensions for the United Nations – The Problems of the Next Decade* (May 1966). The Report suggested that the ordinary work of the General Assembly might be handed over to subsidiary committees of a limited size (under Article 22 of the Charter), each dealing with a particular subject, with varying membership "weighted in favour of those Members with greatest interest or responsibility in the issues involved" (pp. 16–7). (That was the idea used in the writer's essay, *A Working Peace System*, 4th ed. (London, 1946), p. 47). The general principle has been applied at the World Bank and other international institutions, in the Council of Europe and in the European Common Market, etc.

## Regional and Functional Devolution

Looking at the wide sweep of today's international scene two groups of problems, it would seem, could for different reasons be detached from the centre for particular action. One group are the many local issues that have sprung up fast with the creation of the new states: a system of regional devolution may offer great help in dealing with these problems. The other group, at the opposite end of the political spectrum, consists of the grave new global issues, and also some general social and technological issues, that are not amenable to local or partial solution: for these some form of functional devolution seems almost inevitable.

Partly because of the UN's constitution, but especially because of the difficulties in the performance of its organs, the search for relief or additional strength through regional arrangements has spread in the past decade. Just because the regional idea has come into such favour it is essential to distinguish clearly between regional division and regional devolution. A fully integrated regional union would inescapably acquire the nature and ways of a national state and would bring that mood into its part at the UN.[8] As there is little sign of such units coming into being among the new states outside Europe, the UN, moreover, would face a still greater imbalance of power than it does now. While if such regional unions were to spread, one of the effects of their geographical distribution would be to set still harder the ideological division between East and West in Europe; and, more dangerously, the racial division between the West and the coloured continents.[9] Finally, while a number of independent regional units perhaps might help to ease the local conditions of two of the revolutionary trends, the political and the social, they could contribute nothing to the third, the disturbing appearance of new global issues. These would still have to be dealt with through some universal arrangement.

Very different would be the effect of a measure of regional devolution under the authority of the UN. Even old democratic countries have experienced a reassertion of local regional feeling – the United Kingdom in Scotland and Wales, and France in Brittany, etc.; and that in spite of the 'social security' cornucopia, as a reaction to the spreading take-over by the central administrations. Such a 'take-over' is not a possible international policy, with the large number of small new states. At the same

[8] David Mitrany, "European Integration – Federal or Functional", *Journal of Common Market Studies* (December 1965).

[9] It was distressing to hear even the very civilised M. Jean Monnet (in a BBC interview, 10 July 1969) dismiss all economic doubts about the Common Market with the blunt assertion that "European Union is a matter of *civilisation*". No mention of the rest of Europe, none of North America, none of the world at large.

time, interest in active local co-operation – always with a clear rejection of any idea of political union – has been evident in Scandinavia (the Nordic Union), in Central America, in Eastern Africa, in the 'Islamic Crescent' of Turkey, Iran and Pakistan; and elsewhere. Most of the smaller states happen to live in regional clusters[10]; every such group could be provided under the Charter with local institutions reproducing broadly the relevant organs of the UN, with authority to deal in the first instance with regional matters within their competence. Perhaps the most immediate benefit would be one of political education – to develop among these young states and their personnel the sense and the art for political compromise and settlement. Invested with a positive authority for common problems they would have a positive responsibility for solving them; for only if they failed to agree would the matter involved go to the UN's central organs. The new rulers might thus discover that calling a blight 'colonialism' or 'imperialism' will not protect their crops, and calling a seed 'communism' will not increase its yield. Such an arrangement should relieve the UN of many local issues which too often are used for ideological ends, and in time help to make central discussions and decisions at the UN more realistic and responsible.

In the second place, a system of regional devolution could also be used as an indirect remedy for the difficult problem of representation at the UN. In 1954 Mr Dulles had put forward the idea of 'associate membership' for the small states, with a free part in debate but limited voting rights; but once they have tasted full equality any formal reduction in their status would not be easy to put through. Regional devolution, however, may serve as a more acceptable and quite democratic compromise, without the invidious division into classes that is inherent in any system of weighted voting. As the local group would acquire an identity of its own, with positive authority and responsibility for the affairs of the group, the same group identity could be expressed in its having one joint delegation (with rotation among its members) at the UN and elsewhere.[11] And all that

[10] The exception of Switzerland, with her determined neutrality, could be put to good international use, with full membership of the UN, by declaring her permanently neutral on behalf of and under the protection of the UN as the recognised seat of the International Red Cross and other such humanitarian agencies – as in fact she already is – which have done so much to alleviate suffering and anxiety in the two world wars and in other conflicts and calamities.

[11] Students of the subject may be interested in a personal reference. The idea just described of combining a system of regional devolution with one of group representation was developed, precisely for the reasons mentioned here, as long ago as 1917 in a lecture for the first League of Nations Society. Founded in 1916, in the following year the Society arranged a 'circus' of five lecturers (H. N. Brailsford, Professor A. J. Grant, G. Lowes Dickinson, Leonard Woolf and myself) who followed each other at weekly intervals each giving his own lecture

regional action and evolution would remain firmly within the scope and overall authority of the UN and its Charter.[12]

A second line of advance free of ideological obstruction would be through the international assumption of authority for specific issues and activities, through 'functional' arrangements and bodies. In its essence the scope of the 'functional' line of action is two-fold: to take as many issues as possible out of the field of political competition and friction; at the same time, to develop a web of common activities which serving all peoples impartially according to need would gradually build up foundations for a living international society. A recent survey of such work in progress remarked that the concept of "a global partnership to abolish poverty has a decidedly Utopian ring. Yet such a partnership is in the making and provides one of the notable victories for international co-operation in an age marked by national conflict".[13] Apart from the work of the UN with its specialised agencies, that international network now includes over one hundred inter-state agencies and more than 1,500 non-governmental unions and associations – and both groups are growing steadily in response to new problems and needs.

The above quotation refers essentially to the field of welfare, with its deliberate choice of co-operation for the sake of making good use of resources and skills to meet general needs. It is invaluable work socially, but no longer the main part of the story. As was suggested earlier, historically a central characteristic of our time is the appearance of true global problems which cannot be dealt with except through joint international action; and that can only mean through non-political functional arrangements devised for each specific task. Nuclear power and space exploration are outstanding in this range, and so is the problem of the deep sea-bed. At a less political but socially more sensitive level, U Thant has urged the setting up of a global authority with police and enforcement powers to protect man's environment; he described pollution as the gravest everyday

---

in various towns (mostly under the auspices of the Workers' Education Association), at a time when the idea of a League of Nations had begun to arouse general interest, but also some distinct hostility among our audiences. A reduced version of my lecture, without its historical part, appeared in the *Manchester Guardian*, in April 1919, under the title, "Small States and a League of Nations. A Scheme of Devolution".

[12] The advocates of Western Union often refer themselves for support to M. Briand's project for a European Union, in 1928. It is, of course, a false analogy; for the Briand scheme was strictly a scheme of devolution that was to fit and work within the scope of the League of Nations – even to the point of prescribing that the union organs should meet at Geneva at the same time as the Assembly of the League.

[13] Preface to Richard Gardner and Max Millikan (eds.), *The Global Partnership: International Agencies and Economic Development* (New York, 1968), p. 5.

threat to mankind as a whole, and a threat "which did not respect national sovereignty"; and therefore urged that all countries and peoples should be associated from the outset in that common effort. The conference which met in Summer 1970 in Washington, to revise and develop the International Telecommunications Satellite System set up in 1964, was concerned with just such a vital new side of the world community that is coming into being.

And, of course, this way of dealing with the use of satellites reveals the political meaning of this non-political approach. "The functional theory of international organisation, which explicitly stresses the development of agencies devoted to co-operative solution of problems in the economic and social realm, is ultimately concerned with the issue of political and military struggle; functionalism treats the promotion of welfare as an indirect approach to the prevention of warfare. On the whole, international organisation has reflected greater concern with the probability of conflict than with the possibility of co-operation."[14] The functional approach circumvents ideological and racial divisions, as it does territorial frontiers. That was proved when the two leading atomic powers, America and Russia, jointly offered in 1968 a strictly functional scheme through the revised nuclear non-proliferation Treaty. The Treaty is meant to ensure to all UN members full access to the peaceful uses of atomic energy "through an appropriate international body on which non-nuclear states would be represented". What political arrangement, short of a fully-fledged world government, could now provide an answer for both the control and the fair usage of atomic power? What is the political answer for space control? And only in such ways, through common service, can a real and visible equality among states and peoples be approached – the true essence and meaning of 'peaceful change'. Without some such arrangement we are likely to experience before long a scramble for the sea-bed by a few strong countries, more wanton and aggressive than the 'imperialist' scramble for Africa, leaving the bulk of mankind out of it all.[15] Functional arrangements are possible because they are necessary; and the necessity is induced – apart from the older fields of welfare, health and postal communications – by our restless scientific-technological cleverness. Every new invention, every discovery, is apt to breed also a new problem that needs to be jointly

[14] Inis L. Claude, "International Organisation: The Process and the Institutions", *International Encyclopedia of the Social Sciences*, vol. VIII, pp. 34–5.

[15] Already an organisation known as 'Eurocean' has been set up under princely patronage, and with strong business backing from the EEC group, "to exploit the seas around Europe", especially where natural gas and oil are to be found; "great wealth can be won on the ocean beds". (*Daily Telegraph*, 13 August 1970.) – Since then it has been reported that a Russian team has found traces of gold in "the seabed in the Danish Strait and the deepwater section of the mid-Atlantic range". (*Daily Telegraph*, 3 September 1970.)

controlled if the risk of conflict is to be avoided and the invention used for the benefit of all.[16]

Even if some of these new and tangled issues have to be dealt with outside the direct control of the UN, every advance on such lines must contribute something to the development of its international system; both by reducing points of friction which the UN may not be able to absorb, and especially in a positive way by building up the elements of a living world community. There is no conflict between a spreading web of functional international arrangements and the development of any other scheme for a world authority. Indeed, the first could not but help the second; for in acting together on common problems there is always something to be gained and nothing to be lost internationally. Functional arrangements are not temporary extraneous 'contracts' between two or more parties that remain separate in regard to the object of the contract; they are rather joint working partnerships that get solidly woven into the fabric of their social life. In the anxious searching for an accepted international authority it is not an unprincipled or an unwise compromise to lean whenever necessary towards a working democracy rather than a voting democracy.

## Law-Making for the World

The test and the strength of any political community finds expression in the growth of common activities – "the authority of the state is the sum of its functions" – and through that in the continuous process of establishing common rules – the great process of law-making. One paradoxical effect of creating a new international system and at the same time a mass of new and untried sovereign states, is that traditional international law has become impotent as an instrument of law and order. The very existence of the UN, in which they were given an equal standing, has provided these states both with a public voice and a venue for using it to obstruct the application of general rules; admittedly helped in this by the competition between East and West. Under the protection of the UN many new and weak states can and do flout with impunity traditional rules of international conduct as much as the rules of the Charter; and in effect indulge in a display of 'total

[16] The Warsaw Pact Summit Meeting in Budapest, in March 1969, issued a so-called peace appeal for Europe: "No matter how complex the as yet unsolved problems are, they can only be solved through peaceful means, by way of talks and not through the threat to use force . . . By the use of energy, transport, water and air space, as well as in the field of hygiene, great plans which are inseparable from the welfare of the population of the entire continent can be carried out. . . . It would be a practical step in the direction of strengthening European security . . .". This, of course, is a reiteration of the 'co-existence' formula of M. Nikita Khrushchev.

sovereignty' such as no great power would have dared to attempt in the period of so-called 'international anarchy'. One will find plenty of instances in articles in legal and other journals[17]; and the question must be, can a general system of law take root in such lawlessness?

There is on the other hand a new active process of continuous positive law-making through the work of the several organs of the UN, especially the General Assembly. But the lack of political balance has held back and even brought risks also into this natural and necessary process. "There is a danger that bold interpretation of the Charter may place too heavy a strain on the political foundation of the organisation. The problem therefore consists in reconciling the need of allowing a certain scope for the interpretation of the Charter with the necessity to prevent member states from being subjected to entirely new obligations imposed by a majority, for the sole reason of their being in the minority."[18]

In the circumstances the main and most promising line of advance has been the growing body of international administrative law. That is also in the new nature of things, and parallels the rapid growth of administrative law and tribunals within national states. There is a decline in the use of legislative treaties, wrote Mr Oscar Schachter, to the benefit of "operating procedures and practical action. On the whole one must regard that as a desirable trend, as international arrangements which worked even in limited situations would be more conducive to the growth of law than treaties or codes which were not lived up to in practice". And again, there is a gulf between agreement on principles and interpretation and application in particular cases – "often a wide discrepancy between the proclaimed

[17] An outstanding case of international irresponsibility was the wilful closing of the Suez Canal, and the imprisonment and virtual destruction of fifteen foreign merchant ships for no other cause than that they happened to be there when the Canal was closed. Having been built and kept securely open for everyone's use by the 'imperialist' West, the Canal had become a vital social possession of the world at large; the chief sufferers from its closing are indeed the poor states of eastern Africa and south-east Asia. No power would have dared to do such a thing in the nineteenth century without the risk of armed opposition, yet the UN has had to let pass such deliberate damage to international life without protest or sanctions. And equally strangely, even the 'big' states to which some of the ships belonged simply accepted the loss and the outrage.

Again, in some recent cases of sky-jacking, a new and insane political weapon, some members of the UN have actually protected and feted the perpetrators, and again the new majority in the General Assembly were not scandalised by such sovereign irresponsibility and no action was taken. It was left to the private international union of air pilots to press for some protective arrangement with appropriate sanctions. It will be noted that poor countries without a merchant fleet or long-distance airlines of their own have the advantage that they are fairly immune against direct retaliation.

[18] J. A. de Yturriaga, "Non-Selfgoverning Territories: the Law and the Practice of the UN", *Year Book of World Affairs*, 1964, p. 212.

norms and actual conduct".[19] "The progress of international law is dependent on the evolution of an integrated international community", wrote the late Professor Brierly; and that is substantially the very purpose and end of the spreading network of functional organisations. Through their activities they are evolving for their own needs a growing body of rules and standards which are accepted naturally by their members.

As described by Mr Wilfred Jenks, these rules now cover "a wide range of legal problems and relationships which do not arise directly from the mutual relations of states but include the relations of international bodies, their mutual relations and also their relations both with persons in their service and with third parties".

"Moreover, international agreements now increasingly delegate certain regulatory powers to varied types of international bodies, so that the concept includes not only the international agreements as a source of law but also the outcome of the regulatory, quasi-judicial and executive powers they confer" – again paralleling the growing use of delegated legislation in national law-making and administration. "Moreover, international practice now includes the collective as well as the individual acts of states; the former have been greatly increased by the activities of international organisations." "These developments reinforce powerfully the thesis that international law is evolving, at an unsteady pace and in untidy manner, but with no uncertainty of direction, towards a common law of mankind." "It represents an important aspect of the transformation of international law from one regulating the external conduct of states to one which gives expression to the life" of the great universal community.[20]

[19] Oscar Schachter, "Law, Politics and Action in the United Nations" (Hague Academy, *Receuils*, 1966), p. 171.

[20] Wilfred Jenks, *The Proper Law of International Organizations* (London, 1962), pp. 259, 256 and 257. These two distinguished jurists speak also from great practical experience – Mr Schachter as a member of the section of legal affairs at the UN and Mr Jenks now as Director-General of the ILO. Their views are echoed by many academic experts. As Chairman of the annual meeting of the American Society of International Law (Washington, 1965) Professor Urban Whitaker noted that "the Specialised Agencies are developing international law faster than other, more political, organs of the UN system. It is in the technical, less spectacular world of the Specialised Agencies that international law is expanding new frontiers rapidly". Professor Wolfgang Friedmann (Professor of International Law and Director of International Legal Research at Columbia University, N.Y.) wrote a few years ago: "A functional approach to international organisation correlates the development of international law and organisation with political and social realities and tendencies of international life. ... It accepts that this must mean a multitude of legal and international patterns in international organisation, a great variety in their structure in the extent of their powers, and in the influence they exercise in the field assigned to them. There is, of course, no doubt that it is the functional approach which has triumphed in post-war international organisation, resulting in a complex pattern of organisa-

Apart from the legal vacuum caused by disregard of the old general rules and traditions, the trend towards specific administrative law is made inevitable also by the irrelevance of established international law for most of the new problems and the new conditions of international life; just as constitutional and other established rules (such as the right of property, the right to free economic activities, to travel and other individual rights) are falling by the wayside under the benevolent dictates of the planned welfare state. Both sides of this situation are made evident by the ugly new phenomenon of sky-jacking: a relatively minor issue has brought out sharply how helpless general international law is without some specific arrangement resting on specific undertakings by member governments for its application, and containing its own objective sanctions against any breach. A more significant illustration of how new the new world is, is the much graver problem of the deep sea-bed. There is general support for the view that only some special arrangement by and under the UN could deal with it.[21] But agreement will not be easy in the present state of ideological-economic competition. Not only are there no standing rules or precedents to fit the new problems, but perhaps the most respected rule of international law, the 'freedom of the seas', may actually stand in the way of a collective solution. A number of recent acts openly point that way. The Russo-American draft for a "Treaty on the Prohibition of the Employment of Nuclear and other Weapons" on the bed of the oceans (3 April 1970) allows the parties to watch each other's activities, "provided that observation does not interfere with such activities or otherwise infringe rights recognised under international law, including the freedom of the high seas" (Art. III). At the very same time, just because there was no early prospect of collective action, the Canadian Government acting unilaterally assumed powers

---

tions with different objectives, constitutions and powers. What is asserted here is not only that this is the actual pattern of international organisations, but that it is the only possible one at this time, reflecting the actual structure of international relations." *The Changing Structure of International Law* (New York, 1964), p. 276.

[21] The Seventeenth Report of the Commission to Study the Organization of Peace made the following suggestions: "The Commission recommends that under the principle that no nation is allowed to appropriate the sea or seabeds beyond the twelve-mile limit for fish or beyond the continental shelf for minerals the UN take title to these areas. . . . The Commission further recommends that there should be established a special agency of the UN to be called the United Nations Marine Resources Agency. . . . The Commission recommends that the UN agency set up to administer resources seek consent for and take appropriate action leading towards revision of the Convention on the Continental Shelf in order to specify in a non-ambiguous manner the geographic distinction between the continental shelf and the deep sea, so far as the seabed and the minerals in and on it are concerned . . ." (*New Dimensions for the United Nations: The Problems of the Next Decade* (New York, 1966), pp. 44–5).

under the "Arctic Waters Pollution Prevention Act" (8 April 1970) to police the seas up to 100 nautical miles from its coastline, and full defensive rights in the "whole extent of the continental margin" – and bluntly gave notice that it was not prepared to have the Act brought before the International Court of Justice. Now that state of mind has been extended also to the new dimension of space. The UN declaration of principles in regard to space, to which both Russia and America have given their assent, states that the moon and other celestial bodies should be free for exploration by all "in conformity with international law" and not subject to sovereign claims. Does that not restate the doctrine of the 'freedom of the seas' all over again? It does not protect, it abandons space, like the sea-bed, to the few who can, and in effect passes by the claims of the world community.

## The Historical Task

In contemplating the political prospect in the light of the past, the student of international affairs will have to come to the view that "the historical task of our time is not to keep the nations peacefully apart but to bring them actively together"; to aim (as Mr Jenks said) at a "universal community of the world". That is the imperative historical need. In that sense 'peace-keeping' as such – to which students and writers have given so much attention – is essentially irrelevant; and the effort and resources the UN has had to give and is giving to it is merely a measure of how far we have moved away politically from the old 'international anarchy'. And that is very little. The UN was meant to be made in this regard much stronger than the League of Nations, to be provided with a military staff of its own and reliable military help (Articles 42–7 of the Charter.) These have never come into being; and the costly policing operations have proved effective only in a very limited degree in relation to the range and depth of the issue. It has been useful in Cyprus; in the Congo it drew the UN dangerously into extensive military action in a struggle between internal factions. 'Peace-keeping' will not only be ineffective when it is first accepted and then repudiated (Gaza, Suez, etc.), but also unfair to one of the parties and damaging to the standing of the UN. And if the operation were made absolute, or at least if repudiation like acceptance would have to be bilateral, that would commit the UN to chastising the defaulting party forcibly.

Moreover, all that can apply only to quarrels between small states: 'peace-keeping' can never be a task for the UN when great powers are involved, directly or indirectly, as now in the Middle East (where the involvement of Russia and America on opposite sides is uncomfortably close to the confrontation of outside parties, as in the Spanish civil war). 'Peace-keeping' is dramatic, but it has not been a famous victory for the UN, or much of a contribution towards a new world community. "I do not think the UN can be expected to be an effective peace-keeping body" – said an experienced member of the Society of Friends after years of work in the field.[22] It is questionable whether the whole thing is not unfair to the actual position and means of the UN. If the powers now competing ideologically agree to act together, peace-keeping would not be necessary; while if they are at odds, 'peace-keeping' by the UN is both useless and untrue. And even when effective, keeping two armed camps apart is not the same as 'conflict resolution' within a community; the one remains committed to violence, the other to non-violence. Hence any assessment of the task facing us must start from a plain but absolute proposition: that the whole of the traditional view of international politics as based upon and working through power has become impossible. The ultimate test of power is force and its use: when, as now, that force has come to mean nuclear force, uncontrollable in its spread and its effects, power has become too wild to be used, as might an epidemic, as an instrument of policy. And with it the whole body of traditional political theory and of political devices linked to it no longer have relevance for the student or for the statesman.

This situation provides a simple but crucial test for any general proposition and for any particular scheme for international action and organisation: Does it help to move the international stage away from the system of enclosed armed units; does it help to move it towards a system of beneficial common action? The test can be applied fairly to the achievements of the UN in general and in particular during the first twenty-five years of its existence; and it can be applied fairly to the lines of advance briefly discussed above. Perhaps I may quote on this a passage I wrote in a different context:

"A central and vital difference is inherent ,and ineradicable, in their very nature: the UN has internationally a *unifying* role (however imperfectly

[22] Paul Johnson and his wife have devoted their life to the service of peace, formerly in Africa and currently in the Middle East. He said: "Every case of peace-keeping has provided the UN with some experience, but it was left with good intentions without the power to create or require the conditions under which a plan for peace-keeping could be expected to succeed." Moreover, in regard to the various financing methods, each has proved less satisfactory than the one before. "Under the sorts of handicap here enumerated or implied, I do not think the UN can be expected to be an effective peace-keeping body." The task would need either a much stronger UN or a real world government. ("UN Peace-keeping in a Changing World" – Lecture to the Santa Barbara, Cal., UN Association, 19 March 1965).

achieved so far), whereas the EEC or any other regional union while having a unifying role *locally* has of necessity a *divisive* role internationally – in fact, the more effective the first, the sharper the second. [Regarding] 'the twin human predicaments of war and poverty', the EEC might contribute something towards the second, but regionalism as such has nothing to contribute towards the nuclear nightmare, much less towards the new space problem. Beyond a certain point the comparison between an egocentric regional unit and the grand limitless purpose of a universal body becomes meaningless. The 'actor roles' become so different and distant in scope that they no longer belong to the same world of organisation and policy – and of possibilities. One can admire the EEC, but as students we cannot overlook that, internationally speaking, its limits are also its limitations."[23]

The self-evident conclusion was drawn recently by Mr Robert Asher: "International integration can be regional or global. . . . Concentration on the creation of regional machinery without a concurrent strengthening of interregional bonds, however, can produce powerful, intransigent regional blocs that will make integration on a wider scale, or even peaceful *co-existence*, much more difficult."[24] The conclusion should be self-evident because the historical issue is not a change in the mere dimension of political units. Modern history has seen every kind of dimensional variation: provinces have coagulated into national states and states into empires; empires have broken up into states and states into provinces – all of them having one thing only in common, that they stood on the foundation of a limited and fixed territory. And all of them have at all times, whatever their size, relied on force and fighting in the conduct of their 'sovereign' relations. Merely to introduce a new such variation, regional or continental or whatever else, would change the size and stance of the several units but not the nature of their relations; and therefore not the nature of the international system. And indeed, faced with larger and stronger units, the UN would if anything be more incapable to shape their conduct than it can shape the conduct of its more powerful members at present.

Neither the UN nor any re-styled international authority could nurture a peaceful civilised society by presiding over a mass of armed members; any more than 'the king's majesty' could have established a national community of law and order by presiding over a score of be-castled barons with their private feudal armies. But unlike the king, the UN cannot subdue the private national armies by force; nor will it be done by adding new

[23] Carol Ann Cosgrove and Kenneth Twitchett (eds.), *The New International Actors: The UN and the EEC* (London, 1970), p. 51.
[24] In *The Global Partnership*, p. 457–8.

minatory powers to the Charter of the UN.[25] "The Charter of the UN . . . is a framework for organic growth in response to new demands and changing realities . . . an attempt to rewrite its constitution would arrest the continued growth of the UN. . . . The fact is that the Charter is a better instrument for the achievement of UN purposes than any that could be negotiated today."[26] "An increasing number of responsible voices can be heard to say, just as the League of Nations was superseded by the UN, so must the UN now be superseded by something more effective. In so doing they are apt to forget or dismiss the fundamental point that both the League and the UN were created in the aftermath of a world war as part of the precarious peace achieved thereafter, and would not have been created in any lesser circumstances. To create, by anything in the nature of a fresh start, a new world system to avert a third world war would be a task requiring political imagination and determination of an order which neither history nor current experience gives us any right to expect."[27]

A stable international system of law and order could grow only as part of a widening communality of social life, using patiently and persistently every opportunity offered by common needs and global problems to bring them under joint control for common service through common organs. That is how political society has always taken shape and solidified; and that is now the way accepted in every country as in other groupings for giving a new social cast and substance to existing political units. National government now works in a wholly pragmatic way; international government could not work in any other way. Not long ago a student of the future made a comment on that process with reference to the US which is also apposite for the international future:

> "For the new problems, the traditional division into fifty states and a mass of municipalities with their boundaries is 'no longer meaningful'. There is a need for a 'comprehensive overhauling of governmental structures to determine the appropriate size and scope of units that can

[25] Readers who recollect the widespread outcry against the private manufacture of arms after the First World War will heed the lesson of what is going on now. There is little to show for two generations of effort, public and private, in the cause of disarmament; and whatever private manufacture there is, is now almost wholly on behalf and under instruction and control of governments. Nor has this stopped the traffic in arms; rather the mere 'profit motive' has been hardened with a lining of political motive. The sorry spectacle of veto-members of the UN pushing the manufacture of 'improved' weapons and their sale to lesser breeds in competition with each other culminated in even a leftish Labour Government engaging a super-salesman from the world of business to push this sordid trade on our behalf.

[26] Richard Gardner, *In Pursuit of World Order* (New York, 1964), p. 9.

[27] Wilfred Jenks, *The World Beyond the Charter in Historical Perspective* (London, 1969), p. 11.

handle the appropriate tasks'. It would be futile to try to reduce the number of states. 'But all sorts of state functions could be "detached" and taken over by multistate or regional "compacts". ... Even the favorite theme of regionalism would prove no real solution, for the definition of a region is not hard and fast, but varies with different functions: a water region, a transport region, an educational region, and even an economic region has different "overlays" on the map of the US. One must first determine what is to be centralized and what is to be decentralized'."[28]

It would be even more futile merely to try to reduce the number of national states. Nor could the most sanguine observer claim that other kinds of frontal attack on sovereignty and its appurtenances have tamed their nationalist ways. "One displaces only what one replaces" – it may seem strange to quote a Napoleonic dictum in our context, but he had shrewd insights into the problem at his national range. To restrain national sovereignty and to increase international authority are but two sides of the same process; and there is no way of doing it except through a transfer of functions – not of frontiers – from one to the other, pooling sovereignty in whatever degree may be required for each particular task.

## The Present Realities of World Politics

Where do the signs point today? The test is not whether the structure still stands, and its staff are still at work in their offices, but what kind of world in these twenty-five years they have been able to build around them. The vision is not comforting, or promising. "It is a truism to say that the UN after twenty years is quite different from the Organization described in the Charter. It is not the fact of difference that is significant but the degree. In many respects, the UN of today is hardly recognisable from a reading of Charter provisions": conflict between the powers, no peace settlement, arms competition, little useful work on peaceful settlement, the controlling influence of smaller states, emphasis on underdeveloped countries, preoccupation with racial discrimination, independence as a goal regardless of readiness.[29] "When the Charter was drafted, it was contemplated that the great powers would work out an acceptable peace which the UN could maintain. ... But whatever the causes or explanations, the law of

[28] Professor Daniel Bell, "Toward a Communal Society", *Life Magazine*, 12 May 1967. Professor Bell is Chairman of the Department of Sociology, Columbia College, N.Y.; Chairman of the 'Commission for the Year 2000' of the Academy of Arts and Social Sciences; and a member of the President's '1966 Committee on Technology, Automation and Economic Progress'.

[29] Leland Goodrich, *et al.*, *The Charter of the United Nations*, 3rd ed. (New York, 1969), p. 17.

the Charter which was to outlaw the use of force as a means of settling disputes between states has fallen into desuetude."[30] An international organisation such as the League or the UN, "whose power must always depend on prestige and moral influence rather than on force, cannot possibly establish the rule of law if the friends of the accused are able to obstruct the verdict".[31] And both these experienced writers ask for a change in the system of voting to end, in the words of Mr Harlan Cleveland, "the uneasy co-existence of the principle of sovereignty and the fact of grossly unequal power". Yet this problem could be "greatly minimised if the larger states take the lead in developing practices and procedures which encourage and promote the use of the Assembly not as a forum for fighting cold wars but for ending them".

"It is gravely disturbing that many devoted friends have failed to grasp that the future of the UN is threatened as much or more by the neglect of the great powers as by the irresponsibility of the small states."[32] This unity of view from experienced and devoted servants of the international system is supported by yet another. "It is imperative to appreciate the gravity and complexity of the present crisis and the magnitude of the issue at stake. Nor should we deceive ourselves with the fashionable doctrine that the essence of realism is to live in the present rather than to plan for the future. Crisis management, however sophisticated, is no substitute for an organised common peace. . . . The destiny of mankind cannot be left at the mercy of 'game theory' with nuclear wars as the game. The whole future of man now depends on matching the art of government and the organisation of society to the contemporary progress of science and technology."[33]

The UN was based ideally and conceptually on universality of rules, not only of international conduct but of politics in general. That may have been an excessive aspiration; it became a self-defeating aspiration when some eighty new members were added rapidly to the original fifty, many of them with little more unity than the lines of their maps, and most of them in a state of political and social revolutionary gestation. And permeating all that was the East–West ideological conflict (plus the Russo-Chinese one), pressing locally on competing factions, and balking any hope of unity of interpretation and application at the centre even of stated general rules. As things are, the UN may possibly count on fifty odd democracies among its 127 members, with the others shifting uneasily within a variety of dictatorial and 'one-party' regimes, a group which the essential admission of

[30] Benjamin V. Cohen, "The U.N. in its 20th year", *International Organization* (Spring 1966), pp. 185 and 191.
[31] Harold Nicolson, *Perspectives on Peace, 1910–1960* (New York, 1960), p. 41.
[32] Benjamin V. Cohen, *op. cit.*, pp. 204 and 197.
[33] Wilfred Jenks, *The World Beyond the Charter*, p. 12.

Communist China would reinforce powerfully. In such conditions the UN has had to play hard merely to hold its ground at the political level. At the security level it has had no direct hold on the situation, and international security in fact has fallen back into an ominous confrontation of a balance of strength. A city's guardians would not sleep too easily if everyone in town were entitled to carry armed pistols with a promise not to use them. Apart from a willingness to neutralise nuclear power and warfare, there has been no certain sign of any equal readiness to neutralise world politics. Pressure on West Germany and other states to sign the non-proliferation Treaty has gone side by side with the extension of Soviet military and naval 'presence' in the Mediterranean, in the Indian Ocean, and even in the Atlantic. That puts the situation in perspective: the East–West confrontation has been extended, not reduced; and while the West has steadily drawn back, the East has steadily pushed farther into positions beyond anything ventured by Imperial Russia[34]; and still more suggestively, with China's opposite pressure from the East, now with a foothold in East Africa and Aden, and seeking one even in the Persian Gulf. As long as that confrontation persists, the UN cannot hope to gain wider opportunity and more authority for protecting peace in the world at large.[35] Rather the

[34] That may seem to pass over America's military action in Viet-Nam – a miserable episode, which though provoked by Communist pressure on the countries of South-East Asia not only has been costly in human life and resources and American prestige, but could only end in propping up a dubious anti-Communist regime. That was the result in the inter-war period when the West's efforts to 'contain' Soviet pressure ended in supporting a chain of dubious dictatorial regimes along Russia's borders. Both proved badly misjudged reactions to the ideological confrontation; but both demonstrate how lame is the hope for collective security as for better government and human rights while that confrontation goes on. At the same time, when attempting to trace the fate of the international idea since the birth of the UN one cannot leave out the only two truly international acts of that period (assuming the Marshall Plan still to have had ties with the Cold War), both standing to the credit of the United States, and apart from the earlier more general efforts of President Wilson and President Franklin Roosevelt. (i) At the summit meeting in Berlin in 1945, President Truman proposed that all straits and canals which link up open seas should be internationalised. Stalin, no doubt with an eye on the Dardanelles, rejected the idea outright. Winston Churchill refused more diplomatically, from a reluctance to give up control of the Suez Canal. (ii) In 1948, when America was the only country in the world to possess atomic weapons, Mr Truman offered (through the so-called Baruch plan) to put all atomic weapons and development under collective international control. It was perhaps the most critical and most unselfish international act by any state in modern history.

[35] A thoughtful American student predicts that "the UN of 1985 will be a reconciliation system"; "A reconciliation model of politics features bargaining as its main decision-making technique, rather than coercion, ideological fervour, or traditional sanctions"; and the UN "will be a reconciliation system unable to carry out the collective security task as well as does the current UN" (Ernst Haas, *Collective Security and the Future of the International System*, Denver, Col., Monograph Series in World Affairs, vol. 5, no. 1, 1967–68, p. 97).

collective effort has to concentrate on removing as many sensitive sectors of international life as possible from the ambit of confrontation and into the ambit of co-existence through regional self-help (but not 'integrated' *political* regionalism, as that would inevitably be drawn into the politics of confrontation) and joint functional action. These could provide also a measure of law-making and of ordinary policing within the scope of their activities.

The UN is a second attempt to complete the political pyramid within a world system of law and order – both the highest and the most difficult task of the long and troubled effort of political ingenuity and achievement. On such a scale and embracing such a mixture of peoples and conditions it would in any case have to be a working instrument, endlessly adaptable to changing needs and situations. But it so happens that during the UN's own brief life human society has changed in a vaster and faster way than at any other period in history. Writing in 1964 U Thant noted that "the world has changed so rapidly in the last twenty years that it is hard to remember what it was like in the 1920's and 1930's". And Mr Dean Acheson in a BBC radio interview, on 12 June 1970, remarked that the pace of change was more than humanity could stand, "dissolving some of the basic relationships of the past two hundred years". Part of the difficulty is that it is not a straight change. Some changes, the global issues, now are embracing the whole world; at the same time, through national planning the trend shows a regression from the nineteenth century into something like Fichte's *Geschlossener Handelsstaat*. But the human effect, in terms of political outlook and temper, may well be the same from both. The rush and confusion of it all, in Mr Acheson's view, are causing a "deterioration in the quality of our society"; and that cannot fail to affect its prospect. Intended as it was to enthrone a collective political outlook and authority, the UN began life at a time when respect for authority was breaking down everywhere and in all parts of society – in state and industry, in church and in the family; when 'direct action' was replacing argument not only in politics and industry but even in the universities, our centres of enlightenment. These are signs of a wide moral crisis, a crisis of civilisation, and it would have been surprising if the 'permissiveness' which has broken out in every part of life – greeted by so many of the 'élites', the likely or would-be leaders, as a flag of freedom – should not have seeped also into international relations and the behaviour of states, especially the new states and their revolutionary rulers. We have sown much liberty, and are reaping licence. In some degree it is the restlessness of wanting to go fast, and not quite knowing where. As Horace put it in one of his satires, "We are all lost in the woods; the only difference is that we are lost in different directions".

## Winds of Change and the Prospect

That is not altogether unnatural in a period that has to work through and absorb the three-fold revolution discussed earlier in this chapter. It is a period of transition without precedent in history, more complex than the great transition from the medieval to the modern world, in its spread as in its speed and its substance; and in the international sphere with the individual units changing as fast as their mutual problems and relations. Inevitably, and sensibly, both the League of Nations and the UN, as U Thant has written, "were designed as an intermediate base between the international relations of traditional diplomacy . . . and the theoretical, ultimate aim of a world legislature, if not a world government. . . . Both organisations therefore show the weaknesses of a transitional state – great aims with small means, great responsibilities with little authority, great expectations clouded by deep suspicions, and hopes for the future constantly blurred by fears and prejudices from the past".[36] The 'split personality' of the transition has become more sharply defined since 1964, with new means of destruction. When its members show a readiness to reduce and ultimately to drop the use of force, the UN could become an effective joint guardian for keeping order; but as long as the few great powers keep to their armaments, and arm the lesser states, the UN can do nothing – and it should not be burdened and its standing debased with the hollow pretence that it can.[37] Again, when its members will show a readiness to ease their ways of governing, the UN may prove the only effective court for watching that rights and duties are weighed fairly for all people. But as long as a majority of its members, some big and some small, choose to press hard on their subjects, the UN can do nothing – and should not be afflicted with the shaming pretence that its debates and resolutions are inspired solely by devotion to the Declaration of Human Rights. A new international morality expressed in common rules of law and conduct will not grow under the roof of the UN unless its actions and verdicts

[36] "The League of Nations and the United Nations", *U.N. Monthly Chronicle*, vol. 1, no. 1 (May 1964).

[37] In *World Peace through World Law* 3rd. ed. (Cambridge, Mass.), the two distinguished authors, Grenville Clark and Louis B. Sohn, offered "a comprehensive and detailed plan for the maintenance of world peace in the form of a proposed revision of the U.N. Charter"; and in the Introduction in which Mr Clark discussed "practical prospects for the realisation of a genuine peace", he predicted the following time-table:

—by 1965–7 a plan for total and universal disarmament will have been formulated and submitted;

—by 1969–71, ratified by nearly all nations, and into force;

—so that "by 1975 the process of universal and complete disarmament will be well on its way". (xliii–xliv).

can be made to apply to all members and conditions without fear or favour.

The other side of the transition, less dramatic but more true, is turned towards the making of a new society. In military and political issues the UN is blindfolded and hamstrung by the votes of its members. In the wide and growing range of social activities the UN is supported by the plain needs of each case and the professional devotion of its technical staff, as by the interest of the large number of international professional unions and associations; above all, by the sense that all of that work is for the betterment of human life everywhere, and each action a stone towards the building of a peaceful and decent world community. The line which divides these elements in this time of transition thus also makes plain the proper line of advance. Under present conditions the UN can do very little in a direct way to pry loose the outlook and practice of its members from the political ways of the past; and the repeated failure of vain attempts can only weaken faith in the institution as a whole. But as the solid values and altruism of its social services come to be appreciated by the people of the world, it must help in that measure to weaken the hold of a narrow nationalism and turn their eyes towards a more communal future. There is no conflict here between ideal and practice – "the historical task of our time is not to keep the nations peacefully apart, but to bring them actively together". The first in any case the UN cannot do; the other it can do and is doing with greater promise.

How does one sum up the historical moment? To quote the late Professor Hobhouse, it is not the part of the political scientist to predict events, his part is to uncover as best he can "the relation of things"; and that can only mean in the light of things as they are (leaving as beyond his ken the possibility of some great revelation or some great calamity). In that light some of the elements discussed above stand out as central to the prospect of any international system of government.

(i) Throughout history the chief way to political organisation has been through the imposition of some superior authority. That way is not open for the world at large; a common authority could come only by the choice of the half-dozen major powers, supported by some dozen middle states. What are the chances that they will make this choice? For the present it must seem worse than under the old 'balance of power'. Then it was a competition (under the restraint of traditions) for 'imperial' ends, limited in scope and range and in the elements used for that policy; now it is an undefined ideological competition, relentless and unlimited in scope and range and in the means with which it is pressed. The UN can do nothing about that.

(ii) The UN can do nothing for collective security beyond being available as a centre, if and when the powers are willing, where they can be brought together to work out particular agreements (non-proliferation, space, etc.).

(iii) The problem of the mass of new states is merely a side issue: it could be controlled easily if the powers give a lead; it cannot be controlled by the UN as long as their unstable regimes are used as tools in the politics of confrontation.

(iv) The international problem is basically a moral problem: the UN's part is to further the decencies of political intercourse and, as part of that, the treatment of groups and individuals. Something can be done through international rules in particular fields; but it is invidious to launch, and even worse to celebrate grand Declarations when a majority of the UN members rule their people in arbitrary ways.[38]

All these are harsh political barriers raised, mostly deliberately, *against* the coming of a common international system. The UN could not and should not be expected to try to storm them. When they are taken down by those who now man them, the way to a common political system will look more promising.

In such an unhelpful political situation, what positive elements are left that can be used to prepare foundations for a communal future?

(v) As was said above, the most potent factor of our time is the universal social revolution. The whole social field, in its broadest sense, is wide open for beneficial international action. Not only is it a field concerned wholly with giving service for a better life, but one that can be tilled and sown and gathered in unity without waiting on political issues which at present mainly divide. And in giving present service to all who need it, every such action lays down a part of the road that in time may lead to a world community. The sheer evidence that it works will be evidence for the idea of the UN in the minds of men everywhere. The great ideal and work of technical assistance, in all its forms, is part of a true new world, when the political confrontation is bogged down deep in the old international anarchy. Yet for that very reason it is essential to guide that international aid insistently through international agencies; just as the widening of social equality and security in the several states is guided through communal public services.

We do not know what the world will be like even a generation from now. Changes, both constructive and destructive (like the poisoning of air and water and the wrecking of our general environment) are spreading even

[38] Within sight of the UN our time has experienced a new use for frontier walls – not to keep out barbarian invaders, but to shut in the country's own civilised subjects. The people of Czechoslovakia were punished precisely for trying to move towards the Declaration of Human Rights.

wider and faster than the changes since the First World War – and that without war-like action. And perhaps the most troubling question is this: what is all this restless changing doing to our nervous system? Will people want to live at peace when all is stress and noise and instability about them? One thing perhaps can be said in conclusion with some assurance. The prospect of a common international system must depend on the growth of a fair common outlook, gradually replacing the nationalist outlook with its insidious double-talk and double-standards. The needs and the principles are clear; they should be supported when they appear in general relations, but when broken the default should be unhesitatingly exposed. Because of the great strains and dangers pressing on our society this is historically indeed the moment of truth: diplomatic evasions and international hypocrisies will not produce the fruit of a common morality in a world at peace.

# *Appendix I: The Covenant of the League of Nations**

**The High Contracting Parties**

In order to promote international co-operation and to achieve international peace and security

by the acceptance of obligations not to resort to war,

by the prescription of open, just and honourable relations between nations,

by the firm establishment of the understandings of international law as the actual rule of conduct among Governments,

and by the maintenance of justice and a scrupulous respect for all treaty obligations in the dealings of organised peoples with one another,

Agree to this Covenant of the League of Nations.

**Article 1**

1. The original Members of the League of Nations shall be those of the Signatories which are named in the Annex to this Covenant and also such of those other States named in the Annex as shall accede without reservation to this Covenant. Such accession shall be effected by a Declaration deposited with the Secretariat within two months of the coming into force of the Covenant. Notice thereof shall be sent to all other Members of the League.

2. Any fully self-governing State, Dominion or Colony not named in the Annex may become a Member of the League if its admission is agreed to by two-thirds of the Assembly, provided that it shall give effective guarantees of its sincere intention to observe its international obligations, and shall accept such regulations as may be prescribed by the League in regard to its military, naval and air forces and armaments.

3. Any Member of the League may, after two years notice of its intention so to do, withdraw from the League, provided that all its international obligations and all its obligations under this Covenant shall have been fulfilled at the time of its withdrawal.

**Article 2**

The action of the League under this Covenant shall be effected through the instrumentality of an Assembly and of a Council, with a permanent Secretariat.

**Article 3**

1. The Assembly shall consist of Representatives of the Members of the League.

* The texts printed in italics indicate amendments adopted by the League.

2. The Assembly shall meet at stated intervals and from time to time as occasion may require at the Seat of the League or at such other place as may be decided upon.

3. The Assembly may deal at its meetings with any matter within the sphere of action of the League or affecting the peace of the world.

4. At meetings of the Assembly, each Member of the League shall have one vote, and may have not more than three Representatives.

**Article 4**

1. The Council shall consist of Representatives of the Principal Allied and Associated Powers, together with Representatives of four other Members of the League. These four Members of the League shall be selected by the Assembly from time to time in its discretion. Until the appointment of the Representatives of the four Members of the League first selected by the Assembly, Representatives of Belgium, Brazil, Spain and Greece shall be members of the Council.

2. With the approval of the majority of the Assembly, the Council may name additional Members of the League whose Representatives shall always be Members of the Council; the Council with like approval may increase the number of Members of the League to be selected by the Assembly for representation on the Council.

2. *bis. The Assembly shall fix by a two-thirds majority the rules dealing with the election of the non-permanent Members of the Council, and particularly such regulations as relate to their term of office and the conditions of re-eligibility.*

3. The Council shall meet from time to time as occasion may require, and at least once a year, at the Seat of the League, or at such other place as may be decided upon.

4. The Council may deal at its meetings with any matter within the sphere of action of the League or affecting the peace of the world.

5. Any Member of the League not represented on the Council shall be invited to send a Representative to sit as a member at any meeting of the Council during the consideration of matters specially affecting the interests of that Member of the League.

6. At meetings of the Council, each Member of the League represented on the Council shall have one vote, and may have not more than one Representative.

**Article 5**

1. Except where otherwise expressly provided in this Covenant or by the terms of the present Treaty, decisions at any meeting of the Assembly or of the Council shall require the agreement of all the Members of the League represented at the meeting.

2. All matters of procedure at meetings of the Assembly or of the Council, including the appointment of Committees to investigate particular matters, shall be regulated by the Assembly or by the Council and may be decided by a majority of the Members of the League represented at the meeting.

3. The first meeting of the Assembly and the first meeting of the Council shall be summoned by the President of the United States of America.

**Article 6**

1. The permanent Secretariat shall be established at the Seat of the League. The Secretariat shall comprise a Secretary-General and such secretaries and staff as may be required.

2. The first Secretary-General shall be the person named in the Annex; thereafter the Secretary-General shall be appointed by the Council with the approval of the majority of the Assembly.

3. The secretaries and staff of the Secretariat shall be appointed by the Secretary-General with the approval of the Council.

4. The Secretary-General shall act in that capacity at all meetings of the Assembly and of the Council.

5. *The expenses of the League shall be borne by the Members of the League in the proportion decided by the Assembly.*

**Article 7**

1. The Seat of the League is established at Geneva.

2. The Council may at any time decide that the Seat of the League shall be established elsewhere.

3. All positions under or in connection with the League, including the Secretariat, shall be open equally to men and women.

4. Representatives of the Members of the League and officials of the League when engaged on the business of the League shall enjoy diplomatic privileges and immunities.

5. The buildings and other property occupied by the League or its officials or by Representatives attending its meetings shall be inviolable.

**Article 8**

1. The Members of the League recognise that the maintenance of peace requires the reduction of national armaments to the lowest point consistent with national safety and the enforcement by common action of international obligations.

2. The Council, taking account of the geographical situation and circumstances of each State, shall formulate plans for such reduction for the consideration and action of the several Governments.

3. Such plans shall be subject to reconsideration and revision at least every ten years.

4. After these plans have been adopted by the several Governments, the limits of armaments therein fixed shall not be exceeded without the concurrence of the Council.

5. The Members of the League agree that the manufacture by private enterprise of munitions and implements of war is open to grave objections. The

Council shall advise how the evil effects attendant upon such manufacture can be prevented, due regard being had to the necessities of those Members of the League which are not able to manufacture the munitions and implements of war necessary for their safety.

6. The Members of the League undertake to interchange full and frank information as to the scale of their armaments, their military, naval and air programmes and the condition of such of their industries as are adaptable to war-like purposes.

**Article 9**

A permanent Commission shall be constituted to advise the Council on the execution of the provisions of Articles 1 and 8 and on military, naval and air questions generally.

**Article 10**

The Members of the League undertake to respect and preserve as against external aggression the territorial integrity and existing political independence of all Members of the League. In case of any such aggression or in case of any threat or danger of such aggression, the Council shall advise upon the means by which this obligation shall be fulfilled.

**Article 11**

1. Any war or threat of war, whether immediately affecting any of the Members of the League or not, is hereby declared a matter of concern to the whole League, and the League shall take any action that may be deemed wise and effectual to safeguard the peace of nations. In case any such emergency should arise, the Secretary-General shall, on the request of any Member of the League, forthwith summon a meeting of the Council.

2. It is also declared to be the friendly right of each Member of the League to bring to the attention of the Assembly or of the Council any circumstance whatever affecting international relations which threatens to disturb international peace or the good understanding between nations upon which peace depends.

**Article 12**

1. The Members of the League agree that if there should arise between them any dispute likely to lead to a rupture they will submit the matter either to arbitration *or judicial settlement* or to enquiry by the Council, and they agree in no case to resort to war until three months after the award by the arbitrators *or the judicial decision* or the report by the Council.

2. In any case under this article the award of the arbitrators *or the judicial decision* shall be made within a resaonable time, and the report of the Council shall be made within six months after the submission of the dispute.

**Article 13**

1. The Members of the League agree that whenever any dispute shall arise between them which they recognise to be suitable for submission to arbitration

*or judicial settlement*, and which cannot be satisfactorily settled by diplomacy, they will submit the whole subject-matter to arbitration *or judicial settlement*.

2. Disputes as to the interpretation of a treaty, as to any question of international law, as to the existence of any fact which, if established, would constitute a breach of any international obligation, or as to the extent and nature of the reparation to be made for any such breach, are declared to be among those which are generally suitable for submission to arbitration *or judicial settlement*.

3. *For the consideration of any such dispute, the court to which the case is referred shall be the Permanent Court of International Justice, established in accordance with Article* 14, *or any tribunal agreed on by the parties to the dispute or stipulated in any Convention existing between them.*

4. The Members of the League agree that they will carry out in full good faith any award *or decision* that may be rendered, and that they will not resort to war against a Member of the League which complies therewith. In the event of any failure to carry out such an award *or decision*, the Council shall propose what steps should be taken to give effect thereto.

**Article 14**

The Council shall formulate and submit to the Members of the League for adoption plans for the establishment of a Permanent Court of International Justice. The Court shall be competent to hear and determine any dispute of an international character which the parties thereto submit to it. The Court may also give an advisory opinion upon any dispute or question referred to it by the Council or by the Assembly.

**Article 15**

1. If there should arise between Members of the League any dispute likely to lead to a rupture, which is not submitted to arbitration *or judicial settlement* in accordance with Article 13, the Members of the League agree that they will submit the matter to the Council. Any party to the dispute may effect such submission by giving notice of the existence of the dispute to the Secretary-General, who will make all necessary arrangements for a full investigation and consideration thereof.

2. For this purpose, the parties to the dispute will communicate to the Secretary-General, as promptly as possible, statements of their case with all the relevant facts and papers, and the Council may forthwith direct the publication thereof.

3. The Council shall endeavour to effect a settlement of the dispute, and if such efforts are successful, a statement shall be made public giving such facts and explanations regarding the dispute and the terms of settlement thereof as the Council may deem appropriate.

4. If the dispute is not thus settled, the Council either unanimously or by a majority vote shall make and publish a report containing a statement of the facts of the dispute and the recommendations which are deemed just and proper in regard thereto.

5. Any Member of the League represented on the Council may make public a statement of the facts of the dispute and of its conclusions regarding the same.

6. If a report by the Council is unanimously agreed to by the members thereof other than the Representatives of one or more of the parties to the dispute, the Members of the League agree that they will not go to war with any party to the dispute which complies with the recommendations of the report.

7. If the Council fails to reach a report which is unanimously agreed to by the members thereof, other than the Representatives of one or more of the parties to the dispute, the Members of the League reserve to themselves the right to take such action as they shall consider necessary for the maintenance of right and justice.

8. If the dispute between the parties is claimed by one of them, and is found by the Council, to arise out of a matter which by international law is solely within the domestic jurisdiction of the party, the Council shall so report, and shall make no recommendation as to its settlement.

9. The Council may in any case under this article refer the dispute to the Assembly. The dispute shall be so referred at the request of either party to the dispute provided that such request be made within fourteen days after the submission of the dispute to the Council.

10. In any case referred to the Assembly, all the provisions of this article and of Article 12 relating to the action and powers of the Council shall apply to the action and powers of the Assembly, provided that a report made by the Assembly, if concurred in by the Representatives of those Members of the League represented on the Council and of a majority of the other Members of the League, exclusive in each case of the Representatives of the parties to the dispute, shall have the same force as a report by the Council concurred in by all the members thereof other than the Representatives of one or more of the parties to the dispute.

**Article 16**

1. Should any Member of the League resort to war in disregard of its covenants under Articles 12, 13, or 15 it shall, *ipso facto*, be deemed to have committed an act of war against all other Members of the League, which hereby undertake immediately to subject it to the severance of all trade or financial relations, the prohibition of all intercourse between their nationals and the nationals of the Covenant-breaking State, and the prevention of all financial, commercial or personal intercourse between the nations of the Covenant-breaking State and the nationals of any other State, whether a Member of the League or not.

2. It shall be the duty of the Council in such case to recommend to the several Governments concerned what effective military, naval or air force the Members of the League shall severally contribute to the armed forces to be used to protect the covenants of the League.

3. The Members of the League agree, further, that they will mutually support

one another in the financial and economic measures which are taken under this article, in order to minimise the loss and inconvenience resulting from the above measures, and that they will mutually support one another in resisting any special measures aimed at one of their number by the Covenant-breaking State, and that they will take the necessary steps to afford passage through their territory to the forces of any of the Members of the League which are co-operating to protect the covenants of the League.

4. Any member of the League which has violated any covenant of the League may be declared to be no longer a Member of the League by a vote of the Council concurred in by the Representatives of all the other Members of the League represented thereon.

**Article 17**

1. In the event of a dispute between a Member of the League and a State which is not a member of the League or between States not members of the League, the State or States not members of the League shall be invited to accept the obligations of membership in the League for the purposes of such dispute, upon such conditions as the Council may deem just. If such invitation is accepted, the provisions of Articles 12 to 16 inclusive shall be applied with such modifications as may be deemed necessary by the Council.

2. Upon such invitation being given, the Council shall immediately institute an enquiry into the circumstances of the dispute and recommend such action as may seem best and most effectual in the circumstances.

3. If a State so invited shall refuse to accept the obligations of membership in the League for the purposes of such dispute, and shall resort to war against a Member of the League, the provisions of Article 16 shall be applicable as against the State taking such action.

4. If both parties to the dispute when so invited refuse to accept the obligations of membership in the League for the purposes of such dispute, the Council may take such measures and make such recommendations as will prevent hostilities and will result in the settlement of the dispute.

**Article 18**

Every treaty or international engagement entered into hereafter by any Member of the League shall be forthwith registered with the Secretariat and shall, as soon as possible, be published by it. No such treaty or international engagement shall be binding until so registered.

**Article 19**

The Assembly may from time to time advise the reconsideration by Members of the League of treaties which have become inapplicable and the consideration of international conditions whose continuance might endanger the peace of the world.

**Article 20**

1. The Members of the League severally agree that this Covenant is accepted as abrogating all obligations or understandings *inter se* which are inconsistent

with the terms thereof, and solemnly undertake that they will not hereafter enter into any engagements inconsistent with the terms thereof.

2. In case any Member of the League shall, before becoming a Member of the League, have undertaken any obligations inconsistent with the terms of this Covenant, it shall be the duty of such Member to take immediate steps to procure its release from such obligations.

**Article 21**

Nothing in this Covenant shall be deemed to affect the validity of international engagements, such as treaties of arbitration or regional understandings like the Monroe doctrine, for securing the maintenance of peace.

**Article 22**

1. To those colonies and territories which as a consequence of the late war have ceased to be under the sovereignty of the States which formerly governed them and which are inhabited by peoples not yet able to stand by themselves under the strenuous conditions of the modern world, there should be applied the principle that the well-being and development of such peoples form a sacred trust of civilisation and that securities for the performance of this trust should be embodied in this Covenant.

2. The best method of giving practical effect to this principle is that the tutelage of such peoples should be entrusted to advanced nations who, by reason of their resources, their experience or their geographical position, can best undertake this responsibility, and who are willing to accept it, and that this tutelage should be exercised by them as Mandatories on behalf of the League.

3. The character of the mandate must differ according to the stage of the development of the people, the geographical situation of the territory, its economic conditions and other similar circumstances.

4. Certain communities formerly belonging to the Turkish Empire have reached a stage of development where their existence as independent nations can be provisionally recognised subject to the rendering of administrative advice and assistance by a Mandatory until such time as they are able to stand alone. The wishes of these communities must be a principal consideration in the selection of the Mandatory.

5. Other peoples, especially those of Central Africa, are at such a stage that the Mandatory must be responsible for the administration of the territory under conditions which will guarantee freedom of conscience and religion, subject only to the maintenance of public order and morals, the prohibition of abuses such as the slave trade, the arms traffic and the liquor traffic, and the prevention of the establishment of fortifications or military and naval bases and of military training of the natives for other than police purposes and the defence of territory, and will also secure equal opportunities for the trade and commerce of other Members of the League.

6. There are territories, such as South West Africa and certain of the South Pacific Islands, which, owing to the sparseness of their population, or their small

size, or their remoteness from the centres of civilisation, or their geographical contiguity to the territory of the Mandatory, and other circumstances, can be best administered under the laws of the Mandatory as integral portions of its territory, subject to the safeguards above mentioned in the interests of the indigenous population.

7. In every case of mandate, the Mandatory shall render to the Council an annual report in reference to the territory committed to its charge.

8. The degree of authority, control or administation to be exercised by the Mandatory shall, if not previously agreed upon by the Members of the League, be explicitly defined in each case by the Council.

9. A permanent Commission shall be constituted to receive and examine the annual reports of the Mandatories and to advise the Council on all matters relating to the observance of the mandates.

**Article 23**

Subject to and in accordance with the provisions of international Conventions existing or hereafter to be agreed upon, the Members of the League:

(a) will endeavour to secure and maintain fair and humane conditions of labour for men, women and children, both in their own countries and in all countries to which their commercial and industrial relations extend, and for that purpose will establish and maintain the necessary international organisations;

(b) undertake to secure just treatment of the native inhabitants of territories under their control;

(c) will entrust the League with the general supervision over the execution of agreements with regard to the traffic in women and children, and the traffic in opium and other dangerous drugs;

(d) will entrust the League with the general supervision of the trade in arms and ammunition with the countries in which the control of this traffic is necessary in the common interest;

(e) will make provision to secure and maintain freedom of communications and of transit and equitable treatment for the commerce of all Members of the League. In this connection, the special necessities of the regions devastated during the war of 1914-1918 shall be borne in mind;

(f) will endeavour to take steps in matters of international concern for the prevention and control of disease.

**Article 24**

1. There shall be placed under the direction of the League all international bureaux already established by general treaties if the parties to such treaties consent. All such international bureaux and all commissions for the regulation of matters of international interest hereafter constituted shall be placed under the direction of the League.

2. In all matters of international interest which are regulated by general Con-

ventions but which are not placed under the control of international bureaux or commissions, the Secretariat of the League shall, subject to the consent of the Council and if desired by the parties, collect and distribute all relevant information and shall render any other assistance which may be necessary or desirable.

3. The Council may include as part of the expenses of the Secretariat the expenses of any bureau or commission which is placed under the direction of the League.

**Article 25**

The Members of the League agree to encourage and promote the establishment and co-operation of duly authorised voluntary national Red Cross organisations having as purposes the improvemant of health, the prevention of disease and the mitigation of suffering throughout the world.

**Article 26**

1. Amendments to this Covenant will take effect when ratified by the Members of the League whose Representatives compose the Council and by a majority of the Members of the League whose Representatives compose the Assembly.

2. No such amendments shall bind any Member of the League which signifies its dissent therefrom, but in that case it shall cease to be a Member of the League.

# *Appendix II: The Charter of the United Nations**

We the peoples of the United Nations determined

to save succeeding generations from the scourge of war, which twice in our lifetime has brought untold sorrow to mankind, and
to reaffirm faith in fundamental human rights, in the dignity and worth of the human person, in the equal rights of men and women and of nations large and small, and
to establish conditions under which justice and respect for the obligations arising from treaties and other sources of international law can be maintained, and
to promote social progress and better standards of life in larger freedom,

and for these ends

to practice tolerance and live together in peace with one another as good neighbors, and
to unite our strength to maintain international peace and security, and
to ensure, by the acceptance of principles and the institution of methods, that armed force shall not be used, save in the common interest, and
to employ international machinery for the promotion of the economic and social advancement of all peoples,

have resolved to combine our efforts to accomplish these aims.

Accordingly, our respective Governments, through representatives assembled in the city of San Francisco, who have exhibited their full powers found to be in good and due form, have agreed to the present Charter of the United Nations and do hereby establish an international organization to be known as the United Nations.

## Chapter I

## PURPOSES AND PRINCIPLES

### Article 1

The Purposes of the United Nations are:

1. To maintain international peace and security, and to that end: to take effective collective measures for the prevention and removal of threats to the peace, and for the suppression of acts of aggression or other breaches of the peace, and to bring about by peaceful means, and in conformity with the principles of justice and international law, adjustment or settlement of international disputes or situations which might lead to a breach of the peace;

2. To develop friendly relations among nations based on respect for the prin-

* The texts printed in italics indicate amendments adopted by the United Nations.

ciple of equal rights and self-determination of peoples, and to take other appropriate measures to strengthen universal peace;

3. To achieve international co-operation in solving international problems of an economic, social, cultural, or humanitarian character, and in promoting and encouraging respect for human rights and for fundamental freedoms for all without distinction as to race, sex, language, or religion; and

4. To be a centre for harmonizing the actions of nations in the attainment of these common ends.

**Article 2**

The Organization and its Members, in pursuit of the Purposes stated in Article 1, shall act in accordance with the following Principles.

1. The Organization is based on the principle of the sovereign equality of all its Members.

2. All Members, in order to ensure to all of them the rights and benefits resulting from membership, shall fulfil in good faith the obligations assumed by them in accordance with the present Charter.

3. All Members shall settle their international disputes by peaceful means in such a manner that international peace and security, and justice, are not endangered.

4. All Members shall refrain in their international relations from the threat or use of force against the territorial integrity or political independence of any state, or in any other manner inconsistent with the Purposes of the United Nations.

5. All Members shall give the United Nations every assistance in any action it takes in accordance with the present Charter, and shall refrain from giving assistance to any state against which the United Nations is taking preventive or enforcement action.

6. The Organization shall ensure that states which are not Members of the United Nations act in accordance with these Principles so far as may be necessary for the maintenance of international peace and security.

7. Nothing contained in the present Charter shall authorize the United Nations to intervene in matters which are essentially within the domestic jurisdiction of any state or shall require the Members to submit such matters to settlement under the present Charter; but this principle shall not prejudice the application of enforcement measures under Chapter VII.

## Chapter II

## MEMBERSHIP

**Article 3**

The original Members of the United Nations shall be the states which, having participated in the United Nations Conference on International Organization at San Francisco, or having previously signed the Declaration by United Nations of January 1, 1942, sign the present Charter and ratify it in accordance with Article 110.

**Article 4**

1. Membership in the United Nations is open to all other peace-loving states which accept the obligations contained in the present Charter and, in the judgment of the Organization, are able and willing to carry out these obligations.

2. The admission of any such state to membership in the United Nations will be effected by a decision of the General Assembly upon the recommendation of the Security Council.

**Article 5**

A Member of the United Nations against which preventive or enforcement action has been taken by the Security Council may be suspended from the exercise of the rights and privileges of membership by the General Assembly upon the recommendation of the Security Council. The exercise of these rights and privileges may be restored by the Security Council.

**Article 6**

A Member of the United Nations which has persistently violated the Principles contained in the present Charter may be expelled from the Organization by the General Assembly upon the recommendation of the Security Council.

## Chapter III

## ORGANS

**Article 7**

1. There are established as the principal organs of the United Nations: a General Assembly, a Security Council, an Economic and Social Council, a Trusteeship Council, an International Court of Justice, and a Secretariat.

2. Such subsidiary organs as may be found necessary may be established in accordance with the present Charter.

**Article 8**

The United Nations shall place no restrictions on the eligibility of men and women to participate in any capacity and under conditions of equality in its principal and subsidiary organs.

## Chapter IV

## THE GENERAL ASSEMBLY

### *Composition*

**Article 9**

1. The General Assembly shall consist of all the Members of the United Nations.

2. Each Member shall have not more than five representatives in the General Assembly.

*Functions and Powers*

**Article 10**

The General Assembly may discuss any questions or any matters within the scope of the present Charter or relating to the powers and functions of any organs provided for in the present Charter, and, except as provided in Article 12, may make recommendations to the United Nations or to the Security Council or to both on any such questions or matters.

**Article 11**

1. The General Assembly may consider the general principles of co-operation in the maintenance of international peace and security, including the principles governing disarmament and the regulation of armaments, and may make recommendations with regard to such principles to the Members or to the Security Council or to both.

2. The General Assembly may discuss any questions relating to the maintenance of international peace and security brought before it by any Member of the United Nations, or by the Security Council, or by a state which is not a Member of the United Nations in accordance with Article 35, paragraph 2, and, except as provided in Article 12, may make recommendations with regard to any such questions to the state or states concerned or to the Security Council or to both. Any such question on which action is necessary shall be referred to the Security Council by the General Assembly either before or after discussion.

3. The General Assembly may call the attention of the Security Council to situations which are likely to endanger international peace and security.

4. The powers of the General Assembly set forth in this Article shall not limit the general scope of Article 10.

**Article 12**

1. While the Security Council is exercising in respect of any dispute or situation the functions assigned to it in the present Charter, the General Assembly shall not make any recommendations with regard to that dispute or situation unless the Security Council so requests.

2. The Secretary-General, with the consent of the Security Council, shall notify the General Assembly at each session of any matters relative to the maintenance of international peace and security which are being dealt with by the Security Council and shall similarly notify the General Assembly, or the Members of the United Nations if the General Assembly is not in session, immediately the Security Council ceases to deal with such matters.

**Article 13**

1. The General Assembly shall initiate studies and make recommendations for the purpose of:

a. promoting international co-operation in the political field and encouraging the progressive development of international law and its codification;

b. promoting international co-operation in the economic, social, cultural, educational, and health fields, and assisting in the realization of human rights and fundamental freedoms for all without distinction as to race, sex, language, or religion.

2. The further responsibilities, functions, and powers of the General Assembly with respect to matters mentioned in paragraph 1 (b) above are set forth in Chapters IX and X.

**Article 14**

Subject to the provisions of Article 12, the General Assembly may recommend measures for the peaceful adjustment of any situation, regardless of origin, which it deems likely to impair the general welfare or friendly relations among nations, including situations resulting from a violation of the provisions of the present Charter setting forth the Purposes and Principles of the United Nations.

**Article 15**

1. The General Assembly shall receive and consider annual and special reports from the Security Council; these reports shall include an account of the measures that the Security Council has decided upon or taken to maintain international peace and security.

2. The General Assembly shall receive and consider reports from the other organs of the United Nations.

**Article 16**

The General Assembly shall perform such functions with respect to the international trusteeship system as are assigned to it under Chapters XII and XIII, including the approval of the trusteeship agreements for areas not designated as strategic.

**Article 17**

1. The General Assembly shall consider and approve the budget of the Organization.

2. The expenses of the Organization shall be borne by the Members as apportioned by the General Assembly.

3. The General Assembly shall consider and approve any financial and budgetary arrangements with specialized agencies referred to in Article 57 and shall examine the administrative budgets of such specialized agencies with a view to making recommendations to the agencies concerned.

*Voting*

**Article 18**

1. Each member of the General Assembly shall have one vote.

2. Decisions of the General Assembly on important questions shall be made by a two-thirds majority of the members present and voting. These questions shall include: recommendations with respect to the maintenance of international peace and security, the election of the non-permanent members of the Security Council, the election of the members of the Economic and Social Council, the election

of members of the Trusteeship Council in accordance with paragraph 1 (c) of Article 86, the admission of new Members to the United Nations, the suspension of the rights and privileges of membership, the expulsion of Members, questions relating to the operation of the trusteeship system, and budgetary questions.

3. Decisions on other questions, including the determination of additional categories of questions to be decided by a two-thirds majority, shall be made by a majority of the members present and voting.

**Article 19**

A Member of the United Nations which is in arrears in the payment of its financial contributions to the Organization shall have no vote in the General Assembly if the amount of its arrears equals or exceeds the amount of the contributions due from it for the preceding two full years. The General Assembly may, nevertheless, permit such a Member to vote if it is satisfied that the failure to pay is due to conditions beyond the control of the Member.

*Procedure*

**Article 20**

The General Assembly shall meet in regular annual sessions and in such special sessions as occasion may require. Special sessions shall be convoked by the Secretary-General at the request of the Security Council or of a majority of the Members of the United Nations.

**Article 21**

The General Assembly shall adopt its own rules of procedure. It shall elect its President for each session.

**Article 22**

The General Assembly may establish such subsidiary organs as it deems necessary for the performance of its functions.

## Chapter V

## THE SECURITY COUNCIL

*Composition*

**Article 23**[1]

1. The Security Council shall consist of *fifteen* Members of the United Nations. The Republic of China, France, the Union of Soviet Socialist Republics, the United Kingdom of Great Britain and Northern Ireland, and the United States of America shall be permanent members of the Security Council. The General Assembly shall elect *ten* other Members of the United Nations to be non-permanent members of the Security Council, due regard being specially paid, in the first instance to the contribution of Members of the United Nations to the

[1] Amendments to Articles 23, 27 and 61 of the Charter of the United Nations, adopted by the General Assembly on 17 December 1963, came into force on 31 August 1965.
The amendment to Article 23 enlarged the membership of the Security Council from eleven to fifteen.

maintenance of international peace and security and to the other purposes of the Organization, and also to equitable geographical distribution.

2. The non-permanent members of the Security Council shall be elected for a term of two years. *In the first election of the non-permanent members after the increase of the membership of the Security Council from eleven to fifteen, two of the four additional members shall be chosen for a term of one year.* A retiring member shall not be eligible for immediate re-election.

3. Each member of the Security Council shall have one representative.

*Functions and Powers*

**Article 24**

1. In order to ensure prompt and effective action by the United Nations, its Members confer on the Security Council primary responsibility for the maintenance of international peace and security, and agree that in carrying out its duties under this responsibility the Security Council acts on their behalf.

2. In discharging these duties the Security Council shall act in accordance with the Purposes and Principles of the United Nations. The specific powers granted to the Security Council for the discharge of these duties are laid down in Chapters VI, VII, VIII, and XII.

3. The Security Council shall submit annual and, when necessary, special reports to the General Assembly for its consideration.

**Article 25**

The Members of the United Nations agree to accept and carry out the decisions of the Security Council in accordance with the present Charter.

**Article 26**

In order to promote the establishment and maintenance of international peace and security with the least diversion for armaments of the world's human and economic resources, the Security Council shall be responsible for formulating, with the assistance of the Military Staff Committee referred to in Article 47, plans to be submitted to the Members of the United Nations for the establishment of a system for the regulation of armaments.

*Voting*

**Article 27**[2]

1. Each member of the Security Council shall have one vote.

2. Decisions of the Security Council on procedural matters shall be made by an affirmative vote of *nine* members.

3. Decisions of the Security Council on all other matters shall be made by an affirmative vote of *nine* members including the concurring votes of the permanent members; provided that, in decisions under Chapter VI, and under paragraph 3 of Article 52, a party to a dispute shall abstain from voting.

[2] The amendment to Article 27 provided that decisions of the Security Council on procedural matters shall be made by an affirmative vote of nine members (formerly seven) and on all other matters by an affirmative vote of nine members (formerly seven), including the concurring votes of the five permanent members of the Security Council.

*Procedure*

**Article 28**

1. The Security Council shall be so organised as to be able to function continuously. Each member of the Security Council shall for this purpose be represented at all times at the seat of the Organization.

2. The Security Council shall hold periodic meetings at which each of its members may, if it so desires, be represented by a member of the government or by some other specially designated representative.

3. The Security Council may hold meetings at such places other than the seat of the Organization as in its judgment will best facilitate its work.

**Article 29**

The Security Council may establish such subsidiary organs as it deems necessary for the performance of its functions.

**Article 30**

The Security Council shall adopt its own rules of procedure, including the method of selecting its President.

**Article 31**

Any Member of the United Nations which is not a member of the Security Council may participate, without vote, in the discussion of any question brought before the Security Council whenever the latter considers that the interests of that Member are specially affected.

**Article 32**

Any Member of the United Nations which is not a member of the Security Council or any state which is not a Member of the United Nations, if it is a party to a dispute under consideration by the Security Council, shall be invited to participate, without vote, in the discussion relating to the dispute. The Security Council shall lay down such conditions as it deems just for the participation of a state which is not a Member of the United Nations.

## Chapter VI

## PACIFIC SETTLEMENT OF DISPUTES

**Article 33**

1. The parties to any dispute, the continuance of which is likely to endanger the maintenance of international peace and security, shall, first of all, seek a solution by negotiation, enquiry, mediation, conciliation, arbitration, judicial settlement, resort to regional agencies or arrangements, or other peaceful means of their own choice.

2. The Security Council shall, when it deems necessary, call upon the parties to settle their dispute by such means.

**Article 34**

The Security Council may investigate any dispute, or any situation which might lead to international friction or give rise to a dispute, in order to determine whether the continuance of the dispute or situation is likely to endanger the maintenance of international peace and security.

**Article 35**

1. Any Member of the United Nations may bring any dispute, or any situation of the nature referred to in Article 34, to the attention of the Security Council or of the General Assembly.

2. A state which is not a Member of the United Nations may bring to the attention of the Security Council or of the General Assembly any dispute to which it is a party if it accepts in advance, for the purposes of the dispute, the obligations of pacific settlement provided in the present Charter.

3. The proceedings of the General Assembly in respect of matters brought to its attention under this Article will be subject to the provisions of Articles 11 and 12.

**Article 36**

1. The Security Council may, at any stage of a dispute of the nature referred to in Article 33 or of a situation of like nature, recommend appropriate procedures or methods of adjustment.

2. The Security Council should take into consideration any procedures for the settlement of the dispute which have already been adopted by the parties.

3. In making recommendations under this Article the Security Council should also take into consideration that legal disputes should as a general rule be referred by the parties to the International Court of Justice in accordance with the provisions of the Statute of the Court.

**Article 37**

1. Should the parties to a dispute of the nature referred to in Article 33 fail to settle it by the means indicated in that Article, they shall refer it to the Security Council.

2. If the Security Council deems that the continuance of the dispute is in fact likely to endanger the maintenance of international peace and security, it shall decide whether to take action under Article 36 or to recommend such terms of settlement as it may consider appropriate.

**Article 38**

Without prejudice to the provisions of Articles 33 to 37, the Security Council may, if all the parties to any dispute so request, make recommendations to the parties with a view to a pacific settlement of the dispute.

## Chapter VII

## ACTION WITH RESPECT TO THREATS TO THE PEACE, BREACHES OF THE PEACE, AND ACTS OF AGGRESSION

**Article 39**

The Security Council shall determine the existence of any threat to the peace, breach of the peace, or act of aggression and shall make recommendations, or decide what measures shall be taken in accordance with Articles 41 and 42, to maintain or restore international peace and security.

### Article 40

In order to prevent an aggravation of the situation, the Security Council may, before making the recommendations or deciding upon the measures provided for in Article 39, call upon the parties concerned to comply with such provisional measures as it deems necessary or desirable. Such provisional measures shall be without prejudice to the rights, claims, or position of the parties concerned. The Security Council shall duly take account of failure to comply with such provisional measures.

### Article 41

The Security Council may decide what measures not involving the use of armed force are to be employed to give effect to its decisions, and it may call upon the Members of the United Nations to apply such measures. These may include complete or partial interruption of economic relations and of rail, sea, air, postal, telegraphic, radio, and other means of communication, and the severance of diplomatic relations.

### Article 42

Should the Security Council consider that measures provided for in Article 41 would be inadequate or have proved to be inadequate, it may take such action by air, sea, or land forces as may be necessary to maintain or restore international peace and security. Such action may include demonstrations, blockade, and other operations by air, sea, or land forces of Members of the United Nations.

### Article 43

1. All Members of the United Nations, in order to contribute to the maintenance of international peace and security, undertake to make available to the Security Council, on its call and in accordance with a special agreement or agreements, armed forces, assistance, and facilities, including rights of passage, necessary for the purpose of maintaining international peace and security.

2. Such agreement or agreements shall govern the numbers and types of forces, their degree of readiness and general location, and the nature of the facilities and assistance to be provided.

3. The agreement or agreements shall be negotiated as soon as possible on the initiative of the Security Council. They shall be concluded between the Security Council and Members or between the Security Council and groups of Members and shall be subject to ratification by the signatory states in accordance with their respective constitutional processes.

### Article 44

When the Security Council has decided to use force it shall, before calling upon a Member not represented on it to provide armed forces in fulfillment of the obligations assumed under Article 43, invite that Member, if the Member so desires, to participate in the decisions of the Security Council concerning the employment of contingents of that Member's armed forces.

**Article 45**

In order to enable the United Nations to take urgent military measures, Members shall hold immediately available national air-force contingents for combined international enforcement action. The strength and degree of readiness of these contingents and plans for their combined action shall be determined, within the limits laid down in the special agreement or agreements referred to in Article 43, by the Security Council with the assistance of the Military Staff Committee.

**Article 46**

Plans for the application of armed force shall be made by the Security Council with the assistance of the Military Staff Committee.

**Article 47**

1. There shall be established a Military Staff Committee to advise and assist the Security Council on all questions relating to the Security Council's military requirements for the maintenance of international peace and security, the employment and command of forces placed at its disposal, the regulation of armaments, and possible disarmament.

2. The Military Staff Committee shall consist of the Chiefs of Staff of the permanent members of the Security Council or their representatives. Any Member of the United Nations not permanently represented on the Committee shall be invited by the Committee to be associated with it when the efficient discharge of the Committee's responsibilities requires the participation of that Member in its work.

3. The Military Staff Committee shall be responsible under the Security Council for the strategic direction of any armed forces placed at the disposal of the Security Council. Questions relating to the command of such forces shall be worked out subsequently.

4. The Military Staff Committee, with the authorisation of the Security Council and after consultation with appropriate regional agencies, may establish regional sub-committees.

**Article 48**

1. The action required to carry out the decisions of the Security Council for the maintenance of international peace and security shall be taken by all the Members of the United Nations or by some of them, as the Security Council may determine.

2. Such decisions shall be carried out by the Members of the United Nations directly and through their action in the appropriate international agencies of which they are members.

**Article 49**

The Members of the United Nations shall join in affording mutual assistance in carrying out the measures decided upon by the Security Council.

**Article 50**

If preventive or enforcement measures against any state are taken by the

Security Council, any other state, whether a Member of the United Nations or not, which finds itself confronted with special economic problems arising from the carrying out of those measures shall have the right to consult the Security Council with regard to a solution of those problems.

**Article 51**

Nothing in the present Charter shall impair the inherent right of individual or collective self-defence if an armed attack occurs against a Member of the United Nations, until the Security Council has taken the measures necessary to maintain international peace and security. Measures taken by Members in the exercise of this right of self-defense shall be immediately reported to the Security Council and shall not in any way affect the authority and responsiblity of the Security Council under the present Charter to take at any time such action as it deems necessary in order to maintain or restore international peace and security.

## Chapter VIII

## REGIONAL ARRANGEMENTS

**Article 52**

1. Nothing in the present Charter precludes the existence of regional arrangements or agencies for dealing with such matters relating to the maintenance of international peace and security as are appropriate for regional action, provided that such arrangements or agencies and their activities are consistent with the Purposes and Principles of the United Nations.

2. The Members of the United Nations entering into such arrangements or constituting such agencies shall make every effort to achieve pacific settlement of local disputes through such regional arrangements or by such regional agencies before referring them to the Security Council.

3. The Security Council shall encourage the development of pacific settlement of local disputes through such regional arrangements or by such regional agencies either on the initiative of the states concerned or by reference from the Security Council.

4. This Article in no way impairs the application of Articles 34 and 35.

**Article 53**

1. The Security Council shall, where appropriate, utilize such regional arrangements or agencies for enforcement action under its authority. But no enforcement action shall be taken under regional arrangements or by regional agencies without the authorization of the Security Council, with the exception of measures against any enemy state, as defined in paragraph 2 of this Article, provided for pursuant to Article 107 or in regional arrangements directed against renewal of aggressive policy on the part of any such state, until such time as the Organization may, on request of the Governments concerned, be charged with the responsibility for preventing further aggression by such a state.

2. The term enemy state as used in paragraph 1 of this Article applies to any

state which during the Second World War has been an enemy of any signatory of the present Charter.

**Article 54**

The Security Council shall at all times be kept fully informed of activities undertaken or in contemplation under regional arrangements or by regional agencies for the maintenance of international peace and security.

## Chapter IX

## INTERNATIONAL ECONOMIC AND SOCIAL CO-OPERATION

**Article 55**

With a view to the creation of conditions of stability and well-being which are necessary for peaceful and friendly relations among nations based on respect for the principle of equal rights and self-determination of peoples, the United Nations shall promote:

a. higher standards of living, full employment, and conditions of economic and social progress and development;

b. solutions of international economic, social, health, and related problems; and international cultural and educational co-operation; and

c. universal respect for, and observance of, human rights and fundamental freedoms for all without distinction as to race, sex, language, or religion.

**Article 56**

All Members pledge themselves to take joint and separate action in co-operation with the Organization for the achievement of the purposes set forth in Article 55.

**Article 57**

1. The various specialized agencies, established by intergovernmental agreement and having wide international responsibilities, as defined in their basic instruments, in economic, social, cultural, educational, health, and related fields, shall be brought into relationship with the United Nations in accordance with the provisions of Article 63.

2. Such agencies thus brought into relationship with the United Nations are hereinafter referred to as specialized agencies.

**Article 58**

The Organization shall make recommendations for the co-ordination of the policies and activities of the specialized agencies.

**Article 59**

The Organization shall, where appropriate, initiate negotiations among the states concerned for the creation of any new specialized agencies required for the accomplishment of the purposes set forth in Article 55.

**Article 60**

Responsibility for the discharge of the functions of the Organization set forth in this Chapter shall be vested in the General Assembly and, under the authority of the General Assembly, in the Economic and Social Council, which shall have for this purpose the powers set forth in Chapter X.

## CHAPTER X

## THE ECONOMIC AND SOCIAL COUNCIL

*Composition*

**Article 61**[3]

1. The Economic and Social Council shall consist of *twenty-seven* Members of the United Nations elected by the General Assembly.

2. Subject to the provisions of paragraph 3, *nine* members of the Economic and Social Council shall be elected each year for a term of three years. A retiring member shall be eligible for immediate re-election.

3. *At the first election after the increase in the membership of the Economic and Social Council from eighteen to twenty-seven members, in addition to the members elected in place of the six members whose term of office expires at the end of that year, nine additional members shall be elected. Of these nine additional members, the term of office of three members so elected shall expire at the end of one year, and of three other members at the end of two years*, in accordance with arrangements made by the General Assembly.

4. Each member of the Economic and Social Council shall have one representative.

*Functions and Powers*

**Article 62**

1. The Economic and Social Council may make or initiate studies and reports with respect to international economic, social, cultural, educational, health, and related matters and may make recommendations with respect to any such matters to the General Assembly, to the Members of the United Nations, and to the specialized agencies concerned.

2. It may make recommendations for the purpose of promoting respect for, and observance of, human rights and fundamental freedoms for all.

3. It may prepare draft conventions for submission to the General Assembly, with respect to matters falling within its competence.

4. It may call, in accordance with the rules prescribed by the United Nations, international conferences on matters falling within its competence.

**Article 63**

1. The Economic and Social Council may enter into agreements with any of the agencies referred to in Article 57, defining the terms on which the agency

[3] The amendment to Article 61 enlarged the membership of the Economic and Social Council from eighteen to twenty-seven.

concerned shall be brought into relationship with the United Nations. Such agreements shall be subject to approval by the General Assembly.

2. It may co-ordinate the activities of the specialized agencies through consultation with and recommendations to such agencies and through recommendations to the General Assembly and to the Members of the United Nations.

**Article 64**

1. The Economic and Social Council may take appropriate steps to obtain regular reports from the specialised agencies. It may make arrangements with the Members of the United Nations and with the specialized agencies to obtain reports on the steps taken to give effect to its own recommendations and to recommendations on matters falling within its competence made by the General Assembly.

2. It may communicate its observations on these reports to the General Assembly.

**Article 65**

The Economic and Social Council may furnish information to the Security Council and shall assist the Security Council upon its request.

**Article 66**

1. The Economic and Social Council shall perform such functions as fall within its competence in connection with the carrying out of the recommendations of the General Assembly.

2. It may, with the approval of the General Assembly, perform services at the request of Members of the United Nations and at the request of specialized agencies.

3. It shall perform such other functions as are specified elsewhere in the present Charter or as may be assigned to it by the General Assembly.

*Voting*

**Article 67**

1. Each member of the Economic and Social Council shall have one vote.

2. Decisions of the Economic and Social Council shall be made by a majority of the members present and voting.

*Procedure*

**Article 68**

The Economic and Social Council shall set up commissions in economic and social fields and for the promotion of human rights, and such other commissions as may be required for the performance of its functions.

**Article 69**

The Economic and Social Council shall invite any Member of the United Nations to participate, without vote, in its deliberations on any matter of particular concern to that Member.

**Article 70**

The Economic and Social Council may make arrangements for representatives of the specialized agencies to participate, without vote, in its deliberations and in those of the commissions established by it, and for its representatives to participate in the deliberations of the specialized agencies.

**Article 71**

The Economic and Social Council may make suitable arrangements for consultation with non-governmental organizations which are concerned with matters within its competence. Such arrangements may be made with international organizations and, where appropriate, with national organizations after consultation with the Member of the United Nations concerned.

**Article 72**

1. The Economic and Social Council shall adopt its own rules of procedure, including the method of selecting its President.

2. The Economic and Social Council shall meet as required in accordance with its rules, which shall include provision for the convening of meetings on the request of a majority of its members.

## Chapter XI

## DECLARATION REGARDING NON-SELF-GOVERNING TERRITORIES

**Article 73**

Members of the United Nations which have or assume responsibilities for the administration of territories whose peoples have not yet attained a full measure of self-government recognize the principle that the interests of the inhabitants of these territories are paramount, and accept as a sacred trust the obligation to promote to the utmost, within the system of international peace and security established by the present Charter, the well-being of the inhabitants of these territories, and, to this end:

a. to ensure, with due respect for the culture of the peoples concerned, their political, economic, social, and educational advancement, their just treatment, and their protection against abuses;

b. to develop self-government, to take due account of the political aspirations of the peoples, and to assist them in the progressive development of their free political institutions, according to the particular circumstances of each territory and its peoples and their varying stages of advancement;

c. to further international peace and security;

d. to promote constructive measures of development, to encourage research, and to co-operate with one another, and, when and where appropriate, with specialized international bodies with a view to the practical achievement of the social, economic, and scientific purposes set forth in this Article; and

e. to transmit regularly to the Secretary-General for information purposes, subject to such limitation as security and constitutional considerations may require, statistical and other information of a technical nature relating to economic, social, and educational conditions in the territories for which they are respectively responsible other than those territories to which Chapters XII and XIII apply.

**Article 74**

Members of the United Nations also agree that their policy in respect of the territories to which this Chapter applies, no less than in respect of their metropolitan areas, must be based on the general principle of good-neighborliness, due account being taken of the interests and well-being of the rest of the world, in social, economic, and commercial matters.

## Chapter XII

## INTERNATIONAL TRUSTEESHIP SYSTEM

**Article 75**

The United Nations shall establish under its authority an international trusteeship system for the administration and supervision of such territories as may be placed thereunder by subsequent individual agreements. These territories are hereinafter referred to as trust territories.

**Article 76**

The basic objectives of the trusteeship system, in accordance with the Purposes of the United Nations laid down in Article 1 of the present Charter, shall be:

a. to further international peace and security;

b. to promote the political, economic, social, and educational advancement of the inhabitants of the trust territories, and their progressive development towards self-government or independence as may be appropriate to the particular circumstances of each territory and its peoples and the freely expressed wishes of the peoples concerned, and as may be provided by the terms of each trusteeship agreement;

c. to encourage respect for human rights and for fundamental freedoms for all without distinction as to race, sex, language, or religion, and to encourage recognition of the interdependence of the peoples of the world; and

d. to ensure equal treatment in social, economic, and commercial matters for all Members of the United Nations and their nationals, and also equal treatment for the latter in the administration of justice, without prejudice to the attainment of the foregoing objectives and subject to the provisions of Article 80.

**Article 77**

1. The trusteeship system shall apply to such territories in the following categories as may be placed thereunder by means of trusteeship agreements:

a. territories now held under mandate;

b. territories which may be detached from enemy states as a result of the Second World War; and

c. territories voluntarily placed under the system by states responsible for their administration.

2. It will be a matter for subsequent agreement as to which territories in the foregoing categories will be brought under the trusteeship system and upon what terms.

**Article 78**

The trusteeship system shall not apply to territories which have become Members of the United Nations, relationship among which shall be based on respect for the principle of sovereign equality.

**Article 79**

The terms of trusteeship for each territory to be placed under the trusteeship system, including any alteration or amendment, shall be agreed upon by the states directly concerned, including the mandatory power in the case of territories held under mandate by a Member of the United Nations, and shall be approved as provided for in Articles 83 and 85.

**Article 80**

1. Except as may be agreed upon in individual trusteeship agreements, made under Articles 77, 79, and 81, placing each territory under the trusteeship system, and until such agreements have been concluded, nothing in this Chapter shall be construed in or of itself to alter in any manner the rights whatsoever of any states or any peoples or the terms of existing international instruments to which Members of the United Nations may respectively be parties.

2. Paragraph 1 of this Article shall not be interpreted as giving grounds for delay or postponement of the negotiation and conclusion of agreements for placing mandated and other territories under the trusteeship system as provided for in Article 77.

**Article 81**

The trusteeship agreement shall in each case include the terms under which the trust territory will be administered and designate the authority which will exercise the administration of the trust territory. Such authority, hereinafter called the administering authority, may be one or more states or the Organization itself.

**Article 82**

There may be designated, in any trusteeship agreement, a strategic area or areas which may include part or all of the trust territory to which the agreement applies, without prejudice to any special agreement or agreements made under Article 43.

**Article 83**

1. All functions of the United Nations relating to strategic areas, including the approval of the terms of the trusteeship agreement and of their alteration or amendment, shall be exercised by the Security Council.

2. The basic objectives set forth in Article 76 shall be applicable to the people of each strategic area.

3. The Security Council shall, subject to the provisions of the trusteeship agreements and without prejudice to security considerations, avail itself of the assistance of the Trusteeship Council to perform those functions of the United

Nations under the trusteeship system relating to political, economic, social, and educational matters in the strategic areas.

**Article 84**

It shall be the duty of the administering authority to ensure that the trust territory shall play its part in the maintenance of international peace and security. To this end the administering authority may make use of volunteer forces, facilities, and assistance from the trust territory in carrying out the obligations towards the Security Council undertaken in this regard by the administering authority, as well as for local defence and the maintenance of law and order within the trust territory.

**Article 85**

1. The functions of the United Nations with regard to trusteeship agreements for all areas not designated as strategic, including the approval of the terms of the trusteeship agreements and of their alteration or amendment, shall be exercised by the General Assembly.

2. The Trusteeship Council, operating under the authority of the General Assembly, shall assist the General Assembly in carrying out these functions.

## Chapter XIII
## THE TRUSTEESHIP COUNCIL

*Composition*

**Article 86**

1. The Trusteeship Council shall consist of the following Members of the United Nations:

a. those Members administering trust territories;

b. such of those Members mentioned by name in Aritcle 23 as are not administering trust territories; and

c. as many other Members elected for three-year terms by the General Assembly as may be necessary to ensure that the total number of members of the Trusteeship Council is equally divided between those Members of the United Nations which administer trust territories and those which do not.

2. Each member of the Trusteeship Council shall designate one specially qualified person to represent it therein.

*Functions and Powers*

**Article 87**

The General Assembly and, under its authority, the Trusteeship Council, in carrying out their functions, may:

a. consider reports submitted by the administering authority;

b. accept petitions and examine them in consultation with the administering authority;

c. provide for periodic visits to the respective trust territories at times agreed upon with the administering authority; and

d. take these and other actions in conformity with the terms of the trusteeship agreements.

**Article 88**

The Trusteeship Council shall formulate a questionnaire on the political, economic, social, and educational advancement of the inhabitants of each trust territory, and the administering authority for each trust territory within the competence of the General Assembly shall make an annual report to the General Assembly upon the basis of such questionnaire.

*Voting*

**Article 89**

1. Each member of the Trusteeship Council shall have one vote.

2. Decisions of the Trusteeship Council shall be made by a majority of the members present and voting.

*Procedure*

**Article 90**

1. The Trusteeship Council shall adopt its own rules of procedure, including the method of selecting its President.

2. The Trusteeship Council shall meet as required in accordance with its rules, which shall include provision for the convening of meetings on the request of a majority of its members.

**Article 91**

The Trusteeship Council shall, when appropriate, avail itself of the assistance of the Economic and Social Council and of the specialized agencies in regard to matters with which they are respectively concerned.

## Chapter XIV
## THE INTERNATIONAL COURT OF JUSTICE

**Article 92**

The International Court of Justice shall be the principal judicial organ of the United Nations. It shall function in accordance with the annexed Statute, which is based upon the Statute of the Permanent Court of International Justice and forms an integral part of the present Charter.

**Article 93**

1. All Members of the United Nations are *ipso facto* parties to the Statute of the International Court of Justice.

2. A state which is not a Member of the United Nations may become a party to the Statute of the International Court of Justice on conditions to be determined in each case by the General Assembly upon the recommendation of the Security Council.

**Article 94**

1. Each Member of the United Nations undertakes to comply with the decision of the International Court of Justice in any case to which it is a party.

2. If any party to a case fails to perform the obligations incumbent upon it under a judgment rendered by the Court, the other party may have recourse to the Security Council, which may, if it deems necessary, make recommendations or decide upon measures to be taken to give effect to the judgment.

**Article 95**

Nothing in the present Charter shall prevent Members of the United Nations from entrusting the solution of their differences to other tribunals by virtue of agreements already in existence or which may be concluded in the future.

**Article 96**

1. The General Assembly or the Security Council may request the International Court of Justice to give an advisory opinion on any legal question.

2. Other organs of the United Nations and specialised agencies, which may at any time be so authorised by the General Assembly, may also request advisory opinions of the Court on legal questions arising within the scope of their activities.

## Chapter XV

## THE SECRETARIAT

**Article 97**

The Secretariat shall comprise a Secretary-General and such staff as the Organization may require. The Secretary-General shall be appointed by the General Assembly upon the recommendation of the Security Council. He shall be the chief administrative officer of the Organization.

**Article 98**

The Secretary-General shall act in that capacity in all meetings of the General Assembly, of the Security Council, of the Economic and Social Council and of the Trusteeship Council, and shall perform such other functions as are entrusted to him by these organs. The Secretary-General shall make an annual report to the General Assembly on the work of the Organization.

**Article 99**

The Secretary-General may bring to the attention of the Security Council any matter which in his opinion may threaten the maintenance of international peace and security.

**Article 100**

1. In the performance of their duties the Secretary-General and the staff shall not seek or receive instructions from any government or from any other authority external to the Organization. They shall refrain from any action which might reflect on their position as international officials responsible only to the Organization.

2. Each Member of the United Nations undertakes to respect the exclusively international character of the responsibilities of the Secretary-General and the staff and not to seek to influence them in the discharge of their responsibilities.

**Article 101**

1. The staff shall be appointed by the Secretary-General under regulations established by the General Assembly.

2. Appropriate staffs shall be permanently assigned to the Economic and Social Council, the Trusteeship Council, and, as required, to other organs of the United Nations. These staffs shall form a part of the Secretariat.

3. The paramount consideration in the employment of the staff and in the determination of the conditions of service shall be the necessity of securing the highest standards of efficiency, competence, and integrity. Due regard shall be paid to the importance of recruiting the staff on as wide a geographical basis as possible.

## Chapter XVI

## MISCELLANEOUS PROVISIONS

**Article 102**

1. Every treaty and every international agreement entered into by any Member of the United Nations after the present Charter comes into force shall as soon as possible be registered with the Secretariat and published by it.

2. No party to any such treaty or international agreement which has not been registered in accordance with the provisions of paragraph 1 of this Article may invoke that treaty or agreement before any organ of the United Nations.

**Article 103**

In the event of a conflict between the obligations of the Members of the United Nations under the present Charter and their obligations under any other international agreement, their obligations under the present Charter shall prevail.

**Article 104**

The Organization shall enjoy in the territory of each of its Members such legal capacity as may be necessary for the exercise of its functions and the fulfillment of its purposes.

**Article 105**

1. The Organization shall enjoy in the territory of each of its Members such privileges and immunities as are necessary for the fulfillment of its purposes.

2. Representatives of the Members of the United Nations and officials of the Organization shall similarly enjoy such privileges and immunities as are necessary for the independent exercise of their functions in connection with the Organization.

3. The General Assembly may make recommendations with a view to determining the details of the application of paragraphs 1 and 2 of this Article or may propose conventions to the Members of the United Nations for this purpose.

## CHAPTER XVII

## TRANSITIONAL SECURITY ARRANGEMENTS

### Article 106

Pending the coming into force of such special agreements referred to in Article 43 as in the opinion of the Security Council enable it to begin the exercise of its responsibilities under Article 42, the parties to the Four-Nation Declaration, signed at Moscow, October 30, 1943, and France, shall, in accordance with the provisions of paragraph 5 of that Declaration, consult with one another and as occasion requires with other Members of the United Nations with a view to such joint action on behalf of the Organization as may be necessary for the purpose of maintaining international peace and security.

### Article 107

Nothing in the present Charter shall invalidate or preclude action, in relation to any state which during the Second World War has been an enemy of any signatory to the present Charter, taken or authorized as a result of that war by the Governments having responsibility for such action.

## CHAPTER XVIII

## AMENDMENTS

### Article 108

Amendments to the present Charter shall come into force for all Members of the United Nations when they have been adopted by a vote of two-thirds of the members of the General Assembly and ratified in accordance with their respective constitutional processes by two-thirds of the Members of the United Nations, including all the permanent members of the Security Council.

### Article 109[4]

1. A General Conference of the Members of the United Nations for the purpose of reviewing the present Charter may be held at a date and place to be fixed by a two-thirds vote of the members of the General Assembly and by a vote of any *nine* members of the Security Council. Each Member of the United Nations shall have one conference.

2. Any alteration of the present Charter recommended by a two-thirds vote of the conference shall take effect when ratified in accordance with their respective constitutional processes by two-thirds of the Members of the United Nations including all the permanent members of the Security Council.

3. If such a conference has not been held before the tenth annual session of the General Assembly following the coming into force of the present Charter, the

[4] The amendment to Article 109, adopted by the General Assembly on 20 December 1965, came into force on 12 June 1968.
The amendment to Article 109 provided that a General Conference of Member States for the purpose of reviewing the Charter may be held at a date and place to be fixed by a two-thirds vote of the members of the General Assembly and by a vote of any nine members (formerly seven) of the Security Council.

proposal to call such a conference shall be placed on the agenda of that session of the General Assembly, and the conference shall be held if so decided by a majority vote of the members of the General Assembly and by a vote of any seven members of the Security Council.

## Chapter XIX
## RATIFICATION AND SIGNATURE

### Article 110

1. The present Charter shall be ratified by the signatory states in accordance with their respective constitutional processes.

2. The ratifications shall be deposited with the Government of the United States of America, which shall notify all the signatory states of each deposit as well as the Secretary-General of the Organization when he has been appointed.

3. The present Charter shall come into force upon the deposit of ratifications by the Republic of China, France, the Union of Soviet Socialist Republics, the United Kingdom of Great Britain and Northern Ireland, and the United States of America, and by a majority of the other signatory states. A protocol of the ratifications deposited shall thereupon be drawn up by the Government of the United States of America which shall communicate copies thereof to all the signatory states.

4. The states signatory to the present Charter which ratify it after it has come into force will become original Members of the United Nations on the date or the deposit of their respective ratifications.

### Article 111

The present Charter, of which the Chinese, French, Russian, English, and Spanish texts are equally authentic, shall remain deposited in the archives of the Government of the United States of America. Duly certified copies thereof shall be transmitted by that Government to the Governments of the other signatory states.

In faith whereof the representatives of the Governments of the United Nations have signed the present Charter.

Done at the city of San Francisco the twenty-sixth day of June, one thousand nine hundred and forty-five.

# *Appendix III: Membership in the United Nations*

The 127 Member States[1] of the United Nations, and the date of their admission to the Organization, are as follows:

| | |
|---|---|
| Afghanistan | 19 November 1946 |
| Albania | 14 December 1955 |
| Algeria | 8 October 1962 |
| *Argentina | 24 October 1945 |
| *Australia | 1 November 1945 |
| Austria | 14 December 1955 |
| Barbados | 9 December 1966 |
| *Belgium | 27 December 1945 |
| *Bolivia | 14 November 1945 |
| Botswana | 17 October 1966 |
| *Brazil | 24 October 1945 |
| Bulgaria | 14 December 1955 |
| Burma | 19 April 1948 |
| Burundi | 18 September 1962 |
| *Byelorussian SSR | 24 October 1945 |
| Cambodia | 14 December 1955 |
| Cameroon | 20 September 1960 |
| *Canada | 9 November 1945 |
| Central African Republic | 20 September 1960 |
| Ceylon | 14 December 1955 |
| Chad | 20 September 1960 |
| *Chile | 24 October 1945 |
| *China[2] | 24 October 1945 |
| *Colombia | 5 November 1945 |
| Congo (Brazzaville) | 20 September 1960 |
| Congo, Democratic Republic of | 20 September 1960 |
| *Costa Rica | 2 November 1945 |
| *Cuba | 24 October 1945 |
| Cyprus | 20 September 1960 |
| *Czechoslovakia | 24 October 1945 |
| Dahomey | 20 September 1960 |
| *Denmark | 24 October 1945 |
| *Dominican Republic | 24 October 1945 |
| *Ecuador | 21 December 1945 |
| *El Salvador | 24 October 1945 |
| Equatorial Guinea | 12 November 1968 |
| *Ethiopia | 13 November 1945 |
| Fiji | 13 October 1970 |
| Finland | 14 December 1955 |
| *France | 24 October 1945 |
| Gabon | 20 September 1960 |
| Gambia | 21 September 1965 |
| Ghana | 8 March 1957 |
| *Greece | 25 October 1945 |
| *Guatemala | 21 November 1945 |
| Guinea | 12 December 1958 |
| Guyana | 20 September 1966 |
| *Haiti | 24 October 1945 |
| *Honduras | 17 December 1945 |
| Hungary | 14 December 1955 |
| Iceland | 19 November 1946 |
| *India | 30 October 1945 |
| Indonesia | 28 September 1950 |
| *Iran | 24 October 1945 |
| *Iraq | 21 December 1945 |
| Ireland | 14 December 1955 |
| Israel | 11 May 1949 |
| Italy | 14 December 1955 |

* Original member.

[1] The membership list refers to those states who were members of the United Nations on 1 January 1971. Switzerland has preferred not to join the Organization, and some countries which have attained their independence have not sought membership, e.g. Nauru and Western Samoa. The divided states (East and West Germany, North and South Korea, and North and South Viet-Nam) have also not become UN members. Taiwan (Formosa), not the Communist regime on mainland China, fills the Chinese seat at the UN.

| | |
|---|---|
| Ivory Coast | 20 September 1960 |
| Jamaica | 18 September 1962 |
| Japan | 18 December 1956 |
| Jordan | 14 December 1955 |
| Kenya | 16 December 1963 |
| Kuwait | 14 May 1963 |
| Laos | 14 December 1955 |
| *Lebanon | 24 October 1945 |
| Lesotho | 17 October 1966 |
| *Liberia | 2 November 1945 |
| Libya | 14 December 1955 |
| *Luxembourg | 24 October 1945 |
| Madagascar | 20 September 1960 |
| Malawi | 1 December 1964 |
| Malaysia[3] | 17 September 1957 |
| Maldive Islands | 21 September 1965 |
| Mali | 28 September 1960 |
| Malta | 1 December 1964 |
| Mauritania | 27 October 1961 |
| Mauritius | 24 April 1968 |
| *Mexico | 7 November 1945 |
| Mongolia | 27 October 1961 |
| Morocco | 12 November 1956 |
| Nepal | 14 December 1955 |
| *Netherlands | 10 December 1945 |
| *New Zealand | 24 October 1945 |
| *Nicaragua | 24 October 1945 |
| Niger | 20 September 1960 |
| Nigeria | 7 October 1960 |
| *Norway | 27 November 1945 |
| Pakistan | 30 September 1947 |
| *Panama | 13 November 1945 |
| *Paraguay | 24 October 1945 |
| *Peru | 31 October 1945 |
| *Philippines | 24 October 1945 |
| *Poland | 24 October 1945 |
| Portugal | 14 December 1955 |
| Romania | 14 December 1955 |
| Rwanda | 18 September 1962 |
| *Saudi Arabia | 24 October 1945 |
| Senegal | 28 September 1960 |
| Sierra Leone | 27 September 1961 |
| Singapore | 21 September 1965 |
| Somalia | 20 September 1960 |
| *South Africa | 7 November 1945 |
| Southern Yemen | 14 December 1967 |
| Spain | 14 December 1955 |
| Sudan | 12 November 1956 |
| Swaziland | 24 September 1968 |
| Sweden | 19 November 1946 |
| *Syria[4] | 24 October 1945 |
| Thailand | 16 December 1946 |
| Togo | 20 September 1960 |
| Trinidad and Tobago | 18 September 1962 |
| Tunisia | 12 November 1956 |
| *Turkey | 24 October 1945 |
| Uganda | 25 October 1962 |
| *Ukrainian SSR | 24 October 1945 |
| *USSR | 24 October 1945 |
| *United Arab Republic | 24 October 1945 |
| *United Kingdom | 24 October 1945 |
| United Republic of Tanzania[5] | 14 December 1961 |
| *United States | 24 October 1945 |
| Upper Volta | 20 September 1960 |
| *Uruguay | 18 December 1945 |
| *Venezuela | 15 November 1945 |
| Yemen | 30 September 1947 |
| *Yugoslavia | 24 October 1945 |
| Zambia | 1 December 1964 |

[3] The Federation of Malaya joined the UN on 17 September 1957. On 16 September 1963, its name changed to Malaysia, following the admission to the new federation of Singapore, Sabah (North Borneo) and Sarawak. Singapore became an independent State on 9 August 1965 and a Member of the UN on 21 September of that year.

[4] Egypt and Syria were original Members of the UN from 24 October 1945. Following a plebiscite on 21 February 1958, the United Arab Republic was established by a union of Egypt and Syria, and continued as a single Member. On 13 October 1961, Syria, having resumed its status as an independent State, resumed its separate membership in the UN.

[5] Tanganyika was a Member of the UN from 14 December 1961 and Zanzibar was a Member from 16 December 1963. Following the ratification, on 26 April 1964, of Articles of Union between Tanganyika and Zanzibar, the United Republic of Tanganyika and Zanzibar continued as a single Member, later changing its name to the United Republic of Tanzania.

# *Notes on Contributors*

**D. W. Bowett** is President of Queen's College, Cambridge, a lecturer in the Faculty of Law in the University of Cambridge, a Barrister-at-Law of the Middle Temple, and a consultant in international law. He served with the United Nations as a legal officer in New York from 1957 to 1959, and as General Counsel of UNRWA in the Middle East from 1966 to 1968. His publications include *United Nations Forces* (1964), *The Law of International Institutions* (2nd ed. 1970), and numerous articles on international legal and peace-keeping problems.

**Rupert Emerson** is Professor Emeritus of Government at Harvard University and was recently Visiting Professor of Political Science at Yale University and the University of California, Berkeley and Los Angeles. He is a past president of the Far Eastern Association (USA), and of the African Studies Association (USA), and an Honorary Member of the editorial board of *International Organization*. His publications include *State and Sovereignty in Modern Germany* (1928), *From Empire to Nation* (1960), *Africa and United States Policy* (1967), and numerous articles on colonial problems.

**J. E. S. Fawcett** is Director of Studies at the Royal Institute of International Affairs, Vice-President of the European Commission on Human Rights, and Editor of the *International Law Quarterly*. His publications include *The British Commonwealth in International Law* (1963), *International Law and the Uses of Outer Space* (1968), *The Law of Nations* (1968), *The Application of the European Convention on Human Rights* (1969), and numerous articles on international legal problems and human rights.

**Geoffrey L. Goodwin** is Montague Burton Professor of International Relations in the University of London. He served in the Foreign Office from 1945 to 1948, and then joined the staff of the London School of Economics. His publications include *Britain and the United Nations* (1957) and numerous articles on international politics and institutions.

**Ernst B. Haas** is Professor of Political Science and Director of the Institute of International Studies at the University of California, Berkeley. His publications include *The Dynamics of International Relations* (with A. S. Whiting, 1956), *Beyond the Nation State* (1964), *The Uniting of Europe* (2nd ed. 1968), *Tangle of Hopes: American Commitments and World Order* (1969), and numerous articles and monographs on international politics and institutions.

**David Mitrany** was Professor and first Permanent Member of the Institute for Advanced Study, Princeton University, from 1933 to 1958, Visiting Professor at Harvard University, 1930–2, Dodge Lecturer at Yale University,

1932, attached to the Foreign Office, 1939–44, and William Nielson Research Professor, Smith College, Massachusetts, 1950. He was a founding member of the League of Nations Society and a member of the Permanent Conference for International Studies. His numerous publications include *A Working Peace System* (1946).

**F. S. Northedge** is Professor of International Relations in the University of London and a regular broadcaster on current international problems. His publications include *British Foreign Policy: The Process of Readjustment*, 1945–1961 (1962), *The Troubled Giant: Britain among the Great Powers*, 1916–1939 (1966), *Foreign Policies of the Powers* (ed. 1968), *International Disputes* (with Michael Donelan, 1971), and numerous articles on international politics and foreign policy.

**Susan Strange** is a Research Specialist at the Royal Institute of International Affairs with special reference to international economic problems and the role of sterling. She was previously a lecturer in International Relations at University College, London, a UN and Washington Correspondent, and the Economic Correspondent of the *Observer*. Her publications include *The Sterling Problem and the Six* (1967), *Sterling and British Policy* (1971), and numerous articles on international economic problems.

**Kenneth J. Twitchett** is Senior Lecturer in Government and International Affairs at the Bramshill Police College, Basingstoke. He was previously a lecturer in International Relations at the University of Aberdeen. His publications include *The New International Actors: The UN and the EEC* (with Carol Ann Cosgrove, 1970), *International Security: Reflections on Survival and Stability* (ed. 1971), and numerous articles on international politics and colonial problems.

# *Select Bibliography*

THE bibliography is not comprehensive and indicates only some of the articles and books illustrating the various aspects of the United Nations system examined by the contributors to this symposium. Many of the authorities cited by the contributors have been excluded, and preference generally given to material published since 1964. For further bibliographical references the reader is referred to the detailed bibliographies regularly published in *International Organization*, the quarterly journal of the World Peace Foundation, Massachusetts. *The UN Monthly Chronicle*, published by the United Nations Office of Public Information, New York, provides up-to-date, comprehensive, and documented accounts of the Organization's activities and information on the work of its related agencies. The annual September edition of *International Conciliation*, "Issues Before the General Assembly", published by the Carnegie Endowment for International Peace, New York, provides detailed examinations of the United Nations' work and the problems confronting it.

## GENERAL WORKS


BOWETT, D. W., *The Law of International Institutions*, 2nd rev. ed. (London: Stevens, 1970).

CHADWICK, JOHN, *International Organizations*. (London: Methuen, 1969).

CLAUDE, INIS L., Jr., *Swords into Plowshares*, 3rd rev. ed. (New York: Random House, 1966).

COSGROVE, CAROL ANN, and TWITCHETT, KENNETH J., (eds.), *The New International Actors: The UN and the EEC*. (London: Macmillan, 1970).

GOODSPEED, S. S., *The Nature and Function of International Organization*, 2nd rev. ed. (New York: Oxford University Press, 1967).

HINSLEY, F. H., *Power and the Pursuit of Peace*. (London: Cambridge University Press, 1963).

HOFFMANN, STANLEY, "The Role of International Organization: Limits and Possibilities", *International Organization*, X. iii (Summer 1956).

HOFFMAN, STANLEY, "International Organization and the International System", *International Organization*, XXIV. iii (Summer 1970).

JENKS, C. WILFRED, *The World Beyond the Charter*. (London: Allen & Unwin, 1969).

JORDAN, WILLIAM, "Concepts and Realities in International Political Organization", *International Organization*, XI. iv (Autumn 1957).

LUARD, EVAN (ed.), *Evolution of International Organization*. (London: Thames & Hudson, 1966).

LUARD, EVAN (ed), *The International Regulation of Frontier Disputes*. (London: Thames & Hudson, 1970).

MYRDAL, GUNNAR, "Realities and Illusions in Regard to Inter-governmental Organizations", *Hobhouse Memorial Lecture*. (London: London School of Economics, 1955).

PLANO, C., and RIGGS, ROBERT E., *Forging World Order*. (London: Collier-Macmillan, 1967).

*Report of a Study Group on the Peaceful Settlement of International Disputes*. (London: David Davies Memorial Institute of International Affairs, 1966).

REUTER, PAUL, *Institutions Internationales*, 5th ed. (Paris: Presses Universitaires de France, 1967).

YALEM, RONALD J., *Regionalism and World Order*. (Washington, D.C.: Public Affairs Press, 1965).

## THE LEAGUE OF NATIONS

BARBER, A. J., *The Civilizing Mission: The Italo-Ethiopian War*, 1935–36. (London: Cassell, 1968).

BARROS, JAMES, *Betrayal from Within: Joseph Avenol, Secretary-General of the League of Nations*, 1933–1940. (New Haven, Conn.: Yale University Press, 1969).

CECIL, VISCOUNT, *The Great Experiment*. (London: Oxford University Press, 1941).

DEXTER, BYRON, *The Years of Opportunity: The League of Nations*, 1920–26. (New York: Viking Press, 1967).

GOODRICH, LELAND, "From League of Nations to United Nations", *International Organization*, I. i (Winter 1947).

NICHOLAS, H. G., "From League to United Nations", *International Affairs*, Special Issue to mark the Fiftieth Anniversary of Chatham House. (November 1970).

NIEMEYER, GERHART, "The Balance-Sheet of the League Experiment", *International Organization*, VI. iv (Autumn 1962).

THANT, U, "The League of Nations and the United Nations", *UN Monthly Chronicle*, I. i (May 1964).

WALTERS, F. P., *A History of the League of Nations*. (London: Oxford University Press, 1952).

ZIMMERN, ALFRED, *The League of Nations and the Rule of Law*. (London: Macmillan, 1936).

## THE UNITED NATIONS

**General.**

BRUN, ROBERT, *et al.*, *Twenty-five Years After San Francisco*. (Special Issue of *Le Monde diplomatique*, October 1970).

CLAUDE, INIS L., Jr., *The Changing United Nations*. (New York: Random House, 1967).

EAYRS, JAMES, and SPENCER, ROBERT, (eds.), "The UN's Twenty-five Years", Special Issue of *International Journal*, XXV. ii (Spring 1970).

GOODRICH, LELAND M., *et al.*, *Charter of the United Nations: Commentary and Documents*, 3rd rev. ed. (New York: Columbia University Press, 1969).

GREGG, ROBERT, and BARKUN, MICHAEL, (eds.), *The United Nations System and its Functions*. (Princeton, N.J.: Van Nostrand, 1968).

KAY, DAVID A. (ed.), *The United Nations Political System*. (New York: John Wiley, 1967).

HAMMARSKJÖLD, DAG, "Two Differing Concepts of the United Nations Assayed—Introduction to the Annual Report of the Secretary-General on the Work of the Organization, 19th June 1960–15th June 1961", *United Nations Review*, VIII. ix (September 1961).

NICHOLAS, H. G., *The United Nations as a Political Institution*, 3rd rev. ed. (London: Oxford University Press, 1967).

O'BRIEN, CONOR CRUISE, and TOPOLSKI, FELIKS, *The United Nations: Sacred Drama*. (London: Hutchinson, 1968).

PADELFORD, NORMAN, and GOODRICH, LELAND M. (eds.), *The United Nations in the Balance: Accomplishments and Progress*. (New York: Praeger, 1956).

SOHN, LOUIS B., *The United Nations in Action*. (New York: Foundation Press, 1968).

TUNG, WILLIAM L., *International Organization under the United Nations*. (New York: Crowell, 1969).

WILSON, ROBERT R., "The United Nations as Symbol and as Instrument", *American Journal of International Law*, 64. i. (January 1970).

YOUNG, ORAN R., "The United Nations and the International System", *International Organization*, XXII. iv. (Autumn 1968).

**The Political Organs**

ALKER, HAYWARD R., Jr., and RUSSETT, BRUCE M., *World Politics in the General Assembly*. (New Haven Conn.: Yale University Press, 1965).

BAILEY, SYDNEY D., *The General Assembly of the United Nations*, 2nd rev. ed. (New York: Praeger, 1964).

BAILEY, SYDNEY D., "Veto in the Security Council", *International Conciliation*, No. 566. (January 1968).

BAILEY, SYDNEY D., *Voting in the Security Council*. (Bloomington: University of Indiana Press, 1970).

BOYD, A., *Fifteen Men on a Powder Keg: The UN Security Council*. (London: Methuen, 1971).

KEOHANE, ROBERT OWEN, "Political Influence in the General Assembly", *International Conciliation*, No. 557. (March 1966).

KEOHANE, ROBERT OWEN, "Institutionalization in the United Nations General Assembly", *International Organization*, XXIII. ii. (Autumn 1969).

NEWCOMBE, HANNA, ROSS, MICHAEL, and NEWCOMBE, ALAN G., "United Nations Voting Patterns", *International Organization*, XXIV. i. (Winter 1970).

ROWE, EDWARD T., "Changing Patterns in the Voting Successes of Member States in the United Nations General Assembly: 1945–1966", *International Organization*, XXIII. ii. (Spring 1969).

TODD, JAMES E., "An Analysis of Security Council Voting Behaviour", *The Western Political Quarterly*, XXII. i. (March 1969).

**The Secretariat**

BAILEY, SYDNEY D., *The Secretariat of the United Nations*, rev. ed. (London: Pall Mall, 1964).

CORDIER, ANDREW W., and FOOTE, WILDER, (eds.), *Public Papers of the Secretaries-General of the United Nations*, Volume 1, *Trygve Lie*, 1946–1953. (New York: Columbia University Press, 1969).

COX, ROBERT W., "The Executive Head: An essay on Leadership in International Organization", *International Organization*, XXIII. ii. (Spring 1969).

GOODRICH, LELAND M., "The Political Role of the Secretary-General", *International Organization*, XVI. iv. (Autumn 1962).

GORDENKER, LEON, *The United Nations Secretary-General and the Maintenance of Peace*. (New York: Columbia University Press, 1967).

HAMMARSKJÖLD, DAG, "The International Civil Servant in Law and Fact," Lecture delivered at the University of Oxford, May 1961. (Oxford: Clarendon Press, 1961).

KNIGHT, JONATHAN, "On the Influence of the Secretary-General: can we know what it is?", *International Organization*, XXIV. iii. (Summer 1970).

LASH, JOSEPH P., "Dag Hammarskjöld's conception of his office", *International Organization*, XVI. iv. (Autumn 1962).

LIE, TRYGVE, *In the Cause of Peace: Seven Years with the United Nations*. (New York: Macmillan Company, 1954).

ROVINE, ARTHUR W., *The First Fifty Years: The Secretary-General in World Politics 1920–1970*. (Leyden: Sijthoff, 1970).

TOWNLEY, RALPH, *The United Nations: A View from Within*. (New York: Scribner, 1969).

ZACHER, MARK W., "The Secretary-General and the United Nations' Function of Peaceful Settlement", *International Organization*, XX. iv. (Autumn 1966).

ZACHER, MARK W., "The Secretary-General: Some Comments on Recent Research", *International Organization*, XXIII. iv. (Autumn 1969).

ZACHER, MARK W., *Dag Hammarskjöld's United Nations*. (New York: Columbia University Press, 1970).

**Peace-keeping**

ADAMS, T. W., and COTTRELL, ALVIN J., "American Foreign Policy and the UN Peacekeeping Force in Cyprus", *Orbis*, XII. ii. (Summer 1968).

BLOOMFIELD, LINCOLN, *et al.*, *International Military Forces*. (Boston: Little, Brown, 1964); reprint of *International Organization*, XVII. ii. (Spring 1963).

BLOOMFIELD, LINCOLN, "Peacekeeping and Peacemaking", *Foreign Affairs*, XXXXIV. iv. (July 1966).

BLOOMFIELD, LINCOLN, *The UN and Vietnam*. (New York: Carnegie Endowment for International Peace, 1968).

BOWETT, D. W., *United Nations Forces: A Legal Study*. (London: Stevens, for the David Davies Memorial Institute, 1964).

BURNS, E. L. M., "The withdrawal of UNEF and the future of Peacekeeping", *International Journal*, XXIII. i. (Winter 1967–68).

CITRIN, J., *United Nations Peacekeeping Activities*, Monograph Series in World Affairs. (Denver: Denver University Press, 1965–66).

CLAUDE, INIS L., Jr., "United Nations Use of Military Force", *Journal of Conflict Resolution*, VII. ii. (June 1963).

COHEN, MAXWELL, "The Demise of UNEF", *International Journal*, XXIII. i. (Winter 1967–8).

COX, ARTHUR M., *Prospects for Peacekeeping*. (Washington, D.C.: Brookings Institute, 1967).

CURTIS, GERALD N., "The United Nations Observation Group in the Lebanon", *International Organization*, XVIII. iv. (Autumn 1964).

DOXFORD, C. F., "United Nations Peace-Keeping Operations", *Australian Outlook*, XXII. i. (April 1968).

GAGNON, MONA HARRINGTON, "Peace Forces and the Veto: The Relevance of Consent", *International Organization*, XXI. iv. (Autumn 1967).

GOODRICH, LELAND M., *Korea: A Study of U.S. Policy in the United Nations*. (New York: Council on Foreign Relations, 1956).

GORDENKER, LEON, *The United Nations and the Peaceful Unification of Korea: The Politics of field operations, 1947–1950*. (The Hague: Nijhoff, 1959).

HARBOTTLE, MICHAEL, *The Impartial Soldier*, (London: Oxford University Press, 1970).

HEATHCOTE, NINA, "American Policy towards the UN Operation in the Congo", *Australian Outlook*, XVIII. i. (Autumn 1964).

HIGGINS, ROSALYN, *United Nations Peacekeeping 1946–1967: Documents and Commentary. I. The Middle East; II. Asia; III. Africa*. (London: Oxford University Press, vol. I, 1969; vol. II, 1970; vol. III, 1971).

HORN, CARL VON, *Soldiering for Peace*. (London: Cassell, 1966).

JACOBSON, H. K., "ONUC's Civil Operations", *World Politics*, XVII. i. (October 1964).

JAMES, ALAN, *The Politics of Peacekeeping*. (London: Chatto & Windus, 1969).

JAMES, ALAN, *The Role of Force in International Order and United Nations Peacekeeping*. (Ditchley Foundation, 1969).

LALL, ARTHUR, *The UN and the Middle East Crisis*, 1967. (New York: Columbia University Press, 1968).

LARUS, JOEL, (ed.), *From Collective Security to Preventive Diplomacy*. (New York: Wiley, 1965).

LEFEVER, ERNEST W., *Uncertain Mandate: Politics of the UN Congo Operation*. (Baltimore: Johns Hopkins, 1967).

MILLER, LINDA B., *World Order and Local Disorder*. (Princeton N.J.: Princeton University Press, 1968).

NORTHEDGE, F. S., *The Settlement of International Disputes*. (London: David Davies Memorial Institute, 1969).

NORTHEDGE, F. S., and DONELAN, M., *International Disputes: the Political Aspects*. (London: Europa Publications, 1971).

STEGENGA, JAMES A., *The United Nations Force in Cyprus*. (Columbus, Ohio: Ohio State University Press, 1968).

TANDON, YASHPAL, "UNEF, The Secretary-General and International Diplomacy in the Third Arab-Israeli War", *International Organization*, XXII. ii. (Spring 1968).

TWITCHETT, KENNETH J., (ed.), *International Security: Reflections on Survival and Stability*. (London: Oxford University Press, 1971).

VEUR, PAUL W. VAN DER, "The United Nations in West Irian", *International Organization*, XVIII. i. (Winter 1964).

WOLFERS, ARNOLD, "Collective Security and the War in Korea", *The Yale Review*, XLIII. iv. (June 1954). See also WOLFERS, ARNOLD, *Discord and Collaboration*. (Baltimore: Johns Hopkins Press, 1962), Chapter II.

**Colonialism, Trusteeship and Self-Determination**

ALLEN, PHILIP M., "Self-Determination in the Western Indian Ocean", *International Conciliation*, No. 560. (November 1966).

BLUM, YEHUDA Z., "The Composition of the Trusteeship Council", *American Journal of International Law*, LXIII. iv. (October 1969).

DESMITH, STANLEY A., *Exceeding Small: The Future of the US Pacific Trust Territories*. (New York: New York University Press, 1969).

EMERSON, RUPERT, *From Empire to Nation*. (Cambridge, Mass.: Harvard University Press, 1962).

EMERSON, RUPERT, *Self-Determination Revisited in the Era of Decolonization*, Occasional Papers in International Relations Series. (Cambridge, Mass.: Harvard University Press, December 1964).

GARDINIER, DAVID E., *Cameroon: United Nations Challenge to French Policy*. (London: Oxford University Press, 1963).

HAAS, ERNST B., "The Reconciliation of Conflicting Colonial Policy Aims: Acceptance of the League of Nations Mandates System", *International Organization*, VI. iv. (Autumn 1952).

HAAS, ERNST B., "The Attempt to Terminate Colonialism: Acceptance of the United Nations Trusteeship System", *International Organization*, VII. i. (Winter 1953).

HALL, H. DUNCAN, *Mandates, Dependencies and Trusteeship*. (Washington, D.C.: Carnegie Endowment for International Peace, 1948).

JOHNSON, HAROLD S., *Self-Determination within the Community of Nations*. (Leyden: Sijthoff, 1967).

KAY, DAVID A., "The Politics of Decolonization: The New Nations and the United Nations Political Process", *International Organization*, XXI. iv. (Autumn 1967).

MURRAY, JAMES N., Jr., *The United Nations Trusteeship System*. (Urbana, Ill.: University of Illinois Press, 1957).

THULLEN, GEORGE, *Problems of the Trusteeship System: A Study of Political Behaviour in the United Nations*. (Geneva: Librairie Droz, 1964).

TWITCHETT, KENNETH J., "The Racial Issue at the United Nations", *International Relation*, XI. xii. (October 1965).

TWITCHETT, KENNETH J., "The Intellectual Genesis of the League of Nations Mandates System", *International Relations*, III. i. (April 1966).

TWITCHETT, KENNETH J., "The Colonial Powers and the United Nations", *Journal of Contemporary History*, IV. i. (January 1969).

WAINHOUSE, DAVID, *Remnants of Empire: The United Nations and the End of Colonialism.* (New York: Harper & Row, 1964).

WOHLGEMETH BLAIR, PATRICIA, *The Ministate Dilemma*, Occasional Paper No. 6. (New York: Carnegie Endowment for International Peace, October 1967).

WRIGHT, QUINCY, *Mandates Under the League of Nations.* (Chicago, Ill.: University of Chicago Press, 1930).

**Economic Co-operation**

ASHER, ROBERT, *et al.*, *The United Nations and the Promotion of the General Welfare.* (Washington, D.C.: Brookings Institute, 1957).

BLEICHER, SAMUEL A., "UN v. IBRD: A Dilemma of Functionalism", *International Organization*, XXIV. i. (Winter 1970).

COOPER, RICHARD, *The Economics of Interdependence: Economic Policy in the Atlantic Community.* (New York: McGraw-Hill, 1968).

COSGROVE, CAROL ANN, "Help for the 'Have-Nots' ", *Political Studies*, XVII. iv. (December 1969).

COX, ROBERT, (ed.), *International Organisation: World Politics – Studies in Economic and Social Agencies.* (London, Macmillan, 1969).

COX, ROBERT and JACOBSON, HAROLD, *The Anatomy of Influence.* (New Haven, Conn.: Yale University Press, 1971).

FAMILTON, R. J., "East-West Trade and Payments Relations", *IMF Staff Papers*, March 1970.

FRANK, ISAIAH, "International Trade Policy for the Second Development Decade", *International Journal*, XXV. i. (Winter 1969–1970).

FRIEDMAN, IRVING S., "In defence of development", *World Today*, XXII. iv. (April 1966).

GARDNER, RICHARD N., (ed.), *Blueprint for Peace.* (New York: McGraw-Hill, 1966).

GARDNER, RICHARD N., and MILLIKAN, MAX F., (eds.), *The Global Partnership: International Agencies and Economic Development.* (New York: Praeger, 1968); reprint of *International Organization*, XXII. i. (Winter 1968).

GOSOVIC, BRANISLAV, "UNCTAD: North-South Encounter", *International Conciliation*, No. 568. (May 1968).

HAAS, ERNST B., *Beyond the Nation State: Functionalism and International Organization.* (Stanford, Calif.: Stanford University Press, 1964).

HOFFMAN, PAUL, "Progress Report on a Global Partnership", *UN Monthly Chronicle*, IV. iii. (March 1967).

JANNSSEN, L. H., "Events and Trends: The United Nations Conference on Trade and Development", *World Justice*, X. iv. (June 1969).

KINDLEBERGER, CHARLES P., *Power and Money: The Politics of International Economics and the Economics of International Politics.* (London: Macmillan, 1970).

KIRDAR, ÜNER, *The Structure of United Nations Economic Aid to Underdeveloped Countries.* (The Hague: Nijhoff, 1966).

LEGUM, COLIN, (ed.), *The First UN Development Decade and its Lessons for the 1970's*. (New York: Praeger, 1970).

MANGONE, GERARD J., (ed.), *UN Administration of Economic and Social Programmes*, Columbia University Studies in International Organization. (New York: Columbia University Press, 1966).

MEERHAEGHE, M. VAN, *International Economic Institutions*, rev. ed. (London: Stevens, 1968).

MITRANY, DAVID, *A Working Peace System: An Argument for the Functional Development of International Organization*. (London: Royal Institute of International Affairs, 1946).

MONTGOMERY, JOHN D., *Foreign Aid in International Politics*. (Englewood Cliffs, N.J.: Prentice Hall, 1967).

PEARSON, LESTER B., *et al.*, *Partners in Development*. (London: Pall Mall, 1969).

PEARSON, LESTER B., "International Economic Co-operation in a Changing World", *Australian Outlook*, XXIII. ii. (August 1969).

PEARSON, LESTER B., *The Crisis of Development*. (London: Pall Mall, 1970).

RICHARDS, HAMISH, *International Economic Institutions*. (London: Holt, Rinehart and Winston, 1970).

SEWELL, J. P., *Functionalism and World Politics:* A *Study Based on United Nations Programmes Financing Economic Development*. (London: Oxford University Press, 1966).

SHARP, WALTER, *The United Nations Economic and Social Council*. (New York: Columbia University Press, 1969).

SYMONDS, RICHARD, (ed.), *International Targets for Development*. (London: Faber & Faber, 1970).

UNITED NATIONS, *A Study of the Capacity of the United Nations Development System*, 2 vols. (Geneva: United Nations, 1969); *The Jackson Report*.

UNITED NATIONS, ECOSOC's 47th Session, *Report of the Committee for Development Planning on the 4th and 5th Sessions*. (New York: United Nations, 1969); *First Tinbergen Report*.

UNITED NATIONS, ECOSOC's 49th Session, *Report of the Committee for Development Planning on the 6th Session*. (New York: United Nations, 1970); *Second Tinbergen Report*.

WELLS, SIDNEY, "The Developing Countries: GATT and UNCTAD", *International Affairs*, XXXXV. i. (January 1969).

WIGHTMANN, DAVID R., "Food Aid and Economic Development", *International Conciliation*, No. 567. (March 1968).

**Human Rights**

EIDE, B. ASBJÖRN, and SCHOU, AUGUST, (eds.), *International Protection of Human Rights*, Nobel Symposium 7. (New York: Wiley, 1968).

JENKS, C. WILFRED, *Social Justice in the Law of Nations*. (London: Oxford University Press, 1970).

KOREY, WILLIAM, "The Key to Human Rights Implementation", *International Conciliation*, No. 570. (November 1968).

LUARD, EVAN, (ed.), *The International Protection of Human Rights.* (London: Thames & Hudson, 1967).

SAITO, Y., "The Adoption of the Two Treaties on Human Rights at the General Assembly of the United Nations Organization", *World Justice*, X. ii. (December 1968).

**International Law**

AHLUWALIA, KULJIT, *The Legal status, privileges and immunities of the specialized agencies of the United Nations and certain other international organizations.* (The Hague: Nijhoff, 1964).

ASAMOAH, O. Y., *The Legal Significance of the Declarations of the General Assembly of the United Nations.* (The Hague: Nijhoff, 1966).

BLEICHER, SAMUEL A., "The Legal Significance of Recitation of General Assembly Resolutions", *American Journal of International Law*, 63. iii. (July 1969).

CASTAÑEDA, JORGE, *Legal Effects of United Nations Resolutions.* (New York: Columbia University Press, 1969).

CHIU, HUNGDAH, *The Capacity of International Organizations to conclude treaties, and the special legal aspects of the treaties so concluded.* (The Hague: Nijhoff, 1966).

FALK, RICHARD, *Legal Order in a Violent World.* (Princeton, N.J.: Princeton University Press, 1968).

FALK, RICHARD, *The Status of Law in International Society.* (Princeton, N.J.: Princeton University Press, 1969).

FRIEDMAN, WOLFGANG G., "The Relevance of International Law to the Processes of Economic and Social Development", *Proceedings of the American Society of International Law*, 60th annual meeting, Washington, April 1966).

HAMBRO, E. and ROVINE, A. W., *The Case Law of the International Court*, 2 vols. (Leyden: Sijthoff, 1968).

HIGGINS, ROSALYN, *The Development of International Law Through the Political Organs of the United Nations.* (London: Oxford University Press, 1963).

HIGGINS, ROSALYN, "Policy and Impartiality: The Uneasy Relationship in International Law", *International Organization*, XXIII. iv. (Autumn 1969).

HIGGINS, ROSALYN, "The Place of International Law in the Settlement of Disputes by the Security Council", *American Journal of International Law*, 64. i. (January 1970).

IBRAHIM, F. I., *The Power of the International Court to determine its own jurisdiction.* (The Hague: Nijhoff, 1965).

KAHN, SIR MUHAMMAD ZAFRULLA, "Contribution of the Principal Judicial Organ of the United Nations to the Achievement of the Objectives of the Organization", *UN Monthly Chronicle*, VII. vii. (July 1970).

NINČIĆ, DJURA, *The Problem of Sovereignty in the Charter and the Practice of the United Nations.* (The Hague: Nijhoff, 1970).

POLLOCK, ALEXANDER J., "The South West Africa Cases and the Jurisprudence of International Law", *International Organization*, XXIII. iv. (Autumn 1969).

RAJAN, M. S., *United Nations and Domestic Jurisdiction.* (Calcutta: Orient Longmans, 1958).

SIMMONDS, R., *Legal problems arising from the United Nations military operations in the Congo.* (The Hague: Nijhoff, 1968).

SYATAUW, J. J. G., *Decisions of the International Court of Justice: A Digest.* (Leyden: Sijthoff, 1969).

YEMIN, EDWARD, *Legislative Powers in the United Nations and Specialized Agencies.* (Leyden: Sijthoff, 1969).

**The Member States**

BLOOMFIELD, LINCOLN P., "The United States, the Soviet Union, and the Prospects for Peacekeeping", *International Organization,* XXIV. iii. (Summer 1970).

GORDENKER, LEON, "International Organization and the Cold War", *International Journal,* XXIII. iii. (Summer 1968).

MILLAR, T. B., *The Commonwealth and the United Nations.* (London: Methuen, 1967).

STOESSINGER, JOHN G., *The United Nations and the Super Powers.* (New York: Random House, 1965).

KAY, DAVID A., "The Impact of African States on the United Nations", *International Organization,* XXIII. i. (Winter 1969).

KAY, DAVID, *The New Nations in the United Nations,* 1960–67. (New York: Columbia University Press, 1970).

MAGEE, JAMES S., "ECA and the Paradox of African Co-operation", *International Conciliation,* No. 580. (November 1970).

RANA, SWADESH, "The Changing Indian Diplomacy at the United Nations", *International Organization,* XXIV. i. (Winter 1970).

TWITCHETT, KENNETH J., "African Modernisation and International Organization", *Orbis,* XIV. iv. (Winter 1971).

COMBS, JAMES JOSEPH, "France and United Nations Peacekeeping", *International Organization,* XXI. ii. (Spring 1967).

GERMAN SOCIETY FOR FOREIGN AFFAIRS, *The Federal Republic of Germany and the United Nations.* (New York: Manhattan Publishing Co., 1967).

GOODWIN, GEOFFREY L., *Britain and the United Nations.* (London: Oxford University Press, 1958).

H.M.S.O., *Britain and the United Nations.* (London: H.M.S.O., 1970).

NOGUEIRA, FRANCO, *The United Nations and Portugal.* (London: Sidgwick & Jackson, 1963).

BRINKLEY, GEORGE A., "The Soviet Union and the United Nations: the Changing Role of the Developing Countries", *The Review of Politics,* XXXII. i. (January 1970).

DALLIN, ALEXANDER, *The Soviet Union at the United Nations.* (London: Methuen, 1962).

JACOBSON, HAROLD KARAN, *The USSR and the UN's Economic and Social Activities*. (Notre Dame, Ind.: University of Notre Dame Press, 1963).

PETROVSKY, VLADIMIR F., "The Soviet Union and the United Nations", *Vista*, IV. v. (May–June 1969).

RUBINSTEIN, ALVIN Z., *The Soviets in International Organization: Changing Policy Toward Developing Countries*, 1953–1963. (Princeton, N.J.: Princeton University Press, 1964).

WEINER, ROBERT, "The USSR and UN Peacekeeping", *Orbis*, XIII. iii. (Autumn 1969).

ASHER, ROBERT E., *International Development and the US National Interest*. (Washington, D.C.: National Planning Association, 1967).

BLOOMFIELD, LINCOLN P., *The United Nations and US Foreign Policy*, 2nd rev. ed. (London: University of London Press, 1969).

FINKELSTEIN, LAWRENCE S., "The United States and International Organization: The Changing Setting", *International Organization*, XXIII. iii. (Summer 1969).

FINKELSTEIN, LAWRENCE S., (ed.), *The United States and International Organization*. (Cambridge, Mass.: the M.I.T. Press, 1969).

GARDNER, RICHARD N., *In Pursuit of World Order: US Foreign Policy and International Organization*, rev. ed. (New York: Praeger, 1966).

HAAS, ERNST B., *Tangle of Hopes: American Commitments and World Order*. (Englewood Cliffs., N.J.: Prentice Hall, 1969).

ROWE, EDWARD T., "The United States and International Organization", *International Organization*, XXIV. iii. (Summer 1970).

RUSSELL, RUTH B., *The United Nations and United States Security Policy*. (Washington, D.C.: Brookings Institute, 1968).

WEILER, LAWRENCE D. and SIMONS, ANNE PATRICIA, *The United States and the United Nations: The Search for International Peace and Security*. (New York: Manhattan Publishing Co., 1967).